The Helen and Martin Schwartz Lectures in Jewish Studies

Sponsored by the Robert A. and Sandra S. Borns Jewish Studies Program
Indiana University

Sander L. Gilman
Jews in Today's German Culture (1995)

Geoffrey H. Hartman
The Longest Shadow: In the Aftermath of the Holocaust (1996)

Arnold M. Eisen
Taking Hold of Torah: Jewish Commitment and Community in America (1997)

David G. Roskies
The Jewish Search for a Usable Past (1999)

Omer Bartov
The "Jew" in Cinema: From The Golem *to* Don't Touch My Holocaust (2004)

Samuel D. Kassow
*Who Will Write Our History? Emanuel Ringelblum, the Warsaw Ghetto,
and the Oyneg Shabes Archive* (2007)

Hilary Putnam
*Jewish Philosophy as a Guide to Life:
Rosenzweig, Buber, Levinas, Wittgenstein* (2008)

WHEN KAFKA SAYS WE

UNCOMMON COMMUNITIES IN GERMAN-JEWISH LITERATURE

Vivian Liska

INDIANA UNIVERSITY PRESS
Bloomington and Indianapolis

This book is a publication of

Indiana University Press
601 North Morton Street
Bloomington, IN 47404-3797 USA

http://iupress.indiana.edu

Telephone orders	800-842-6796
Fax orders	812-855-7931
Orders by e-mail	iuporder@indiana.edu

Earlier versions of some of the material in this book have been published previously. Portions of chapters 1 and 2 were published in *The Yale Journal of Criticism* 13, no. 2 (2000): 343–60. © Yale University and The Johns Hopkins University. Reprinted with permission of The Johns Hopkins University Press. Parts of chapter 3 appeared in "La grand décision et la petite différence," *Europe: revue littéraire mensuelle* 923 (2006): 63–78. A briefer version of chapter 4 was published in Vivian Liska and Mark Gelber, eds., *Theodor Herzl between Europe and Zion,* Conditio Judaica 67 (Tübingen: Niemeyer Verlag, 2007), 161–73. Chapter 6 was published in *Transversal: Zeitschrift des Centrums für jüdische Studien* 2006: 43–55. Most of chapter 8 was published in *New German Critique* 91 (2004): 24–36. Chapter 10 was published in Frank Stern and Maria Gierlinger, eds., *Die deutsch-jüdische Erfahrung: Beiträge zum kulturellen Dialog* (Berlin: Aufbau-Verlag, 2003), 147–63. Chapter 13 is a revised version of "Ein Meridian wider die Zeit: von Paul Celan zu Franz Kafka," in *Kafka und die Weltliteratur,* ed. Manfred Engel, et al. (Göttingen: Vandenhoeck and Ruprecht, 2006), 210–34. Parts of chapter 15 were published in *Arcadia* 38, no. 2 (2003): 329–34. Vivian Liska thanks the editors for permission to reprint this material.

The paper used in this publication meets the minimum requirements of American National Standard for Information Sciences—Permanence of Paper for Printed Library Materials, ANSI Z39.48-1984.

Manufactured in the United States of America

Library of Congress Cataloging-in-Publication Data

Liska, Vivian, date
  When Kafka says we : uncommon communities in German-Jewish literature / Vivian Liska.
    p. cm. — (The Helen and Martin Schwartz lectures in Jewish studies)
  Includes bibliographical references and index.
  ISBN 978-0-253-35308-5 (cloth : alk. paper) 1. Kafka, Franz, 1883–1924—Criticism and interpretation. 2. Austrian literature—20th century—History and criticism. 3. German literature—20th century—History and criticism. 4. Jewish authors—Austria. 5. Jewish authors—Germany. 6. Group identity in literature. 7. Identity (Psychology) in literature. I. Title.
  PT2621.A26Z76917 2009
  833'.912—dc22

                                                                              2008043198

1 2 3 4 5   14 13 12 11 10 09

Contents

PART 5. KAFKA'S COMPANIONS

Abbreviations

Introduction: Uncommon Communities

> If the writer is in the margin of or at some distance from his fragile community, this situation puts him only more in the position to express another possible community and to forge the means for another consciousness and another sensibility.
>
> —Deleuze and Guattari 1986, 17

In his diary entry from 8 January 1914, Franz Kafka writes: "What have I in common with Jews? I have hardly anything in common with myself and should stand very quietly in a corner, content that I can breathe" (1975, 622).[1] The beginning of this diary entry could not be more straightforward. "What have I in common with . . . ?" is a question that can be regarded as the starting point of all queries about an individual's belonging to a cultural, ethnic, or religious community. Kafka's question suggests that he will go on to reveal his relationship with the Jewish community, or what would, today, be viewed as an aspect of his "Jewish identity." By the end of the passage, however, it becomes clear that these expectations will not be met. While Kafka's question is simple, his response is not. What might seem, at first glance, a reluctance, if not a refusal to be part of a community, turns out to be a symptom of a lack of inner wholeness and coherence associated with what is generally called the "modern crisis of identity." In what follows, it is clear that Kafka does not turn to either of two familiar positions from which the modern individual confronts collectivities. He is not interested in pitting individualism against the exigencies of a community—a favored nineteenth-century approach. Nor does he look in the opposite direction, to the possibility that the self-alienated modern individual might find refuge in the embrace of a group, an impulse associated with anti-individualist, conservative, or nationalist reactions to modernity. Instead, Kafka conjures up an all-encompassing estrangement and, in a puzzling image, describes the conclusions he should draw from this condition.

Kafka's sense of alienation appears to lead to a state of isolation and utter despondency of which he is often seen as the ultimate embodiment. The end of the passage, however, leaves even this conclusion in doubt. While his initial question can be firmly situated in a cultural, religious, political context, his response does not address the requirements of those discourses. It ends with a metaphor, a literary image that remains open to multiple, even contradictory readings. This passage has been cited both as evidence of his dismissal of Jewish concerns *and* as an expression of regret for not being part of the community. To be sure, it is difficult to determine the tone and meaning of the concluding image: "I should put myself quietly into a corner, content that I can breathe." The image seems to suggest Kafka's shame and guilt about his inability to be part of a community, to have any identity at all, but it remains unclear if irony undermines this call for a self-castigation evoked by the image of a child's punishment of being "put in a corner." Alternatively, or even in concert with the irony, this corner could also, tragically, describe the place where Kafka feels he should position himself, painting himself into a corner, into a dead end, where nothing but bare life stripped of all existential substance and support can subsist. It is, however, also possible to see this corner as a point farthest removed from the center, yet still part of the room, its ultimate margin, where he might finally catch some air and breathe. These and other readings are conceivable, and there is no way to know how desirable or undesirable Kafka considered the identification with "Jews" to be.

With his suggestive but ultimately indeterminate last image, Kafka responds to his question in the language of literature. The response can be neither readily conceptualized nor translated into a political or ideological message, because rather than trying to present a clear, fixed answer, he moves into a realm where ambiguity does not need to be avoided. In the end, Kafka feels that he "*should* quietly put [himself] into a corner." What he actually does is only implicit in this image. Not content simply to breathe—or else equating breathing with writing— he produces literature, novels and stories, fragments, letters, and diary entries, which provide no single and definitive answer to his initial question but allow for an exploration of its implications in uncommon ways. From the perspective of this corner, he opens opportunities to engage in the quest for literature's own potential to forge "another possible community," "another consciousness and another sensibility" (Deleuze and Guattari 1986, 17).

Both Kafka's fiction and his non-fictional work—his letters and diaries—depict many and diverse groups and collectivities, which are sometimes explicitly called "communities," but, as in the diary entry discussed above, it often remains unclear how he relates to or assesses these groups. An ambivalence toward collectivities in general and toward the Jewish community in particular can be found throughout his work, starting with his early diary entries about Zionism and the Yiddish theater and culminating in the loving yet subtly critical depiction of the mice people portrayed in "Josefine, the Singer," one of his last major stories. In a famous letter to Max Brod, Kafka situates his own generation of Prague Jews writing in German in an interstitial space without grounding: "[T]heir hind legs were still mired in their father's Jewishness and their thrashing forelegs found no new ground. The ensuing despair became their inspiration" (1958, 337).[2] A similar conflict is exhibited by many German-Jewish authors throughout the past century. As in the case of Kafka, a wavering and often tormented relationship to Judaism and the Jews underlies their work and becomes a source of inspiration. The social, cultural, and historical contexts of this ambivalence, its biographical, political, and psychological motivations and its literary forms, ranging from tragic pathos to sarcastic or grotesque provocation, are multiple and varied, and give rise to creative visions that add to the richness of this literature and its continuing relevance.

This book focuses on works by twentieth-century authors writing in German who, by choice or fate, are situated "in the margin of or at some distance from" (Deleuze and Guattari 1986, 17) their Jewish community. The book's aim is not to provide a survey of modern German-Jewish literature but to explore paradigmatic instances in which these authors' marginal position generates unconventional literary approaches toward communities and selves and the relationship between them. The essays, moreover, highlight the literary means by which these authors convey both the attractions exerted by groups and collectivities—safety, security, solidarity, a sense of meaning and direction—and the dangers associated with them. These dangers consist primarily in the homogenizing and self-serving confinement of the group's members, the constriction of their cultural or political horizon, and the denigrating exclusion of "others," those who do not belong.

This book also examines the authors' attempts to portray and affirm alternative modes of togetherness and to suggest instances of relations, alliances, and shared experiences that avoid and counteract these dangers. Far from proposing ideas of community that can be used directly for political or ideological aims, these works depict uncommon communities or transmit the conditions for such alliances, which may or may not make the concrete parameters of their German-Jewish context explicit. These communities are called "uncommon" in a double sense of the word: they are not only unusual, as the simple meaning of the word suggests, but they are uncommon because they question the foundation of community based on a principle of identity and sameness, of "having something in common." The works discussed in this book draw provisional collectivities that are neither self-enclosing nor exclusionary, and from a variety of standpoints they formulate a critique of closed communal entities as well as the myths, traditions, and beliefs by which such communities legitimize themselves. Concomitantly, they display various degrees of skepticism toward ideals involving a fixed, collective identity. They do not, however, promote the increasingly popular notion that identities can be invented out of nothing, constructed from scratch, and discarded at

will. Even in their most radical critique of the community from which they feel—
to various degrees—estranged, they continue to acknowledge the formidable and
often terrifying impact of its history, tradition, and fate on their lives and works.

As the focus on individual works and the close attention to specific poems or
passages indicate, the readings in this book emerge from the conviction that these
instances of uncommon communities do not exist independently of their literary
expression and the interpretative act that discerns them. Contrary to a widespread
practice in cultural studies and political theory that invokes literary texts only to
subsume them under pre-existing concepts and categories, the underlying premise of this book is that literary texts resist this kind of translation. Rather than
embracing or rejecting communities, Kafka's short diary entry, as well as all of
the works featured in the following essays, reveal complex, conflicting, and polyvalent, multi-interpretable relations to communities in general and to the Jewish
collectivity in particular. In some way, all of the authors discussed in this book
ask Kafka's question: "What do I have in common with Jews?" Each responds dif-
ferently, but like Kafka, each answers "in the language of literature," a move that
sets their responses apart from theories that currently address issues of collective
identity and concepts of community, including those theories that may be close in
spirit to the complex attitudes toward communities disclosed in this book.

During the last decades of the twentieth century, the search for uncommon
forms of community arose in different theoretical contexts (Herbrechter and
Higgins 2006). Among them, poststructuralist theories called traditional communitarian impulses into question. While these theories were also critical of enlightened modernity's individualism, they simultaneously attempted to rescue the
notion of community from totalitarian associations. Citing a few titles will suffice
to indicate the nature of these theories: *The Unavowable Community* (Blanchot
1983), *The Inoperative Community* (Nancy 1986), *The Community of Those Who
Have Nothing in Common* (Lingis 1994), *The Coming Community* (Agamben 1993).
In general, these works and others propose communal configurations in which a
mutual interdependence and exposure would not preclude but would rather enable individual specificity and create communities not subject to an exterior or
pre-existent definition. In accordance with the focus of this book, these theories
oppose any communion or fusion based on a unified, institutionalized, and exclusionary common ground, a sharply defined goal, and a clear conceptualization
of itself. Unlike the communities discussed here, however, these approaches often
pursue an ideal of provisional affiliations entirely devoid not only of a "common
space, time or identity" (Korhonen 2006), but also of all traces stemming from a
shared past, upbringing, tradition, language, religion, or history. This ideal of a
community that relinquishes all intrinsic bonds ignores or denies the ambivalences, dilemmas, and torments conveyed at the end of Kafka's diary entry and in
the other texts discussed in this book.

The uncommon communities referred to in the subtitle manifest themselves
at different levels and are uncommon in a variety of ways. They can be found in the

language, the narrative stance, the poetic address, or the imaginary world of the texts discussed in this book. Some are unusual, precarious, contradictory "we's" voiced by a protagonist, a narrator, or a lyrical persona; others are depictions ranging from couples to circumscribed groups. Some of these communities, despite all their efforts, cannot quite shield themselves from intruders, and others cannot completely close and unify their own ranks. At a different level, and less literally, such communities are conveyed in descriptions of fictive, imaginary, and poetic alliances that defy all conventional expectations of unity or communion. There are associations in which the participants share nothing but the insight into their own estrangement. There are friends who do not know each other and antagonists who turn out to be allies against a common enemy. There are hostile exchanges that disclose or reach a shared vision and monologues that reveal discordant, dissonant voices. At another level, uncommon communities can develop out of the ways in which these works relate to older texts, transforming their myths, traditions, and beliefs about how communities ought to be constituted into new visions of being together. Repeatedly, uncommon communities are formed between the living and the dead: there are impossible communions arising from a desperate poetic conjuration of the departed and others in which the voices of the dead address us. At yet another level, uncommon communities can arise from elective affinities between author and reader, and from the closeness a writer or poet feels toward his or her precursor. There, unlikely correspondences come into view, alliances across ruptures that are described as unbridgeable, or, in one instance, a bond so threatening that it results in an outright refusal to read on. Furthermore, there are communities of readers who debate—and disagree—about works and authors, foremost among them Kafka. These communities extend not only beyond different loyalties and ideologies, languages and places, but also beyond generations, pointing to the lineage of readers of an author or a work through the ages and ultimately to the transmission of literature as such.

To what extent can the authors discussed in this book be regarded as an uncommon community? At first sight, they form a community only because they can all be called twentieth-century German-Jewish writers, a not particularly uncommon grouping.[3] For some the term designates the "Jewish contribution to German literature" and for others "Jewish literature in the German language" (Kilcher 1999, 485–89). In the context of this book, which centers on ambivalences toward fixed identities and questions of belonging, neither of these designations is appropriate.[4] In a letter to Max Brod from June 1921 Kafka places his writings "in the small world of German-Jewish literature" (1958, 336), a world he defines in terms of multiple impossibilities, where the very idea of a firm place and solid ground becomes questionable. In another letter, this time to his fiancée Felice, Kafka writes: "Couldn't you, by the way, also tell me what I really am? In the last issue of the *Neue Rundschau* 'The Metamorphosis' is mentioned and dismissed on good grounds, adding something like: 'K's art of story-telling has something archetypically German.' By contrast, Max [Brod] writes in his article: 'K's stories are among the most Jewish documents of our time'" (1982, 719–20).[5] German-Jewish literature should indeed not be regarded as a fixed and definable category or essence, but as the result of a focus, a set of questions asked in the process of reading and interpreting individual texts.[6]

The complexity of the communal relations reflected on in this book is intimately linked to the German-Jewish (or Austrian-Jewish) cultural, historical, and literary context in which this literature arose. This context, often for tragic reasons, contributed to generating a lucid awareness of the attractions and dangers of communitarian allegiances. Although almost all of the chapters address instances of communities within an explicitly Jewish context, the focus here lies less on the particular relation these authors have with the Jewish community than on the implications of the way they configure communities as such. Still, such abstractions and assumptions of continuities throughout the twentieth century may conceal as much as they reveal, and one must be sensitive to distinctions between the different periods in which the works were written: the first decades of the twentieth century, the aftermath of World War II, and the latter part of the twentieth century.

At the turn of the past century the change from the predominant model of community, an "organic" entity based on "kinship, language and religion," to a "mechanistic formation of society, based on reason, law and politics" (Isenberg 1999, 5) triggered major political and theoretical discussions. In the German-Jewish context, a concern with communities featured prominently in intra-Jewish debates concerning assimilation and acculturation as well as cultural and political Zionism. These debates were, at the time, played out in the discrepancies and difficult relations between Eastern Jews living in the *shtetls* of Poland, Russia, and Hungary who were seen as representatives of the traditional communitarian model, and Western, assimilated Jews living in German cities who were considered to be the paradigmatic agents of modernity.[7] Considering the authors discussed here (Kafka, Theodor Herzl, Else Lasker-Schüler) it becomes apparent that a strict division between modern and anti-modern tendencies—between progressive, individualistic, and cosmopolitan Jews on the one hand and traditionalist Jews desirous of remaining within or returning to communal folds on the other—is impossible. Instead, this division between modern and anti-modern, worldly and communitarian, was often experienced within the lives and visions of individual Jews as a continuing cultural and existential dilemma.

In the aftermath of the war, when the illusory nature of assimilation and a German-Jewish symbiosis had become evident, the terms of this dilemma changed. Jews had become the major victims of the most murderous "we" in history. The national socialists, who wanted to shape their new Germany after the model of a large, homogeneous, and exclusionary community, did not differentiate between urban assimilated Jews and those living in eastern Europe. The Jews had become a "community of fate" (*Schicksalsgemeinschaft*) against their will and beyond all divides, and the literature written by the survivors was inevitably dominated by the common theme of mourning and remembrance. But traces of the ambivalence between communitarian impulses and a radically modernist, individualist, and private attitude remain. They inform the differences in the poetics of commemoration to be found in the works written in the immediate post-war years and discussed here (works by Paul Celan, Nelly Sachs, and Ilse Aichinger).

Toward the end of the twentieth century, very different political and historical circumstances also engendered new discourses about communal belongings. In the course of a critique of modernity's universalist ideals and what came to be widely regarded as its consequence, an imperialist drive toward global mastery, theories such as postcolonialism, multiculturalism, and cultural studies partly rehabilitated the notion of a collective identity and, especially for members of minority cultures, an emphasis on common roots. At the same time, these theories insisted on the necessity of affirming multiple belongings and various forms of *métissage* that would undo clear boundaries and demarcations between ethnic groups, communities, and national allegiances. In this context, "Jewishness" came, for some, to "stand for a form of historical and racial *inbetweenness*" (Bhabha 1995, 14) and Jewish literature for the paradigmatic "diasporic writing" that affirms its foreignness as a counterpart to all forms of "territorialization" and nationalism. To some extent, this attitude toward communal alliances can be found in the works of the "second generation" authors discussed in this book (Robert Schindel, Doron Rabinovici, Robert Menasse). However, "Jewishness" does not figure in their works as a light and easy "hybridity" (Herzog 2002), a term often associated with "inbetweenness." Instead, they formulate their ambivalent identification with Jews in terms of a conflict between their criticism of closed communities and their loyalty toward the victims of the Holocaust. Amid doubts about the actual disappearance of anti-Semitism in their environment, they search for literary forms that would manifest their tentative new alliances with their non-Jewish environment, their uneasy relationship with Jewish groups and institutions, and their distancing from the generation of German-Jewish authors in the immediate post-war period. They affirm their bonds with "the Jews" in terms of a commitment to remember Jewish suffering, but, aware that they are, at the most, "secondary witnesses," they are reluctant to invoke the victimhood of the previous generation for a legitimation of exclusionary communitarian impulses and goals in the present. Nevertheless, in view of both the past and the present, they sense that a distance, however invisible, between them and their non-Jewish environment remains.

Although the authors discussed in this book lived and wrote in different historical and social contexts and vary in their views about "what they have in common with Jews" or in their respective approaches to communities in general, they all ask Kafka's question and give ambivalent answers. At first glance, the three pre-war authors—Kafka, the "Jewish son" and master modernist from Prague, for whom literature was his whole existence; Herzl, the Viennese dandy, the self-styled hero of Jewish nationalism and author of journalistic essays, rather insignificant plays, and occasional short stories; and Lasker-Schüler, the eccentric bohemian poet who roamed the artists' cafés of Berlin and created her persona in equal measure in Hebrew ballads and Arabic legends—seem to have little in common. While all three were born into families belonging to the assimilated Jewish bourgeoisie, they could not differ more in literary stature, poetic sensibility, and intellectual or ideological orientation. Yet, even if their actual views concerning their affiliation with the community of Jews or their respective approaches to communities in general differ, these writers all speak from a peripheral position and reflect upon this position in their work.

For obvious reasons, the differences in context and source of their allegiance to Jews are not as wide for the three authors writing in the immediate aftermath of the Holocaust: Paul Celan, the Romanian-born author of the preeminent poetic oeuvre in the German language after 1945, whose parents were killed by the Nazis and who drowned himself in the Seine in 1970; Nelly Sachs, the Nobel laureate who grew up in Berlin, survived the war in Swedish exile, and repeatedly suffered from severe depression; and Ilse Aichinger, the Austrian author of difficult, experimental poetry, radio-plays, and short prose, whose only novel, *Herod's Children,* published in 1946, is inspired by her experiences as the daughter of a Jewish woman and a Nazi sympathizer in Vienna during the German occupation.

The three contemporary Austrian writers, Robert Schindel, Robert Menasse, and Doron Rabinovici, are even closer in spirit and existential situation. Although they come from very different intellectual backgrounds—Schindel started out as a radical leftist activist and experimental poet, Menasse as a philosopher and Hegel expert, and Rabinovici as a historian of Vienna during the war years—they all address, adopt, *and* distance themselves from their Austrian-Jewish historical, cultural, and literary legacy. Although they too pose queries as to what they "have in common with Jews," these writers ask Kafka's question in a new form. Schindel, in a 1995 essay on "Judaism as Memory and Resistance," insists on the necessity of a communion with the murdered Jews, but at the same time wonders: "What is it that links me to my humiliated, tortured, deported, gassed and shot ancestors? I'm ignorant of religious and national scriptures [. . .] Foreign, my roots are truly foreign to me" (1995b, 146).

One figure has, so far, remained unmentioned: Hannah Arendt. While a political thinker and not an author of literature, she did deal extensively with literary figures—foremost among them Rahel Varnhagen, Heinrich Heine, Stefan Zweig, and Franz Kafka—and their relationship to their Jewish origins. Moreover, in her philosophical writings she addresses questions of belonging and exclusion and of alternative forms of togetherness in ways that are deeply marked by her own conflicted relationship to the Jewish community. Her famous response to Gershom Scholem's rebuke for showing insufficient love for the Jewish people is a particularly poignant instance of a complex attitude to Jewishness as a collectivity: "I have never in my life 'loved' any people or collective— . . . I indeed love 'only' my friends." This reply, however, has to be read side by side with a passage in the same letter in which she affirms her Jewishness as a total self-evidence—"a matter of course, beyond dispute or argument" (in Young-Bruehl 1982, 369).

This book is organized concentrically in regard to Kafka. Its starting point, an investigation of Kafka's attitude toward communities in general and the Jewish community in particular, largely takes the book's title literally, while the three subsequent sections move toward a more metaphoric and, in the final section, more mediated understanding of Kafka's "we." The first section, "Kafka's Communities," lays the groundwork for the argument underlying this book as a whole. The three chapters here literally explore the effects of Kafka's use of "we" and "us" in several shorter texts, aphorisms, and diary entries. The focus is on the function and effect of instances in which Kafka, who is often considered the ultimate representative of the modern individual—lonely, forlorn, isolated—uses the first-person plural and alternatively speaks as the representative of a collectivity or a group. The first of these essays links passages in Kafka's writings that deal explicitly with Jewish issues to others that reflect in more general terms on the dynamics of closure and exclusion in communities as such. The second chapter analyzes the rhetorical moves of his "Speech on the Yiddish Language" and the crucial role of his contradictory use of the pronoun "we." The last chapter in this section consists of a close reading of Kafka's enigmatic story "A Little Woman" and shows that he conceives of his writing self as engaged in an ongoing battle with imagined or internal antagonists who nonetheless turn into allies against a nameless, opaque, and uniform enemy. While there is nothing intrinsically Jewish about this situation, it illustrates the depth of Kafka's suspicions about homogeneous entities—including his own self—and sheds light on the meaning of his words "I have scarcely anything in common with myself," correlated with his question "what do I have in common with the Jews?" These essays of course explore only a small fraction of the instances where Kafka says "we" in his fictional and non-fictional writings. Contrary to Marthe Robert's contention that "Kafka rarely says 'we'" (1979, 74), the first-person plural pervades his stories, fragments, diary entries, and letters. "The Problem of Our Laws," "Investigations of a Dog," "Josefine, the Singer," "Building the Great Wall of China"—to name only a few—are written predominantly from the perspective of a "we." All these instances deserve to be explored separately, and the occurrences analyzed in this book are merely examples illustrating the intricacy of the first-person plural in Kafka's writings.

Although the order of the chapters in this book is not chronological but rather thematic, it nevertheless marks the Holocaust as a caesura. Following "Kafka's Communities," the second section, "Revisiting the Common Ground," analyzes works written in the first decades of the twentieth century and explores representations of collective identity in a sense similar to the one highlighted in the Kafka essays. The "common ground" revisited in these chapters refers either literally to place and territory or metaphorically to values and traditions. The first of these chapters deals with Theodor Herzl's barely known late philosophical tales in which the ageing founder of political Zionism questions his former ideals of heroic leadership and embraces the values of common men and a more pragmatic and differentiated conception of national unity. The chapters on Else Lasker-Schüler retrace her imaginative and provocative transformations of biblical figures and the role she assigns to poetry in creating bonds across ethnic and religious borders.

The third section, "Communities of Fate," discussing works written in the immediate aftermath of the Holocaust, emphasizes literary approaches to communitarian belonging in light of questions primarily related to a collective memory of the catastrophe. Close readings of individual poems by Paul Celan reveal how his reinvention of a poetic language after the Holocaust derives from a "crossing through" and "crossing out" (*durchkreuzen*) of traditional literary tropes and metaphors. This poetic gesture corresponds to a refusal of commonplaces accompanying his sense of radical uprootedness and loss of communal bonds, with the exception of those linking him to the dead. Unlike Celan, Nelly Sachs, to whom the last chapter in this section is devoted, reverts to a romantic poetics based on the idea of the poet as mouthpiece of a people and repeatedly invokes a unified and unifying "we." Read, however, against the grain of their traditional appearance, her poems reveal an awareness of the artificial construction of this continuity as nothing but a messianic hope.

Part 4, "Contentious Commemorations," focuses on controversial modes of remembering the Holocaust and on the self-definitions and cultural interrelations of the groups—Jewish and non-Jewish—involved in these "acts of memory" in works by contemporary Austrian writers. Although Aichinger, born in 1921, belongs to an earlier generation than the other authors discussed in this section and draws on a poetics that is, in many ways, closer to that of Celan and Sachs, she shares with the younger authors a concern with the effect of the political and cultural realities of her time on forms of remembering—and forgetting—the Holocaust. The closed and exclusionary community Aichinger demystifies is the postwar group of German writers known as *Gruppe 47* and its claims of a radically new beginning after the catastrophe. Like Celan and Sachs, Aichinger pledges allegiance to the memory of the dead, more particularly to the young Christian resistance fighters Sophie and Hans Scholl. The essays on contemporary Austrian novelists demonstrate the complexities of their relationship to the Jewish survivors of the previous generation, to the non-Jewish children of the perpetrators, and to the notion of communal identity altogether.

The final section returns to Kafka, but approaches his work through investigations of its reception by, impact on, and inspiration for other authors and thinkers. This section explores literary and theoretical readings of Kafka's work that articulate in strikingly different ways their specific affinity with the writings of their predecessor, more particularly with the ambiguity of his "we." Terrified by the destabilizing effect of Kafka's prose, Aichinger pretends to keep away from his texts, but by that same token affirms their impact and echoes his ambivalence toward closed communities. Celan, in several masterfully encrypted references, evokes an imaginary communion with his precursor across the historical divide that marks his poetry. The last chapter addresses Arendt's straightforwardly political approach to Kafka in her reading of *The Castle* as a statement about the need for Jews to close ranks in the face of a hostile society and in her later critique of an escape from politics and history that she believes to be implied in Kafka's parable "He." In pointing to the subtler but no less effective powers of literature to open up alternative visions for an "uncommon community" of readers across the generations, this final chapter also forms an epilogue to the whole book.

Although this book represents a very personal journey, it was shaped by many encounters and exchanges and by the intellectual company of exceptional fellow travelers. I wish to express my gratitude to all those colleagues and friends who, in countless conversations, offered insight and advice on different aspects of this book: Stanley Corngold, Mark Gelber, Geoffrey Hartman, Geert Lernout, Eva Meyer, John Neubauer, Thomas Nolden, Katrien Vloeberghs, Bernd Witte, and Irving Wohlfarth. I want to thank Martin Chalmers and Esther Kinsky for their fine translations of poems, primary texts, and passages of my own writing, Lee Ann Sandweiss and Nathan Van Camp for their assistance with the manuscript, and Luc Acke for his help with matters big and small. This book would not have come into existence without Nancy K. Miller, who helped me see the pattern in the carpet and inspired some of the key concepts of this book. I am most grateful to Alvin H. Rosenfeld, who offered me the opportunity to publish it in his series under the expert guidance of Janet Rabinowitch. This book is dedicated to Nathalie, Jacques, Tamara, and Daphne, and most of all to Charles, who, for more than three decades, stood by me *contre vents et marées*.

PART ONE

KAFKA'S COMMUNITIES

When Kafka Says We

In his diary entry from 29 October 1921, Kafka writes of "this borderland between loneliness and community" (D, 396)[1] in which he dwells. This territory was the only country Kafka ever truly inhabited. His stories, letters, and diary entries draw and redraw the contours of this land, revealing at its borders two extreme modes of being in the world: a condition of isolation and hermetic self-enclosure on the one hand and a state of total group cohesion on the other. Emblematic images of both are among the most poignant elements of Kafka's legacy: here is the one, "lonely like Franz Kafka,"[2] excluded, without protection, and at the remotest distance of human contact; there, in a vision more terrifying still, are the many locked into each other, identical and interchangeable, constituting opaque instances of impenetrable unity. The borderland between loneliness and communal life reveals Kafka's longings in both directions and his alternating flights from one to the other. In his life, he experiences this land as paralysis, emptiness, and living death. In his work, however, this region transforms into a language of force and movement that runs up against borders, confounding inside and outside, same and other, I and we. In Kafka's writing, the lifeless desert is not the area in between, but that which lies beyond both borders: the most radical forms of solitude and of community, autonomous separateness and homogeneous unison.

Undoubtedly, Kafka's yearning to belong and to gain the self-confidence that accompanies belonging drew him to the community of Jews, and his aversion to conformism kept him from adhering to it fully. Beyond this personal vacillation, one recognizes in Kafka's borderland a move away from the individualism of modernity, and more specifically of the assimilated *Westjuden* on the one hand, and from the seductions of communal ideologies on the other. Yet it is impossible to recuperate his work for any ideology, including Zionism, and also impossible to see his writing in terms of an omnipresent, politically conceived flight, what Deleuze and Guattari call a "deterritorialization" directed against fascism, Stalinism, and capitalism alike. Both views are simplifications that miss Kafka's specific insight into the attractions and dangers of closed and homogeneous collectivities. The *lignes de fuite* that Deleuze and Guattari detect everywhere in his work, these vanishing lines that prevent Kafka's writing from settling on firm ground, describe only one of its movements. The battles Kafka fought happened in confrontations at borders, where lines meet, touch, and hook into each other, where contrary forces wrestle with each other like the interlocked bodies of the adversary but interdependent neighbors he describes in one of his dreamlike diary entries (D, 272–73). If these battles ultimately do not deliver firm conclusions—one would hardly go to Kafka for that—they do sharpen the questions, and occasionally, through sheer pressure against the obstacles, they point, like Walter Benjamin's "Destructive Character," toward a way "where others encounter walls and mountains" (2002a, 542).

Just as there are many entrances to the burrow of Kafka's work—the opening remark of Deleuze and Guattari's Kafka book (1986, 3)—there are several ways of approaching the relationship between Kafka and the Jews. A first and unquestionably indispensable approach reconstructs Kafka's actual involvement with Jewish, particularly Zionist, movements of his time on the basis of historical and biographical evidence. The purpose of such a reconstruction, a more accurate understanding of Kafka as a person or as a paradigmatic example of a Western Jewish intellectual in central Europe at the beginning of the twentieth century, is important and has inspired many outstanding accounts of Kafka's complex and oscillating interest in Judaism and Zionism. Ritchie Robertson's study (1985), especially his research into the historical discussion of the tension between *Gesellschaft* and *Gemeinschaft*, society and community, in Kafka's time, is undoubtedly a prerequisite for a better understanding of the context of Kafka's writings about communal configurations. Similarly, Giuliano Baioni's (1994) tracing of the conflict between Kafka's self-castigating existence as the paradigmatic occidental Jew ("der westjüdischste aller Juden" [Kafka 1983, 294]), his attraction to a communal engagement, and his guilt-ridden indulgence in his solitary vocation as a writer illuminates the circumstances in which Kafka's reflections on collective identities came into being. More recently, Iris Bruce (2007) has reconstructed Kafka's involvement in the cultural Zionism of his day and has convincingly demonstrated the presence of corresponding themes and motifs in his literary works. However, efforts to go beyond these and other existing biographical studies about Kafka's actual relationship to Judaism and Zionism are forced into esoteric perspectives or limited to discoveries of marginalia.

The second approach consists of allegorical interpretations of his texts and their use as an inventory of analogies with structures in some way related to Judaism. Fragments of recognizable Judaica amid the gaping abstractions of Kafka's texts undoubtedly invite readings of the castle, the court, the imperial message, and the law as God, the Torah, or Jerusalem, of the stories' paraphernalia as kabalistic, Hassidic, or messianic icons, of their descriptions of various struggles as confrontations between God and his people, this people and its others, this people and itself, *Ost-* and *Westjuden,* assimilated Jews and Zionists, not to mention the different shades of Zionism. Impressive as many of these translations of Kafka's text into the different registers of Judaism are, the sheer number of possible alternatives leaves the search for the ultimate hermeneutic criteria open and questions of interpretative accuracy unanswered.

Replacing these approaches with an eye to the relevance of Kafka's relation to Jewish issues for an understanding of his attitude to collective identities in general is a third, maybe more compelling, though not necessarily less controversial perspective on the question. In reading his fiction, one has no verifiable way of identifying what the different groups and communities in Kafka's fictional texts might refer to, and any attempt to assign them specific correspondences in the real world reveals only the choices and concerns of the reader. Rather than trying to match the images of communities and collectivities in these texts to particular instances in reality, it may therefore be more promising to focus on the internal and external dynamics at work in Kafka's communal configurations as such. The situation is somewhat different with his non-fictional writing. His letters and diaries, unlike his literary work, do explicitly mention Jewish "realities," but any attempt to go beyond a reconstruction of the biographical development of his attraction to Jewish instances and movements will have to choose from the manifold, more or less explicit, and often contradictory statements Kafka made on the issue in the course of his life. Reducing these contradictions to changes of mind at different phases of Kafka's life may illuminate his individual development, but it barely addresses larger concerns. A different approach considers that it is precisely in those sometimes disturbing ambiguities and hesitations *within* his statements that the most valuable insights can be discovered. They are to be found in Kafka's personal writings as well as in his fiction wherever he reflects on the seductions and traps of collective ideals and communal forms of life. They may be most strikingly significant where Kafka, whose name became a byword for the ultimate experience of solitude, says "we."

A Diary Entry

The first of Kafka's diary entries mentioning Zionism, his critical review from 26 March 1911 of Max Brod's novel *Jüdinnen,* is written entirely from the perspective of a "we." In this review, Kafka voices three objections to the novel: in his view, the book lacks a solution to the Jewish question, a non-Jewish observer, and a young male leading figure. "In Western European stories," he writes in the first critique, "as soon as they even begin to include any groups of Jews, we are now almost used immediately to hunting for and finding under or over the plot the solution to the Jewish question too. In the *Jüdinnen,* however, no such solution is indicated [. . .]" (D, 45). "Offhand," he continues, "we recognize in this a fault in the story, and feel ourselves all the more entitled to such a criticism because today, since Zionism came into being, possibilities for a solution" are at hand (D, 46). This "we": is it a pluralis majestatis and nothing more? If we take this first criticism directed at Brod's novel as a straightforward expression of Kafka's conviction, he appears as an unequivocal defender of Zionist thought who expects literature to present answers serving the cause. Yet, the tone of the passage indicates that underneath these seemingly uncomplicated judgments, there is an internal dialogue taking place: the hesitant beginning, the awareness that the critical reading of the novel may be dictated by habit and established expectation, and mainly the word "offhand" ("kurz entschlossen") introducing Kafka's seeming criticism of the book's lack of a solution to the "Jewish problem" reveal a skepticism toward the rashness and self-righteousness with which Kafka imagines that a "we" with which he obviously does not wholly identify would find fault with Brod's novel.

The second criticism Kafka directs at Brod's novel reinforces this undercurrent of ambiguity. The "fault" of the insufficiently addressed solution to the *Judenfrage,* he writes, "has an other origin," namely the absence, in *Jüdinnen,* of "non-Jewish observers who, in other stories draw out the Jewishness so that it advances toward them in amazement, doubt, envy, fear, and finally is transformed into self-confidence" (D, 46). This passage seems to imply that it is only in the presence of a non-Jewish outsider's perspective that Jewishness can and may "draw itself up to its full height" (D, 46) ("sich in seiner ganzen Länge aufrichten"). "This is indeed what we demand," Kafka continues; "we don't accept any other way of dissolving the Jewish masses" (D, 46; translation slightly modified). Hartmut Binder understands this passage as an atypically ideological statement written under the influence of a review of Brod's book by the Zionist Hugo Herrmann, who insists that a hostile non-Jewish presence in the novel would be necessary to justify the Zionist cause (Binder 1979a, 376). Giuliano Baioni disagrees with Binder, explaining Kafka's statements as a pragmatic preemption of a critical reaction to the book, namely that non-Jewish readers will not understand the Jewish world of the novel because it does not include a non-Jewish point of view with which they could identify (1994, 41). Baioni's interpretation minimizes the significance of Kafka's statement in order to strengthen his argument that Kafka's attraction to Judaism resided in his perception of it as a self-enclosed world: "Kafka always looks at Judaism from within and experiences it as a completely autonomous world" (1994, 41). This view is contradicted by the almost offensive metaphor with which Kafka illustrates his critique of Brod's novel and which is left out by both Binder and Baioni: Jewishness, Kafka writes, should manifest itself in its full grandeur only under the eyes of an antagonistic observer ("ein gegensätzlicher Zuschauer"); just as the convulsive starting up of a lizard under our feet on a footpath in Italy delights us greatly, again and again we are moved to bow down, but if we see them at a dealer's by hundreds crawling over one another in confusion in the large bottles in which otherwise pickles are usually packed, then we don't know what to do. (D, 46)

Kafka insists that this image has a more general validity: just like any other kind of identity, Jewishness ("das Jüdische") is a source of fascination and delight only as an unpredictable, mobile appearance drawn out by the presence of an outsider, not as a self-sufficient, enclosed entity. In the German original, the last words of this quotation are more explicit: "so wissen wir uns nicht einzurichten" (2002c, 161); then we cannot settle, cannot be at home there. But who is "we?" If one draws the parallel between Kafka's statement about the way Jewishness should show itself, and the simile by which he illustrates it, the "we" by which Kafka identifies here with the solitary wanderer on an Italian footpath would correspond to the non-Jewish observer, the "gegensätzlicher Zuschauer," and Jewishness to the lizard, whereas the rest of the text invites the assumption that Kafka uses "we" to reflect on the Jewish question from the inside. No wonder there is no place to settle on firm ground: there is hardly a homeland for such an elusive, contradictory "we." Although the text does not resolve this ambiguity of perspective, it highlights the precariousness of its position.

Kafka's choice of words in this passage must have seemed too controversial to the translator of the *Diaries:* "eine andere Auflösung der Judenmassen erkennen wir nicht an" (2002c, 160)—the literal "we don't accept any other way of dissolving the Jewish masses" is rendered as "no other principle for the organization of this Jewish material seems justified to us" (D, 46). The only "solution to the Jewish question" Kafka seems to have in mind here is the dissolution of "Judenmassen"—Jewish masses, which most probably refer to the closed and homogeneous communities of *Ostjuden.* This "autonomous" Jewish community should dissolve and be replaced by another kind of Jewishness, one that *does*—proudly, possibly even defiantly—face the eye of an external observer. It is only under his gaze that it may fully redress itself. Zionism, the passage implies, can perform this task, but it can fulfill it only if it is closer to the "convulsive starting up of a lizard" than to a bottle of vegetables: rather than a tightly closed mass-gathering of identical members, Kafka imagines it here as a movement toward self-confidence both dependent on and uninhibited by an encounter with a challenging, maybe even antagonistic other.

The phrasing of the last lines of the entry, where Kafka expresses his third, somewhat obscure critique of Brod's novel—that it oddly enough can do without the "prominent youth, who attracts the best to himself" (D, 46)—confirms this view. The charismatic youth whom Brod's novel can surprisingly omit, Kafka conjectures, is one who could lead the members of the community "in schöner radialer Richtung an die Grenzen des jüdischen Kreises" (2002c, 161), "along a beautiful radius to the margins of the Jewish circle" (D, 46). In this image, the direction is centrifugal, the face of the youthful leader turned outward. It invites a comparison with a very different image of unification that makes its repeated appearance in Kafka's writings: the "Reigen," a round dance or, less literally, a ring.

The Ring

In a famous passage from "Beim Bau der chinesischen Mauer" ("Building the Great Wall of China" [2007, 113–24]),[3] we read:

> Wie groß und reich und schön und liebenswert ihr Land war, jeder Landsmann war ein Bruder, für den man eine Schutzmauer baute und der mit allem was er hatte und war sein Leben lang dafür dankte, Einheit! Einheit! Brust an Brust, ein *Reigen des Volkes,* Blut, nicht mehr eingesperrt im kärglichen Kreislauf des Körpers, sondern süß rollend und doch wiederkehrend durch das unendliche China. (2002a, 342; emphasis added)

> every fellow countryman was a brother for whom they were building a protective wall and who was thankful all his life, thankful with everything that he had and was: unity! unity! breast on breast, a round dance of the people, blood no longer confined in the meager circulatory system of the body, but rolling on sweetly and yet returning to its source through the infinity of China. (KSS, 115)[4]

In spite of its obvious exaggeration, its atypically exalted parataxis, and its suggestion of a total subjection to the brotherhood, this masterful rendering of the idea of an organic "Volksgemeinschaft" (community of a people) has often been read as an enraptured expression of Kafka's ideal. Hartmut Binder even takes this passage as a proof of Brod's intuition that Judaism was gradually and silently getting hold of Kafka: "The praised cohesion of the people and the blood in the empire of the East is obviously an image of the unity of the people which he found among Eastern Judaism and which seemed to him a guarantee of a happy life" (1979a, 505).[5] There are several similar images of unity and wholeness in Kafka's work, but it is questionable whether any of them can be taken as a direct expression of his hopes. It is more likely that these passages constitute precisely the ground of ambiguity where the ideal of a homogeneous community is simultaneously an object of longing and an instance of terror.

In "Forschungen eines Hundes" ("Researches of a Dog" [KSS, 132–61]), the narrating dog lovingly describes the solidarity of the "Hundeschaft" (dogdom) as the greatest happiness one can yearn for: "die Sehnsucht nach dem grössten Glück, dessen wir fähig sind, [das] warme Beisammensein" ("longing for the greatest happiness we are capable of: warm togetherness" [KSS, 133]), and compares it to the indifference and hostility of other creatures; yet, in twice using the hardly attractive image of the dogs as a collectivity living all in one heap—"Alle auf einem Haufen!"—Kafka evokes an image similar to that of the bottle of lizards crawling over one another in the earlier diary entry. Despite the ambivalent tone here, the description of this communion still carries a note of longing which culminates in the dog's question: "Warum tue ich es nicht wie die anderen, lebe einträchtig mit meinem Volke und nehme das, was die Eintracht stört, stillschweigend hin [. . .] und bleibe immer zugekehrt dem, was glücklich bindet, nicht dem, was uns immer wieder unwiderstehlich aus dem Volkskreis zerrt" (2002b, 488). In Stanley Corngold's translation: "Why won't I behave like the others, live in harmony with my kind [. . .] and turn forever toward what binds us happily together and not toward what, time and time again, irresistibly, of course, tears us out of the circle of our kind" (KSS, 133).[6] The English version, which otherwise corrects significant errors in older translations, by syntactic necessity uses the first-person plural both for the experience of that which binds the people ("binds us happily together") and for that which drives the dog away from its circle ("tears us out"). Significantly, the German uses "us" only the second time ("was glücklich bindet, nicht dem, was uns immer wieder unwiderstehlich aus dem Volkskreis zerrt"). The plural "we" applies here precisely where the dog is alone in being driven away from the community, because his self is split and torn by contradictory impulses. This paradox captures the ambivalence accompanying his desire of desertion.

The description of the community of seven dogs in "Forschungen eines Hundes," presented by the narrating dog as an incident in his youth (and convincingly interpreted by several critics as an autobiographical reminiscence of Kafka's earlier attraction to the actors of the Yiddish theater who embodied for him the epitome of a unified *Volksgemeinschaft*), repeats the image of the ring found in "Beim Bau der chinesischen Mauer":

> Das Heben und Setzen ihrer Füsse, bestimmte Wendungen des Kopfes, ihr Laufen und ihr Ruhen, die Stellungen, die sie zu einander einnahmen, die *reigenmässigen* Verbindungen, die sie miteinander eingingen. (2002b, 490; emphasis added)

The "way they raised and set down their feet, certain turns of their head, their running and their resting, the attitudes they assumed toward one another, the combinations they formed with one another like a round dance" (KSS, 134). These round dance–like constellations are created by figures of interrelatedness performed with "grossartiger Sicherheit" (2002b, 491) (magnificent certainty), and could be read in a positive sense as a sign of desirable self-confidence. But the image of the ring, implying a closed circle, seems to gain a clearly negative connotation in another short prose text where Kafka addresses the constitution of a community in its most explicit form.

The title of the text, "Eine Gemeinschaft von Schurken" (A Community of Scoundrels), given to it by Max Brod, does not do justice to the complexity of Kafka's first sentence: "There was once a community of scoundrels, that is to say, they were not scoundrels, but ordinary people, the average. They always stood by each other" (2002b, 42). Only a few lines long, the text captures the mechanism of homogenization on which not only an evil community, as Brod's title implies, but every closed community depends. If one of its members commits a crime, or rather transgresses the rules—which is, "again, nothing scoundrel-like, but something usual, the ordinary" ("wie es gewöhnlich, wie es üblich ist")—and thereby breaches the unity of the community, he confesses, and "they then analyzed it, judged it, demanded expiation, pardoned, etc. It was well intended, the interests of the individual and of the community were met and the penitent was given the complement of the color he had shown" (2002b, 43).[7] In order to ensure the wholeness of the community and to reestablish its harmony, the distinction created by the individual act—which does not have to be an actual crime, "something scoundrel-like" ("etwas Schurkenhaftes"), but simply any form of differentiation—must be effaced in a process that reintegrates the action of the individual into the whole. Any "color" the individual has shown will be neutralized through the addition of its complementary color until the difference is wiped out: "So they always stood by each other, and even after death they did not desert the community, but rose to heaven dancing in a ring" (2002b, 43). The round dance, the closed circle in which all faces turn toward each other and refuse the acknowledgment of any distinction as well as anything that lies outside the circle, will be destroyed in the face of the heavens, the absolute. This negative assessment of a tightly closed community sheds doubts on interpretations that turn Kafka's occasional longing to belong into his ideal of human interrelation; it rather answers the question of Kafka's dog in "Researches of a Dog": "Why won't I behave like the others, live in harmony with my kind" (KSS, 133).

There can be little doubt about the text's implicit condemnation of the community's behavior. The narrative situation seems to be equally clear: an impersonal, omniscient speaker talks in the tone of a fairy tale and from the distance of wisdom about a community, about "them." But a closer look reveals that this unified perspective is disturbed: "There was once a community of scoundrels, that is to say, they were not scoundrels, but ordinary people, the average" (2002b, 42). And then again: "When for example one of them committed something scoundrel-like, which again was nothing scoundrel-like, but something usual, the ordinary." Twice the speaker shifts his judgment from a negatively connoted expression to a neutral one. He thereby describes precisely what happens as one crosses the threshold from outside to inside: the critical outside view dissolves, and from inside the rules and values of the community become naturalized, become "obvious," the "usual," the "average"; they become—the common. Significantly, this insight is itself not presented as a moral judgment. Instead, the narrator, who seemed so distant and neutral and so unified in a first reading, goes through the process of this change of points of view himself. Switching perspectives with treacherous smoothness, he doubles up into two voices that henceforth accompany the text; crossing the boundaries of the community with barely more than a little "actually," a "d(as) h(eisst)," he is both outside and inside, bystander and member, judging and participating in the round dance. He thereby partakes in the formation of a different figure, one that simultaneously points inward and outward, one that joins the singular and the plural in a different "we."

Community

Another short text, called "Gemeinschaft" (Community) by Max Brod (Kafka 2002b, 313–14) and (mis)translated as "Fellowship" by Tania and James Stern (Kafka 1976, 435–36),[8] can be seen as a quasi-symmetrical counterpiece to "Eine Gemeinschaft von Schurken." Both texts reveal and undo the mechanisms used by a closed community to insure its cohesion, but unlike the latter, which is concerned with the process of internal neutralization of difference and dissent, "Gemeinschaft" deals with a community's delimitation from its outside. The narrator of the story is a "we" and speaks as a member of a community of five friends. He tells about the origins of the group and of its persistent refusal to accept a sixth one who tries to join them:

> We are five friends, one day we came out of a house one after the other, first one came and placed himself beside the gate, then the second came, or rather glided through the gate like a little ball of quicksilver, and placed himself near the first one, then came a third, then the fourth, then the fifth. Finally we all stood in a row. People began to notice us, they pointed at us and said: Those five just came out of that house. Since then we have been living together; it would be a peaceful life if it weren't for a sixth one continually trying to interfere. (KCS, 435)

These first lines of the text simultaneously affirm and undermine the "founding myth" of the little *Gemeinschaft*. The five indeed came out of the same house, but this common "origin" does not ensure or justify their cohesion. The speaker introduces himself in the first-person plural, but when he enumerates the members of the group, he becomes impersonal. Instead of saying "first, or second, or third [. . .] I came," he uses the impersonal form, implying the disappearance of his individuality: the members of the group have become interchangeable. It is only after having been identified from the outside that the group becomes a community. The speaker is well aware of the difference between the actual constitution of the community and its perception from the outside: he knows that one day, meaning any day, the friends came out of a house, meaning any house, and that they form a row for no obvious reason. It is only when the people outside, who notice them, begin to use the definitive form and say that those five just came out of that house that they turn into a unity. The image of the "Quecksilberkügelchen," the little ball of quicksilver to which one of the members of the group is compared, perfectly renders the total dissolution of the individual in the community. This osmosis without residue suggests that a quasi-natural law is holding the group together. The rest of the text gradually and relentlessly unmasks this pretense and reveals the cruel mechanism behind this seemingly natural cohesion.

The group depends on the people who perceive it for its constitution; it depends on the rejection of the sixth for its delimitation and its perpetuation: the definition of the community's contours cannot be achieved once and for all. It is through the process of a continual rejection of another that the community ensures its survival. The core of the text is constituted by a lengthy, pseudo-logical explanation as to why the group refuses to let the sixth join them.

> He doesn't do us any harm, but he annoys us, and that is harm enough; why does he intrude where he is not wanted? We don't know him and don't want him to join us. There was a time, of course, when the five of us did not know one another, either; and it could be said that we still don't know one another, but what is possible and can be tolerated by the five of us is not possible and cannot be tolerated with this sixth one. In any case, we are five and don't want to be six. (KCS, 436)

What starts out as an apologetic account of the group's existence and mode of action imperceptibly turns into a warning about the manipulation that can be involved in creating and maintaining a community. As the text proceeds, it unmasks this community's fundamental self-lie. It becomes obvious that a common origin is insufficient to hold the community together. In the absence of any internal bond, the only means for insuring the cohesion of the group is its violent practice of exclusion. Kafka undermines the arguments the speaker brings forward in defense of the community's practice through several subtle, essentially linguistic strategies: he blurs passive and active modes so that the group's perception of the outsider as a disturbance is turned into his performance of a disturbing action. (This can be perceived more clearly in the original: "Er tut uns nichts aber er ist uns lästig, das ist genug getan" [2002b, 313].) Furthermore, the speaker's explanation of the group's rejection of the sixth seems to be built according to a perfect logical causality, but a closer look reveals its entirely tautological nature: "we reject him because we don't know him [. . .] we don't know each other either but what's possible for us is not possible for him [. . .] In any case, we are five and don't want to be six" (my translation). Finally, his defense of the group's legitimacy has no other foundation but the conservation of the status quo: "It is also pointless for the five of us, but here we are together and remain together." In these images, little is left of Kafka's admiration or envy of communal life. Instead, they show its darkest side: when the credibility of actual common concerns fails and the sheer drive to herd together takes over, the community lives through the existence of the pariah.

That the rejection of the sixth one is nothing but a means of holding the group together is confirmed in a further pseudo-argument by the speaker, in which he refers to an obscure common past to justify the group's behavior: "A new combination we don't want, just because of our experiences" (KCS, 436). The appeal to previous experiences remains entirely elliptical: the only experience we know of on the basis of the text is precisely the process of exclusion itself. Deviously, the speaker preempts alternatives. He incorporates the refusal of any dialogue with the sixth one into the final argument. Like all the others, it tautologically turns back on itself: "Long explanations would amount to accepting him in our circle, so we prefer not to explain and not to accept him" (KCS, 436).

And then, the last line: "But however much we push him away, back he comes" (KCS, 436). These last words of the text can be read in different ways: one can, like Binder, believe that they suggest a "triumph of justice" in the face of the discriminatory behavior of the five, or at least the continual presence of a fortunate hindrance to the final fulfillment of the group's goals, the riddance of the other. But one can also leave the speaker's misleading point of view behind and take the perspective of the one who is excluded: why, after all, does he persist in his efforts? Read from this perspective, one can then sense in those last words the outsider's desperate knocking at the door and his hopeless hope to be admitted. In view of the borderland in which Kafka set up his tents, those last words leave both perspectives open. They show in one glance the senselessness and terror inherent in the constitution of such a community as well as the equally senseless longing to be part of it. Above all, this ending joins the views of those inside and those outside of the circle, revealing the inextricable entanglement of their concerns and the mutual interdependency of their existences. Binder concludes, "So they are, in the end, neither five nor six" (1979b, 365). Indeed, in those last words, the "we" the text started out with no longer refers to a defining number but to a situation of uneven yet indispensable togetherness.

An Other "We"

"I have seldom, very seldom crossed this borderland between loneliness and community," Kafka writes in his diary; "I have even been settled there longer than in loneliness itself" (D, 396; translation modified). Being "lonely like Franz Kafka" is not to be equated with isolation and seclusion. His borderland makes room for various perspectives, ranging from the phantasms of a sentimental participation in the Big Jewish Family to a cold assessment of the mechanisms of exclusion on which the cohesion of a community depends. More intensely even than in solitude, Kafka lived in the difficult situation of one who recognizes the temptations and terrors of saying "we." Yearnings to belong to a greater entity are kindled by a promise of relief from the torments of being torn, of being nobody and nowhere. Kafka's writing recognizes this promise but unmasks it as an illusion. True, there is no ground beneath one's feet in the borderland that Kafka experienced in all its torments, but beyond the borders, where the movement between attraction and flight comes to a halt, these contradictory forces coalesce and close themselves into a trap. This seems to leave no alternatives open. Yet, Kafka's writing occasionally sets out a counterpoint to this bleakness. Undoing claims of entity and wholeness and pointing at the interdependency of what is dissimilar, even antagonistic, Kafka's work opens up perspectives on alternative and unexpected ties across frontiers. Making the strange familiar, it creates links between foreign grounds and widens the horizon of possibilities; making the familiar strange, it dissolves unquestioned bonds and self-righteous certitudes. At the crossing of these movements, there is a different "we" and an other community, one in which impermeable walls turn into porous partitions that connect as they divide.

Shooting at the Audience:
Kafka's Speech on the Yiddish Language

In the first words of his diary entry cited in the introduction of this book, "What do I have in common with Jews? I have hardly anything in common with myself" (D, 252), Kafka combines his sense of himself as a Jew with a description of his fractured sense of self, and beyond that, with a skeptical questioning of unity and wholeness altogether. Given this attitude, how should one understand Kafka's repeatedly expressed enthusiasm for just those manifestations of Jewishness that are most likely to be associated with a pre-modern community and a commitment to traditional modes of togetherness—the Yiddish theater, Yiddish writing, the Yiddish language? And what does it mean when, in this context, Kafka says "we"? Explanations that see little more than a compensation for his own state of mind are inadequate and miss the much more complex role Kafka assigns to Yiddish.

In a letter to Milena, Kafka describes himself as "the most Western Jewish of all Western Jews"—for Kafka the quintessence of the modern individual—and declares that as a consequence he has "not been granted a single quiet second" (1983, 294). This assertion is in conspicuous contrast to a statement made on a different occasion, in which Kafka describes the way of life of Western Jews—a group among whom he evidently reckons himself—in the following terms: "*Our* western European circumstances are, if *we* consider them with a cautious fleeting glance, ordered in this way; everything takes its quiet course. *We* live in a virtually joyful harmony. . . ."[1] Kafka is here speaking of "western European circumstances," but given the context of these words—an address in the Jewish Community House in Prague—it is undoubtedly the "Western Jewish" circumstances in particular that he has in mind. In the contradiction between the letter's description of his own self-alienation and restlessness on the one hand and the ordered, "quiet course" and "joyful harmony" of this "we" on the other, one can recognize the ambivalences of Kafka's "borderland between loneliness and community" (D, 396; translation slightly modified). Kafka's description of the "western European circumstances" is taken from what came to be known as his "Rede über die jiddische Sprache" ("Speech on the Yiddish Language"), a text in which this borderland comes alive and conveys a compelling example of Kafka's "we."

Kafka's "Speech on the Yiddish Language" (2002a, 188–93) is his introduction to a recital of Yiddish poems by his friend Yitzchak Löwy, leading actor of the Yiddish theater group, on 18 February 1912 in Prague:

> Before the first verses by the Eastern Jewish poets I would first like to say to you, ladies and gentlemen, that you understand much more Yiddish than you think. Not that I fear for the impression that will be made on each one of you this evening, but I want this effect to be set free when it deserves to be. This cannot happen, however, as long as some among you are so afraid of Yiddish, that one can almost see it written on your faces. And I'm not even talking about those who look down on Yiddish. But fear of Yiddish, fear with a certain amount of distaste at bottom, is comprehensible after all.
>
> Our western European circumstances are, if we consider them with a cautious fleeting glance, ordered in this way; everything takes its quiet course. We live in a virtually joyful harmony, understand one another when it is necessary, get by without one another when it suits us, and understand one another even then. Who, from within such an order of things, could understand the confused jargon of Yiddish or who would even wish to do so?
>
> Yiddish is the youngest European language, only four hundred years old and actually much younger even than that. It has not yet developed linguistic forms of the clarity we require. Its expression is short and quick. It has no grammar books. Admirers try to write such grammar books, but Yiddish goes on being spoken; it doesn't come to rest. The people don't leave it to the grammarians. It consists only of foreign words. These, however, are not at rest in it, but retain the urgency and liveliness with which they were taken in. Migrations pass through Yiddish from one end to the other. Within Yiddish all this German, Hebrew, French, English, Slav, Dutch, Romanian, and even Latin is marked by curiosity and frivolity, and it takes some strength to hold the languages together in this state. Which is why no reasonable person would think of turning Yiddish into a world language, however justified that might appear to be. Only the cant of thieves borrows from it gladly, because it needs coherence less than individual words. Also, because Yiddish was for so long a despised language.
>
> But then again fragments of familiar linguistic rules prevail in this bustle of language. For example, in its beginnings Yiddish derives from the period when Middle High German was changing into New High German. There were forms which were not fixed: Middle High German took one form, Yiddish the other. Or Yiddish developed Middle High German forms more consistently than New

High German itself; for example the Yiddish *mir seien* develops more naturally out of the Middle High German *sin* than does the New High German *wir sind* (we are). Or Yiddish kept the Middle High German forms in spite of the New High German. Once something had arrived in the ghetto, it didn't manage to get away so quickly. So forms like *Kerzlach' Blümlach, Liedlach* remained.

And now the dialects of Yiddish pour into this linguistic construction of chance and laws. Indeed, the whole of Yiddish consists only of dialect, even the written language, although agreement has largely been reached on spelling. With all this, ladies and gentlemen, I think I will have convinced you for the moment, that you will not understand a word of Yiddish.

Don't expect any help from the explanations of the poems. If you're not even capable of understanding Yiddish, no on the spot explanation will help you. You will at best understand the explanation and realize that something difficult is coming. That will be all. I can for example tell you:

Herr Löwy will now, as indeed he will, recite three poems. First "Die Grine" by Rosenfeld. *Grine,* those are the greenhorns, the newly arrived immigrants in America. In this poem a small group of such Jewish immigrants walk down a street in New York with their dirty baggage. Of course a crowd gathers, stares at them, follows them, and laughs. The poet, angered at the sight, takes these street scenes as an occasion to address Jews and humanity. One has the impression of the group of immigrants pausing as the poet speaks, although they are far away and cannot hear him. The second poem is by Frug and is called "Sand and Stars." It is a bitter interpretation of a biblical promise which says we shall be like the sand by the shore and the stars in the sky. Now, we are already trodden underfoot like the sand; when will the words about the stars come true? The third poem is by Frischmann and is called "The Night is Still." At night a pair of lovers meets a pious scholar going to the prayer house. They are alarmed, are afraid of being betrayed; later they reassure one another.

Now, as you see, nothing has been achieved by these explanations. Sewn up inside these explanations, you will in the course of the reading look for what you already know, and what is really there, you will not see. Fortunately everyone who knows the German language is also capable of understanding Yiddish. Because seen from a great distance the surface comprehensibility of Yiddish is constituted by German; that is an advantage over all other languages. It is only just, therefore, that it also has a disadvantage compared to them all. Namely, Yiddish cannot be translated into German. The links between Yiddish and German are so delicate and significant that they must tear when Yiddish is brought back to German, which means that it is not Yiddish that is brought back, but something insubstantial. Through translation into the French language, for example, Yiddish can be communicated to the French; through translation into German it is destroyed. *Toit* for example is simply not *tot* (dead) and *Blüt* is by no means *Blut* (blood).

But it is not only from this distance of the German language, that you, ladies and gentlemen, can understand Yiddish; you may come a step closer. It is not so long ago that the familiar everyday language of German Jews, depending on whether they lived in town or country, rather more in the East than the West, appeared as a more or less remote initial stage of Yiddish, and many shades of it have remained. Hence the historical development of Yiddish could just as well have been followed on the surface of the present as in the depths of history.

You come very close to Yiddish nevertheless, when you consider that within you, apart from knowledge, there are also forces at work and points of contact with forces which enable you to understand Yiddish empathetically. Only here can the commentator's explanations help, reassuring you, so that you no longer feel excluded and also realize that you should no longer complain about not understanding Yiddish. That is the most important thing, since with each complaint, understanding recedes. But sit still, and then you are suddenly in the midst of Yiddish. But once Yiddish has taken hold of you—and Yiddish is everything, word, Hassidic melody, and the very being of this Eastern Jewish actor himself—then you will no longer recognize your earlier tranquility. Then you will feel the true unity of Yiddish so powerfully that you will be afraid, though no longer of Yiddish, but of yourself. You would not be able to bear this fear alone, if from this language you did not at the same time draw a self-confidence which withstands the fear and is even stronger than it. Enjoy it, as much as you can! Then when it fades away, tomorrow and later—and how could it remain attached to the memory of a single evening of a reading!—then I wish that you will also have forgotten your fear. Because we did not want to punish you.

(Translated by Martin Chalmers for this book)

Kafka's "Speech on the Yiddish Language" has repeatedly been interpreted either as a sign of his nostalgic feelings of Jewish belonging (Beck 1971; Isenberg 1999, 1–19)[2] and a provocative strategy to bring the Jewish public of Prague to "abandon the individualism that arose with assimilation" (Baioni 1994, 52), or as an enlightened Jew's own derogatory and at best folkloric view of Yiddish language and culture (Robin 1989, 52).[3] However, the virtuoso rhetoric of the speech reveals, instead, an attempt to unsettle those Western Jews he addresses in his talk: to make them aware of the illusory nature of the "quiet" and "harmony" of their existence, to reveal to them the emptiness and triviality of their conformist "western European" existence, and to convey to them his own restlessness and uncertainty. Yiddish, in Kafka's talk, is not simply a matter of nostalgia for the supposedly greater authenticity of the Eastern Jewish theater group but rather a means of perturbing his assimilated Jewish environment. Kafka uses his commentary on Yiddish as an instrument of disturbance, with which he would like to shake up the Jewish establishment surrounding him. Read in this light, his "Speech on the Yiddish Language" is not to be considered an exceptional affirmation of a strong Jewish identity,[4] unrelated to the rest of his work, but a literary text driven by the same fundamental thrust we find in many of his writings.

Marthe Robert's remark that Kafka rarely says "we" and that "when he does so, it is rarely without ambiguity" (1979, 74) is taken from her comments on Kafka's diary entry of 5 October 1911 in which he recalls, "Some songs, the expression 'Yiddische Kinderlach', some of this woman's acting (who, on the stage, because she is a Jew, draws us listeners to her because we are Jews, without any longing for or curiosity about Christians) made my cheeks tremble" (D, 65). To Robert these words and the use of the first-person plural evoke Kafka's experience of a real community in the presence of the Jewish theater group and of his "deeply felt response to the maternal call of the actress" (1979, 74). At this moment, writes Robert, Kafka takes his place "parmi les *jüdische Kinderlach* de la grande famille qu'il a desertée" (1979, 74) (among the Jewish children of the big family he has deserted).

Undoubtedly this diary passage captures one of those exceptional moments in which Kafka shared in a feeling of community based on purely internal bonds. In the recollection of his trembling cheeks, the quotation conveys the entirely emotional, if not sentimental, and at any rate uncontrollable effect the encounter with Judaism and Yiddish had on him that evening. If, however, one compares this experience with the complexity of Kafka's "Speech on the Yiddish Language," written a few months later, it becomes clear that this moment can hardly be translated into a dominant idea or an ideal. About Kafka's introduction to Yitzchak Löwy's recital of Yiddish poems, Robert writes: "If this speech were not the admirable text we know it to be, it would still be of inestimable value because of the harmony which it establishes, not only between Kafka and himself, between himself and the Jews, between Western Jews and Yiddish, but also between himself and the German language." But is "harmony," *accord,* really what the text is about? The rhetoric of the text speaks a different language. The encounter Kafka stages in his speech between all the instances mentioned by Robert can more readily be described as a confrontation. Its rhetoric lays bare and widens the divisions running through and between these entities, so that even the internal wholeness of each one of them is challenged. The text does indeed mention "die wahre Einheit des Jargon," "the true unity of Yiddish," but Kafka's description of Yiddish, the function he ascribes to it, and the way he addresses his audience are evidence less of an inclusive embrace than a provocative assault on the complacency and composure of the public attending the reading, essentially composed of the German-speaking, assimilated Jewish establishment of Prague.

Shortly before his talk, Kafka writes in his diary that he "will give a good talk, this is certain," and that, on the evening itself, it "will come straight out of me as though out of a gun barrel" (D, 180). A few days after the recital he remembers not only the "proud, unearthly feeling" he had during his speech, but also his "coolness in the presence of the audience" (D, 181). Kafka expects there to be a deep unease among his listeners that evening and confronts them with their repression of their own status as parvenus. To them Yiddish embodies an earlier, more primitive stage of "civilization" which they themselves have left behind, regard with contempt, and would like to make contact with only from a great distance. Indeed, after a treacherously gentle beginning, in which Kafka reassures his listeners that they will understand much more Yiddish than they think, and in which he pretends to have complete understanding for their fear of the "Jargon," he holds up a mirror to their sterile and empty lives: "Everything takes its quiet course. We live in a virtually joyful harmony, understand one another when it is necessary, get by without one another when it suits us, and understand one another even then." Significantly, Kafka switches here from the first-person singular, which he used at the beginning of his speech, to the plural "we." What Kafka expects from the encounter between the public—among whom he counts himself—and Yiddish is a disruption of the false "joyful harmony" in which relationships between people are based entirely on necessity, self-interest, and mutual indifference.

In his introduction to the recital evening Kafka is evidently not merely interested in convincing his audience of the value of Yiddish. The complex construction of the speech shows that it is itself conceived as an invitation to an experience designed to produce a true self-awareness in the listeners, if not a transformation of their basic outlook and way of life.

Some of the characteristic features of Yiddish that Kafka chooses to emphasize here seem almost calculated to displease his largely bourgeois audience. At first, surely with provocative intent, Kafka associates Yiddish with youthful frivolity, with restlessness and lack of clarity, with a disregard for order and laws, with strangeness, with wandering and social marginalization. Immediately after, however, he does take care to stress that Yiddish is subject to grammatical rules; in fact, he quickly makes Yiddish altogether respectable by showing that it, like modern German, derives from Middle High German and is even more consistent and "conservative" than modern German, the language held in such high regard by Prague's educated Jewish middle class. But at that point, by going on to describe Yiddish as a mixture of "chance and laws," he further underlines its subversive anarchy, since his formulation suggests that in Yiddish regularity can no longer be distinguished from the unpredictable. When he then states that the cant of thieves draws on Yiddish, that Yiddish consists solely of words from foreign languages and that it has retained the nomadic spirit of its past, Kafka seems deliberately to be making it difficult for his audience to feel comfortable with this language. Within Yiddish, Kafka continues, all national languages from which it borrows are seized by such a powerful centrifugal force that a great countervailing force is required in order to hold them all together. In emphasizing this dangerous explosive power Kafka is again clearly not trying to make Yiddish palatable to his listeners as a kind of harmless folkloric tradition. He presents it instead as dynamic, heterogeneous, and mobile, threatening to disrupt the order in which the members of his audience have established themselves. For all its linguistic rules, in the end, the Yiddish of Kafka's description remains this "confused jargon" and a powerful challenge to the way of life of the Western Jewish audience. Even the way in which Kafka then describes the relation of Yiddish to the respected German language is anything but "harmonious." He suggests that Yiddish cannot be translated into German, although it is possible to translate it into French or other languages. It is also no accident, rather an allusion to the Germanic aesthetics of heroism admired by many assimilated Jews, that he chooses the words *Blut* (blood) and *Tod* (death) to demonstrate this impossibility. The umlauts in the Yiddish *Blüt* and *Toit* inevitably "twist" and soften the pathos-filled sound these words have in German.

Kafka's warning that introductory explanations of the poems to be read by Löwy can hardly contribute to their understanding is intended to have a similar undermining effect. That this poetry and its language are ultimately not at the disposal of pure reason and should be received by drawing on all the emotions available to a person represents a further challenge to these listeners with their bias to intellect and reason. Consequently, Kafka's elucidations of the poems to be recited by Löwy also remain brief and dry, seemingly adapting to the expectations of his audience. His intention of creating disquiet in his listeners can nevertheless be discerned even in the choice of poems he presents and the aspects he picks out and recounts: neither the story of the derided, dirty immigrants of "Die Grine" by Rosenfeld, nor Frug's lament about the continuing diaspora existence, nor the pair of evidently secret lovers, surprised by the Talmud scholar close to a synagogue in the poem by Frischmann, correspond to the values of the established Jewish bourgeoisie whom Kafka is addressing.

In the middle of the speech the provocative description of Yiddish and of the poems climaxes in a triumphant sentence that stands in complete contrast to the initial reassuring statement. Kafka says he hopes that "I have convinced you for the moment, ladies and gentlemen, that you will not understand a word of Yiddish." Only after Kafka has made something strange and uncanny of Yiddish, something that cannot easily be integrated into the ordered existence of his addressees, does he gradually lead them closer to Yiddish again. Step by step the method by which he literally lures his listener into a trap becomes evident: "Seen from a great distance . . . ; not only from this distance . . . you may come a step closer . . . you come very close. . . . But sit still, and then you are suddenly in the midst of Yiddish. But once Yiddish has taken hold of you . . . then you will no longer recognize your earlier tranquility." Kafka clearly wants to sensitize his assimilated audience to the power of Yiddish. Yet the ultimate aim of his speech, which in his diaries he so proudly describes as something that gave him a feeling of strength that he never felt before, lay not so much in convincing his audience of an idea or an ideology but in shaking up the "quiet course" of things in which it has established itself. The culmination of the introduction is indeed likely to have echoed in his listeners' minds longer than mere praise of Yiddish would have done. Kafka predicted this at the end of his speech. With great subtlety bordering almost on cynicism, Kafka discharges his audience and leaves it to experience the Yiddish recital: "But once Yiddish has taken hold of you—and Yiddish is everything, word, Hassidic melody, and the very being of this Eastern Jewish actor himself—then you will no longer recognize your earlier tranquility. Then you will feel the true unity of Yiddish so powerfully that you will be afraid, though no longer of Yiddish, but of yourself." In a *tour de force* Kafka is preparing his readers for an experience that will no longer appear strange and distant but will convey to them the frightening sense of having "barely anything in common with themselves" (D, 252). It will estrange them from themselves and thereby from their own illusory equanimity and self-satisfaction. The accompanying fear would be unbearable, Kafka continues, if it did not also imply a new self-confidence, a state that would put an end to the secret feelings of inferiority of their parvenu existence, and also to their delusion of the supposedly calm order of things. Kafka at least professes to wish for his audience that these two effects of the Yiddish recital evening will resonate together. Because otherwise it could be that Kafka has only put fear into them. Can we believe Kafka at the end when he again reassures his audience with the words, "We didn't want to punish you"?

If one looks at the speech as a whole, then, it is hardly possible to speak, as Marthe Robert does, of a harmonious reconciliation between Western Jews and Yiddish or between Yiddish and German. And what about that other *accord* Robert mentions, the one between Kafka and himself? In the last sentence of the text Kafka unexpectedly uses the first-person plural again: "Denn strafen wollten *wir* Sie nicht"—"Because *we* didn't want to punish you." Here Kafka places himself in the camp of the Jewish actor, identifying with him: the last words of the address suggest that his introduction, together with Löwy's performance, is indeed intended to leave a powerfully unsettling memory in the minds and lives of the listeners. A few paragraphs earlier, however, did Kafka not say "we" when he talked about the way in which modern individuals live side by side in indifference and isolation? The intersection of these two contradictory "we's" describes not only his uneasy borderland of opposing longings and fears, but also the hope for another kind of community which Kafka's speech suggests to his audience. This hope is directed at the possibility underlying his relentless conveying of the fathomless precariousness of human existence, that this condition is not to be covered up by easy certainties and an established mode of life, but can be made bearable in the attempt to share it with others.

An Alliance of Foes: Kafka and the Feminine

> There is the possibility that you could go on
> living in this fashion, only guard such a way of life
> against women. Guard it against women, but in the
> "in-this-fashion" they are lurking already.
>
> —D, 406

A man who wishes to ensure his peace and quiet, his stability and self-sufficiency, is confronted by a troubling creature. He tries to ward it off, but it eludes his control. The man fights the disturbing figure with all the means at his disposal and denies to the very end that the latter has any effect on him. The intensity of his resistance, however, testifies to the opposite and is accompanied by a profound feeling of insecurity that takes on a life of its own and can no longer be reversed. His obsession with the menacing figure and his means of defense come to dominate him and destabilize him to the point where he starts resembling the unsettling creature. In this process it becomes evident that the initial solidity of the man was never anything more than pretense. The man, who nevertheless pursues his efforts to stay in control, is drawn into an ongoing struggle. The revelation that the disquiet generated by the troubling creature is inherent in the man's own being suggests the end of his poised mastery, and points to its always illusory nature. However, this disclosure also initiates the possibility of the man's salvation and uncovers the redemptive features of the ongoing struggle itself: the deferral of the end, the forestalling of the literal settling of differences, the postponement of the ultimate amalgamation of the two antagonistic forces into a closed unity. This struggle takes place within Kafka's "borderland between solitude and community"

(D, 396, translation slightly modified) and wards off both his isolation on the one hand and a threatening collective entity on the other. In their continuous battle the adversaries indeed prove to be allies in the face of such a third party: a powerful, self-identical, and undifferentiated collectivity. In contrast to this totalizing and homogeneous unity, the hostile alliance of the battling opponents—the man and the troubling creature—is simultaneously the origin of the man's salvation: it prevents closure and permits the persistence of a state of life-sustaining suspense.

This figure runs through Kafka's work in numerous variations and with a variety of emphases, from his early "Description of a Struggle" to his final aphorisms, sketches, and diary entries. In "The Worry of the Father of the Family," Odradek, a mobile, toy-like spool, shakes the confidence of the paterfamilias, who tries in vain to remain master in his own house. As he loses his grip, he gains an illuminating insight into his finitude. In "The Top," the philosopher, observing the children's toy, finds himself unable to grip the object, that is, to grasp its essence. He himself loses control and turns into a spinning top but, it is suggested, thereby regains life. In "The Burrow," the undecided struggle against a troubling intruder becomes the ubiquitous principle that creates the burrow in the first place. The bouncing balls tormenting the elderly bachelor Blumfeld, the old mole-like animal of "In Our Synagogue," are triggers of disturbances disrupting all that is solid, resisting all efforts to dismiss them, but ultimately opening up self-enclosed spaces. As we demonstrated earlier, traces of this figure can be found even in non-literary texts such as the "Speech on the Yiddish Language." Confronted by Yiddish, the assimilated Western Jewish audience, living in apparent self-confidence, calm, and harmony, experiences an unsettling but transformative destabilization, which, it is suggested, ought to stay with them forever. In his final diary entry Kafka describes the dynamic of his own writing in a similar way:

> More and more fearful as I write. It is understandable. Every word, twisted in the hands of the spirits—this twist of the hand is their characteristic gesture—becomes a spear turned against the speaker. Most especially a remark like this. And so *ad infinitum*. The only consolation would be: It happens whether you like it or not. And what you like is of infinitesimally little help. More than consolation is: You too have weapons. (D, 423)

The increasing insecurity of writing is caused by the antagonistic challenge of "spirit hands" (*Geisterhände*), which inhabit the words of the writer and turn against him. The attempt to "grasp" the resulting fear, to conceptualize it and get a grip on it, itself directly activates the dynamic of the struggle. This is particularly true of "a remark like this," a writing that tries to capture—evidently in vain—the elusive process of writing described in this very passage. Revealed in this cryptic logic is the endlessness of the writing process itself. The consolation—"it happens whether you like it or not"—derives from this lack of control itself: in the limits of his own power, which bring about a surrender of will, the writer is relieved of the strain of his mastery. Yet this gesture of laying down his arms is superseded by one more twist: "More than consolation is: You too have weapons." With these words the writer accepts the conditions given to him by the spirit hands and engages in the struggle. United in their discord they—the I and the antagonistic spirit hands—write in opposition to the true enemy, who would put an end to their "saving" struggle. This struggle achieves a deferment of the finality that would bring writing to an end, which, for Kafka, would be synonymous with death.

The action of the spirit hands takes the form of a "twist," a "movement." Common to all unsettling beings in Kafka's writings—Odradek, the top, the balls, and the rest—is a constitutive mobility. It makes these beings uncontrollable, but also guarantees the dynamic of the confrontation and prevents the final determination of the antagonism in terms of rigid antitheses. It is also this mobility that is transmitted to the narrator or protagonist, who originally imagines himself to be static and stable. At times, the creature's impact expresses itself in terms of the man's direct self-observations of his own increasing restlessness; usually, however, he is unaware of it and its only manifestation occurs in the man's mode of expression. The infiltration of the opponent's restlessness into the speech or the behavior of the narrator or protagonist corresponds to the action of the spirit hands in Kafka's description of his own writing as a saving struggle with a menacing opponent—saving because it is undecided and ongoing, and thereby postpones the end.

For all the similarities, this figure takes many guises, depending on the source of the disturbance. In the confrontation with disturbing objects, the transfer of the unrest is less complex than when the source of the destabilization is personified. This is especially true whenever the threatening being assumes a female form and introduces the pre-existing and overdetermined social, psychological, and symbolic discourses of femininity into the confrontation between the antagonistic players.

Kafka's texts situate the feminine between the conventional poles of everyday normality and an uncanny sublime. Women invariably seduce, dazzle, disturb the hero with their call, which either is rooted in ordinary life or emerges from a mythical primeval world. Bound to the quotidian, women stand for conformity and stability; arising from a mythical source, they embody a menacing, creaturely form of being that represents a deadly danger for the rational subject. Kafka's female figures are frequently found at the intersection of these two spheres or in the area of transition between them. In both cases they represent a radical challenge to the male protagonist. Kafka's ideas of femininity often echo the polarities of stereotypical discourses, but the idiosyncrasy of his writing performs a transformation of traditional ascriptions. The most complex mode of this transformation occurs as a metaphoric transfer of the feminine to the process of writing itself.

In a letter dated 24 November 1912 Kafka implores his fiancée Felice to stop writing to him at night: "Nightshifts are the privilege of men everywhere in the world, even in China" (1982, 118).[1] The quotation points to Kafka's description of his own writing process. Parthenogenesis, the birth of the author out of his own work, takes place in the course of writing at night, as described by Kafka in his diary entries on the genesis of "The Judgment": the story, which he wrote at one sitting during the night of 22–23 September 1912, from ten o'clock at night to six o'clock in the morning, has "come out of me like a real birth, covered with filth and slime" (D, 214). In invoking a cultural tradition implemented "everywhere in the world" in order to discourage Felice from writing at night, he excludes real women from this process while the motif of the birth of the work transfers femininity to the male creator of the text and its emergence. A similar "feminization" of writing and of his visions takes place in the story "A Little Woman" (1992, 202–209).[2]

Kafka's late story "A Little Woman" has not, so far, attracted much attention, and if noticed at all it has usually been interpreted as a case study of neurosis or paranoia (Lange-Kirchheim 1986, 180–93; Nicolai 1996, 89–115; Kaus 2002). Assuming a "healthy psyche" as a goal, these interpretations at best—that is, when they do not entirely confuse the author with the narrator—allow that Kafka has clear-sightedly described a pathology—persecution mania, repression of drives, inability to form relationships—from which the author supposedly wanted to distance himself through his writing. Such interpretations seem obvious in many respects. They do not, however, do justice to the complexity of the story, because they proceed from an expectation of normality and from this standpoint pronounce an implicit judgment on the protagonist which the story itself both encompasses and undermines. As in numerous other works by Kafka, normality, conformity, and a healthy psyche are personified as static figures challenged in their self-confident authority through confrontation with a destabilizing antagonist. As in other texts, there occurs a separation between an "absolute" enemy from which these expectations of stability emanate, and a being, generated in the text, against which the male protagonist battles. In "A Little Woman," as in other instances, the struggle with this creature is simultaneously a disturbance and a salvation, and here too, the antagonistic dynamic of the struggle postpones an ultimate judgment, finality, and death. In this story the instance of disturbance is a little woman, also called "my little judge" (LW, 207), who is allied in some mysterious fashion with the "real" ruling instance of judgment called "world" or "public" (Öffentlichkeit), which with its "*great* powers" could condemn the narrator "for good and all" (LW, 204). It is precisely the man's antagonistic interaction with the little woman that stands in the way of this finality. In the face of the "great," self-subsistent instance— "public" or "world"—the man and the little woman prove to be allies. The "little woman" becomes both threat to his desire for mastery and source of a struggle that ultimately protects him from some final verdict and keeps him alive. In this "antagonistic alliance" between the speaking man and the "little woman" Kafka enacts a paradigmatic scene of the struggle generating his writing. In this story, too, the "little woman" pervades the discourse of the speaker. "In the heat of battle [. . .] getting completely out of hand" (LW, 205–206), her impact transgresses the boundaries of the narrator, who would like to ward off her effect on him, but the constant disquiet arising from their hostile alliance is a protection against a final decision that would bring his activities to a halt and end his discourse.

Almost nothing happens in the story. In a single obsessive monologue, uninterrupted by any external voice or view from outside, located neither in time nor space, a man describes his futile struggle against a little woman who incessantly and apparently without any reason takes out her anger on him, while he would desperately like to hold on to his way of life:

> This little woman is highly dissatisfied with me, she always finds something objectionable in me, I am always doing the wrong thing to her, I annoy her at every step; if a life could be cut into the smallest pieces and every scrap of it could be separately assessed, every scrap of my life would certainly be an offense to her. (LW, 202)

The man's monologue consists for the most part of contradictory self-justifications. It is not immediately clear which accusations these are meant to counter, since the origin of the vexation that fuels the woman's anger remains unknown to him—and to the reader. The monologue consists, then, of various attempts to neutralize the woman's rage: "I did once try to point out to her how one might put an end to this perpetual resentment of hers, but my very attempt wrought her to such a pitch of fury that I shall never repeat it" (LW, 203). Out of the rhetorical drive set in motion to this end, there emerges a catalogue of options to end this situation, but ultimately none seem possible or have the power to change anything. This impasse arises out of Kafka's game with falsely logical conclusions that call into question the bases of rationality and expose reason itself as a monumental justification machine running wild and getting nowhere: it is made of pseudo-analytical conclusions, unexplained contradictions, false naturalizations, unproven denials, untrustworthy protestations of innocence and accusations of guilt of the opposing party, dubious inversions, and tautological arguments, which give the impression of speaking the language of logic and nevertheless break all its rules. The man's monologue is a model example of Kafka's "immobile assaults" (D, 122)[3] (*stehender Sturmlauf*), this movement in writing that with sheer unbounded energy immediately takes back every statement just made only to take it up again with a barely perceptible shift, often to retract it yet again still in the same sentence. In a seemingly quiet moment in which he is "confident that she won't be able to convince anyone else" of his guilt, he muses:

> So perhaps I can feel quite reassured, can I? No, not at all; for if it becomes generally known that my behavior is making her positively ill, which some observers, those who most industriously bring me information about her, for instance, are not far from perceiving, or at least look as if they perceived it, and the world should put questions to me, why am I tormenting the poor little woman with my incorrigibility, and do I mean to drive her to death, and when am I going to show some sense and have enough decent human feelings to stop such goings-on—if the world were to ask me that, it would be difficult to find an answer. (LW, 204)

Imaginary questions by an inexistent interlocutor result in the impossibility of answers. Circular arguments pile up to such an extent that they become an end in themselves and the aim of the exercise gets out of sight. In the case of "A Little Woman," this aim itself leads into a circular argument: the point of the entire argumentation is "to stay quietly where I am" (LW, 206), to leave everything as it is and to protect the narrator's own mode of existence against any change whatsoever. However, apart from the mode of the monologue itself, nothing is known of this existence. Because of the practical absence of "reality-particles," of a temporal and spatial context, and because of the exclusively internal perspective of the narrator, the whole story depends on the way it represents the struggle in the narrator's monologue itself. The futile attempt of the man to gain control over the disturbing creature raging against him *is* the man's story and existence. It thus becomes evident that nothing else is at stake here but the never-ending justification for such a self-justifying monologue—and its writing itself.

In ever-new variations the narrator reports the dissatisfaction, the anger, the wrath, the suffering of the little woman, only to deny again and again their significance and importance, and above all their effect on him. This process takes place through two contrary developments: an explicit affirmation of a poised distance from the disturbance—"I am becoming calmer about the whole affair now that I think I can perceive how unlikely it is to come to any crisis" (LW, 207)—and an implicit, intensifying disquiet manifest in the course of the text itself—"The fact that I have, all the same, grown somewhat uneasy has nothing to do with the real significance of the affair" (LW, 208). This increasing unrest is given a female connotation, conveying the woman's "real" presence onto the narrator's mode of expression. If at the beginning the narrator still occasionally tries to see things from the woman's point of view and to consider the possibility of his guilt or responsibility for her anger, he gradually sets in motion a rhetoric excluding her perspective and his possible contribution to the situation. In the early paragraphs the narrator at first seems to accept the woman's perspective: "Now the little woman is highly dissatisfied with me, she always has some fault to find with me, I am always doing her an injustice, I annoy her at her every turn" (LW, 202). Step-by-step the perspective shifts and the man's denial of the impact made by the little woman becomes increasingly assertive. At first the narrator speculates on his possible guilt, his responsibility, the need to change. Admittedly from the start each of these thoughts leads into contrary protestations. Yet as the story goes on even these beginnings of an attempt to see the woman's anger from her point of view disappear, and with them the perspective of the woman altogether. The self-justifications appear to have their effect and the narrator starts believing his own account of the situation. In the final paragraphs his only interest is in the state, or rather, the pacification of his own unease. The more he wants to convince himself of his control of the situation, of his "calm" in the face of the little woman, the more evident his own destabilization becomes; and the more he denies the effect of the furious woman on him, the more his form of expression corresponds to her agitated behavior. While the "real" woman is "excluded" in this way, she, or at least her manner of being and expression, finds a way into the narrator's discourse. His attempts at rationalization, like the raging woman herself, "get out of hand" at the same time as he distances himself ever more frequently from what he calls "the matter." With no true meeting between the man and the woman taking place, there also occurs here, in defiance of all the man's retractions, a gradual adoption, in the process of writing, of the attributes of the disruptive figure by the speaker—not least those associated with her femininity.

In the course of the man's considerations as to whether the situation has developed and changed over time, he makes his opinion of the gender difference explicit: "And on closer reflection it does appear to be quite generally the case that those changes which the state of affairs seems to have undergone in the course of time are not changes in the matter itself, but merely developments in my attitude towards it, in so far as this attitude has been growing, on the one hand, calmer, *more manly* [*männlicher*], while on the other, as I have to admit, a certain agitation has been creeping into it, under the influence of the constant shocks, petty though they may be" (LW, 207, emphasis added). The views of the narrator correspond to stereotypical gender differences: male means "calm," firm, addressing the essentials without distraction, while restlessness, precisely that inner agitation, therefore, which increasingly takes hold of the man, has in this constellation an unequivocal female connotation. At this point, however, it becomes clear from the man's monologue that the woman's behavior—the so-called "matter"—remains unchanged, and only the opinions of the man are subject to the most violent and contradictory fluctuations. While in the opening lines a particular degree of mobility is ascribed to the woman, it is the man's monologue that "performs" this mobility and this to an increasing extent, even as he protests his calmness. Here Kafka, as so often, takes a concept at its word: in the text "mobility" is actualized in gestures of the body.[4] Gestures appear from the very beginning, and ever more emphatically as the story continues, as the little woman's most conspicuous mode of expression. In the first paragraph she is described by her bodily movements: "She likes to put her hands on her hips and abruptly turn the upper part of her body sideways with a suddenness that is surprising" (LW, 202). It is striking that the story also concludes with a gesture, but this time it is the narrator's own. These final lines enact the impact of the little woman on the monologue of the narrator and the transfer of the feminine onto the act of writing and the level of the text itself.

The anger of the little woman is boundless whenever she is confronted by the speaker: her almost mythical rage pervades everything and threatens to overwhelm all the means of defense at the man's disposal. This mythic dimension of the little woman is evident in the initial description of her appearance and her movements:

> The impression that her hand makes on me I can only convey by saying that I have never yet seen a hand which has the individual fingers so clearly marked off from one another as in her case; and yet her hand has by no means any anatomical peculiarities, it is a perfectly normal hand. (LW, 202)

Objectively "normal," she is nevertheless perceived by the narrator as an almost witch-like figure with claw-like hands, threatening to grab him and drag him away. She shares many attributes with the mythical women in Kafka's "The Silence of the Sirens," in addition to the claws: her form of expression is silence accompanied by a language of gestures. The yearning and entranced gestures of the silent Sirens are, although unconscious, their most powerful weapon. Similarly, the prevailing expression of the little woman is gestural. Her movements, which convey no symbolic meaning, are emphasized from the beginning: "She likes to put her hands on her hips and abruptly turn the upper part of her body sideways with a suddenness that is surprising" (LW, 202). In a key passage the narrator interprets the movements of the little woman in terms similar to those used for the Sirens, as a "compensation" for silence and as a weapon in the struggle against the rationalizing, controlling man: "So with her woman's cunning she tries a middle course; silently, only by the outward signs of a secret sorrow does she seek to bring this affair before the public court" (LW, 203). While the narrator himself becomes tangled up in the rationalization mechanisms of his words, the little woman counters these words in a different language, a creaturely language that belongs entirely neither to nature nor to culture—that is, neither controlled nor dictated from the outside—but represents the articulation of a primary state of being without meaning, a language that does not speak or argue but performs and reveals.

In the middle of the story the language of the narrator is contrasted with the gestures of the woman, and it is here that the word "we" appears in the text for the first and only time. After the narrator has described his characteristic habit of "whispering a gentle word of warning to anyone whose howls of rage got completely out of hand," he continues, "In this fashion, naturally, we shall never come to an understanding" (LW, 206). In this fashion: that is, with his words and her gestures an understanding between them is impossible. There immediately follows a description of the woman consisting of nothing but gestures:

> I shall go on stepping out of my house, perhaps in the joyful hours of early morning, only to meet that disgruntled face, disgruntled on my account, that morose curl of the lip, that searching look which knows in advance what it will find, which sweeps over me and misses nothing, however fleeting the glance may be, that bitter smile furrowing the girlish cheek, that plaintive raising of the eyes to heaven, that planting of the hands on the hips to gain support, and then that turning pale and trembling which accompanies the outburst of fury. (LW, 206)

Words do not help the man against this theatrical expressiveness. Consequently, in the next paragraph the narrator hurries to a friend, in order to *talk* over the matter with him, but the friend's advice is powerless, telling him nothing new—nothing gets through because the narrator has long been spellbound by his gesticulating, disturbing opponent. It is that remnant of "creaturely nature" that cannot be repressed by his rationalizations and that finally emerges in the nar rator's own monologue. In the penultimate paragraph he reveals that he has "all the same, grown a trifle uneasy" and that this unease expresses itself "as it were in a purely physical way" (LW, 208). The anger of the little woman has indeed constantly manifested itself in a purely physical way, and at the beginning her "symptoms" are also explicitly called "physical." In the preceding paragraph the narrator indulges in the idea that "any other man" would long ago have recognized this suffering little woman "as a leech, and noiselessly crushed [her] under his heel well out of public earshot" (LW, 208). However, though a physical gesture, this imaginary act of violence does not emulate the mode of expression of the gesticulating woman and is, significantly, still ascribed to "another man," an alter ego of the narrator. Not until the final sentence are the narrator's body and gestural language brought into the picture:

> So from whatever angle I consider it, it always becomes apparent—and from this I will not budge—that if only I keep this little matter just lightly concealed with my hand I shall remain free for a long time to go on living my life as hitherto, untroubled by the world, despite all the raging of this woman. (LW, 209)

The part of the body carrying out this gesture, the hand, is also the one that in the very first paragraph was emphasized in relation to the little woman; it is the hand with which the spirits, in Kafka's diary entry, turn against the writer with a characteristic "twist"; and it is ultimately the narrator's hand—and the writing hand of the author—to which this very story owes its existence.

The hands of the woman described at the beginning of the story, those hands whose fingers are so peculiarly marked off from one another, are distinguished from the hand of the narrator: his hand only "lightly" covers up "this little matter," in contrast to the violent crushing by the boots of the hypothetical "other man." The hand, in these last lines, like the story itself, only pretends to hide and repress the raging woman: she shines through the narrator's half-open fingers with all the evidence of Kafka's art.

The gesture of the hand described in these last lines turns out to be the condition for the continuation to live "as hitherto." The partial "concealment" of "this little matter" describes the process that takes place throughout the story: in the words "lightly concealed" and "little matter," the narrator evidently plays down—and thereby partly represses—a threat that can hardly be so light and small if it has the power to put an end to "living his life as hitherto." From this vantage point the whole story can be reread as the admission of the futility of the attempt to cover up the threat of the little woman, to minimize and master it. In the end, the ultimate goal of the narrator is revealed: the "untroubled" perpetuation of his previous way of life that consists of nothing else but the struggle with the little woman itself. The sole condition for this continuation, these last lines tell us, is the *concealment* of the matter, but—and here is the final twist—this occurs in precisely the gesture of the hand that also enacts the process of writing—which, in the end, is the act of *disclosing*—the "matter." This final circular, or rather, aporetic figure might suggest that the story as a whole, this "little parable of non-arrival" (Corngold 2004, 124), maintains a perfect machinery of self-preservation, in which, apart from the perpetuation of writing, nothing happens. Yet something does happen: the disclosure of the dynamic of the process of writing itself. In essence it is contained in the structure of the final sentence: "I shall remain free [. . .], untroubled by the world, and go on living my life as hitherto, despite all the raging of this woman" (LW, 209). In these last lines, "the world," the enemy that could emit the final verdict, the sentence that would end his struggle, is literally separated from "this woman" by the words indicating the man's hope to continue "as hitherto." The separation of "world" and "woman" into two very different adversaries takes place at the level of the sentence structure rather than in the content: the *meaning* of these last words merely suggests the hope to go on living as before, regardless of *both* world and woman. But such a reading disregards the linguistic form disconnecting these two instances: the separation is established in the phrase "to go on living my life as hitherto"—which is nothing other than the enactment of the "light concealment with my hand," that is, writing itself. This writing—and literally the structure of the sentence—effects the detachment of his "little" adversary from the all-powerful, hostile enemy. Finally, the man can continue in his ways if he remains protected from the world. The little woman, however, is another matter: despite her raging—that is, *against and only with her,* can he go on living. Like the spirit hands in Kafka's last diary entry, her raging makes possible the postponement of the final sentence, the endlessness of the struggle—and writing itself.

United in the struggle, the man and his little woman mark the threshold between the closed space of the self and the hostility of the public world. This threshold is the location of Kafka's writing. No doormen and no henchmen keep guard here, but raging, silent, gesticulating women. To the extent that they are part of the public world it is necessary to defend writing against them, to fight for it and protect it, because only by writing, only in this fashion can Kafka live. But "in the 'in-this-fashion' they are lurking already" (D, 406).

PART TWO

REVISITING
THE COMMON GROUND

A Vision out of Sight: Theodor Herzl's Late "Philosophical Tales"

At times, minutiae sprung from the poetic imagination can capture a shift in the needs and hopes of a nation better than sociological inquiries and political programs. One such instance is the well-known little scene drawn by the Israeli poet Yehuda Amichai (1967) in which a man—presumably the poet—is sitting on the steps near the gate at David's Citadel and puts down two heavy baskets beside him. A group of tourists stand around their guide, who points at the man: "You see the man over there with the baskets? A little to the right of his head there's an arch from the Roman period. A little to the right of his head." "But he's moving, he's moving!" the man says to himself, and concludes: "Redemption will come only when they are told, 'Do you see that arch over there from the Roman period? It doesn't matter, but near it, a little to the left and then down a bit, there's a man who has just bought fruit and vegetables for his family'." Amichai's inconspicuous little scene has become part of the Israeli literary canon and has been praised as an illustration of the poet's "unflagging zest for the tangible particulars of the ordinary world."[1] For some, however, the shift in emphasis encouraged in Amichai's lines goes well beyond the expression of an individual poetic sensibility and can be perceived as a sign of the dwindling belief in the grand ideals and the world historical force that once fueled the Zionist endeavor. For traditional Zionists, the insistence on the primacy of a basket of vegetables over a monument bearing witness to former triumphs, of the cares and concerns of everyday life over past heroic acts, might be seen as a threat to the pride and vigor of the nation. Yet, far from questioning the Zionist cause, Amichai's miniature can be read as a confirmation of the vitality of its aims and as a vision of its ultimate fulfillment.

Two details in Amichai's text support this view. The poet's call for a change of perspective occurs after the emphatic remark that the man is "moving, he's moving!" This exclamation points to the fact that the man cannot be used as a point of reference for the historical monument, as a mere means to get the arch into focus, because, unlike the static historical remnant, he is alive. His movements, the changing givens and circumstances of his life, necessarily alter his distance and relation to the arch. Amichai's image can be translated into a larger picture. It is precisely in a living society and for a nation on the move, one that undergoes continuous transformations, that the relevance and impact of the past are subjected to change and require constant revisions and reassessments. Furthermore, one would be mistaken if one were to read the man's final reflection as an invitation to give up greater perspectives and bow to the basic necessities of the day. Amichai's story does not call for a demise of visionary hopes but, on the contrary, evokes a *redemption,* the vision of an ideal state of being that is yet to come. Just as a Hassidic belief famously invoked by Walter Benjamin suggests that the coming of the messiah does not involve any violent change but only a slight readjustment of the world—"dass er nicht mit Gewalt die Welt verändern wolle, sondern nur um ein Geringes sie zurechtstellen werde" (2002b, 811)—so does Amichai intimate that salvation may not require more than a minute change in the focus of a sight.

The figure of Theodor Herzl has, in many ways, become a monument, an arch of triumph in its own right. In Israel, his portrait adorns the walls of official buildings and offices, he figures on stamps, coins, and telephone cards, and his grave is a site of pilgrimage for tourists and Zionists nostalgically longing for uplifting heroic ideals. His photograph behind the seat of the head of parliament keeps referring the politicians of today to the myth of Zionism's founding father. At the same time, and as befits a mythical figure, the concrete particulars of Herzl's life and work have receded into oblivion. In several passages in his writings Herzl himself refers to his project—if not to himself—as a statue or a bronze sculpture in which his living person will have left traces comparable to the fingerprints of an artist (1976, 106).[2] He envisioned that, as founding figure of the Jewish state to come and as a magnanimous benefactor of humanity at large, he would eventually become a legend and a revered icon of world history. He expresses this prophecy most succinctly in one of his diary entries from 16 June 1895, at the time when he started believing—or encouraged himself to believe—that his ambitious project could actually materialize: "Ich glaube, für mich hat das Leben aufgehört und die Weltgeschichte begonnen" (T, 116) (I think for me life has ended and world history has begun). In Herzl's diary this line stands alone, and in the absence of comments one is led to hear the solemn tone of this statement. But some of his more intimate diary reflections indicate that he was well aware of the dangers inherent in such self-aggrandizing mystification: "Mich vor Selbstüberschätzung,

Hochmuth und Narretei hüten, wenn's gelingt. Wenn's misslingt, hilft mir die Literatur" (T, 49) (To guard myself from overestimating myself, from arrogance and foolishness in case it succeeds. In case it does not, literature will help me). It is true that in his political and official writings Herzl does not mention the dangers of casting himself as a heroic persona. As still another diary entry shows, he omits this concern very consciously from the political sketches of his project: "Manches in diesen Aufzeichnungen wird lächerlich, übertrieben, verrückt erscheinen. Aber wenn ich, wie in meinen literarischen Arbeiten Selbstkritik geübt hätte, wären die Gedanken verkrüppelt geworden" (T, 84) (Some of these [political sketches] will seem ridiculous, exaggerated, mad. But it would have crippled my ideas if I had exerted self-criticism there as I did in my literary works). Herzl obviously believed that the ideational and rhetorical *élan* needed to carry out his grand visionary project would be hampered by open displays of self-doubt or hesitation. Literature, however, was another matter. The distinction he makes between his political and his literary writings points to one of the key functions Herzl assigns to his fictional prose. He repeatedly delegates to literature the role of consolation in case his grand project should fail or conceives of it as a wellspring of ideas untamed by pragmatic considerations. However, literature undoubtedly has, for Herzl, more than such a compensatory or inspirational function. Far from being merely a psychological "help," a comfort for his ego in case of failure and in the face of defeat, or a laboratory for his visionary imagination, it is a reservoir of doubts, hesitations, and afterthoughts. This is particularly true for his late self-reflections about his own ambition of becoming a heroic player on the stage of world history and of the ideal of public or heroic life in general.

The opposition between "Leben" and "Weltgeschichte," between life and world history, that Herzl so strikingly evokes in his diary entry of 16 June 1895 leaves no noteworthy traces in his political writings and is only rarely mentioned in his later diary entries. He obviously considered the implicit conflict or incompatibility between the two modes of existence and their respective domains, the private realm of ordinary life and the global public sphere, unfit for the legend he set out to become. It is to literature, more particularly to the philosophical tale, that Herzl turns to explore the implications of this conflict.

In 1900 Herzl published seventeen stories in a volume entitled *Philosophical Tales.* Between 1900 and 1902 he wrote four additional philosophical tales and included them as a closing chapter in his collection of minor writings, *Feuilletons* (1911), which he himself selected and ordered two years before his death. While most of the stories published in the earlier volume, like his novel *Old New Land,* can be read as literary enactments and affirmations of his political and diplomatic activities in those years, those last tales reconsider in often complex ways the terms of this commitment. Half a decade after the ominous diary entry announcing his departure from "life" and his grand entrance on the scene of world history, Herzl—certainly under the impact of the first signs of ageing and a sense that his "hopes for practical success have now disintegrated" (1985, 980)[3]—makes the contrast between *Leben* and *Weltgeschichte* the central topic of his philosophical tales.[4]

It is not surprising that Herzl turns to literature, and more particularly to the philosophical tale, to address this topic. On the very first page of his diary, in a passage where he wonders whether his ideas for the project of a Jewish state will become a "monument for humanity" or merely a source of delight and entertainment for himself, he concludes: "Und vielleicht zwischen diesen Möglichkeiten: für die Literatur" (T, 3) (And maybe between these possibilities: for literature). Literature, for Herzl, is situated between monumental, historical reality and purely personal musings and therefore lends itself particularly well to reflections about the relationship between these two realms. Gisela Brude-Firnau believes that Herzl turned to literature in order "to compensate for the multiplicity of reality through the medium of fiction."[5] Possibly, his "philosophical tales" point in the opposite direction: rather than being seen as attempts to overcome and master a reality that resists bending itself to his will, they can be shown to embrace the indomitable multifariousness of reality in ways that his other writings could not. His choice of the designation "philosophical tales" may have been inspired by Voltaire's "Contes Philosophiques," more particularly his most famous, *Candide,* which Herzl quotes in his diary. His four late philosophical tales, all written between 1900 and 1902, in the same period as *Old New Land,* can undoubtedly be read as mid-life reassessments of his own personal successes and failures, choices and errors. However, the medium he chooses for these reflections, and their curious mixture of allegorical tableau and realistic narrative, points beyond purely biographical or psychological concerns to insights that shed light on aspects of Herzl's thinking that have so far remained underexposed.

The tone, literary mode, and stylistic register of Herzl's four philosophical tales are far from unified. The first tale, "Epaphroditus," narrates a fictionalized episode of a factual moment in Roman history. The second, "Däumerle und Bäumerle oder die Zukunft" (Däumerle and Bäumerle or the Future), is a humorous allegorical tale with both satirical and moralizing undertones. The third, "Die linke Glocke" (The Left Bell), stands in the tradition of the home-comer's story and the popular genre of the *Lügengeschichte,* the liar's tale. The last, "Die Brille" (The Spectacles), is cast as a nostalgic letter written to a former classmate. In spite of these differences, these stories are linked by several common denominators: all four relate a decisive turn in the life of a middle-aged or ageing man and involve the perspective of one who looks back on former triumphs and defeats, on past decisions, dreams, and choices. The plots of all four tales hinge, to different degrees, on the narrative device of dramatic irony. The surprise caused by an unexpected and ironic turn in the story reenacts the turn taken by the respective protagonists and releases the philosophical insight promulgated in the story. However, unlike in parables or traditional fables, these insights are not merely nuggets of truth or arguments dressed up as stories. Their literary value derives from the nuances and the suggestiveness that convey Herzl's self-questioning of issues that remained for him unresolved.

As philosophical tales these stories invite the translation of specific figures and events into general insights while at the same time retaining the "reality effect" (Roland Barthes), the sense of contingency and ambiguity that prevents them from petrifying into mere prescriptive principles and precepts. This dual nature—both concept and narrative—inherent in the very notion of the philosophical tale perfectly suits the topic of these stories. They dramatize the tension, but also blur the line, between private life and public role, between heroism, might, and glory and the experience of life's compromises, contingencies, and contradictions.

Epaphroditus

The first of Herzl's philosophical tales, "Epaphroditus," imagines the last days of the mighty Roman dictator Sulla. Still at the height of his power, this shrewd and ruthless ruler unexpectedly resigns. Just as even his strongest rivals, Marius and Cinna, have given up hope of challenging his position, Sulla withdraws from his public functions, turns his back on politics, and travels southward to the seashore, where he indulges in the common joys of life, in food, wine, women, music, dance, and spectacle. He relishes the excitement of cities and the beauty of sunsets, rejoices in the fleeting and intense experiences of the senses and—as his self-chosen nickname Epaphroditus indicates—wholeheartedly devotes himself to the cult of the love goddess Aphrodite. He deems himself the happiest of mortals, considers himself protected from the wrath of his enemies, and mocks those who continue to strive for power and glory. One day, on the occasion of a gladiators' fight in the circus, a beautiful woman standing behind him puts her hand on his shoulder. Sulla turns around and is instantly infatuated by her. After demonstrating her superiority and coldness by lowering her thumb and thereby deciding on the death of the wounded gladiator, the woman runs off and disappears. Before leaving the arena to pursue this seductive stranger, Sulla turns to Pompeius and reaffirms that he is the happiest of men and only wants to discover one more thing: how to die a happy death. He also warns Pompeius about a group of former rivals who have invited him for dinner. Sulla predicts that these power-thirsty men will try to involve him in their evil plotting. Pompeius disregards Sulla's warning and is indeed caught up in a conspiracy against Sulla. The former dictator's rivals do not believe that he has really given up his power. Convinced that Sulla's retreat into privacy is merely a strategic move to mislead his enemies, they decide to kill him. Meanwhile, Sulla has joined the beautiful woman, who turns out to be Fannia, Caesar's mistress. It also turns out that her seduction of Sulla is a trap. The conspirators pressure Pompeius to join them and rush off to Fannia's bedroom to kill Sulla, but they come too late: the "Epaphroditus" has died minutes earlier in the arms of Caesar's beautiful mistress, finding the happy end he sought. "Now," concludes Pompeius in referring to Sulla's desire to know what a happy death is, "Now he knows" (F, 265).

Herzl's story can be read autobiographically. One can then see in it the fantasy of a politician who, at the height of his glory but besieged by enemies, escapes them by willingly relinquishing his power and retreating into privacy. Herzl may very well have identified himself with the historical Roman leader Sulla, who is described as a handsome and charismatic self-made man with aristocratic leanings and as a deft leader of his people. It is also plausible that Herzl, in this little story, invents an alternative to the ambitions that dictated his own life in those years. Having failed in his private life and fearing defeat in his political endeavors he may have sought recourse in literature to imagine the possibility of deliberately giving up on his earlier ambitions. But there may be more to Herzl's story than this.

"Epaphroditus" is based on an actual episode in Roman history, the conflict in 88–87 BC between the *optimates,* the aristocrats commanded by Lucius Cornelius Sulla, and the *populares* representing the pro-plebeians led by Marius. The rivalry between Sulla and Marius drove the Roman republic into a civil war after the former had returned victorious from the Italian wars. Sulla was made *dictator rei publicae constituendae,* commanded horribly bloody attacks on Marius's men, and then efficiently reorganized the government (essentially by limiting the powers of magistrates, censors, and army commanders), the legislature, and the juridical system. Herzl's story is to a large extent a faithful retelling of existing historical accounts of Sulla's life. It is more than likely that Herzl's source is Plutarch's *Life of Sylla.* Not only large parts of Herzl's plot but also many details, excerpts of dialogues, character traits, and events in "Epaphroditus" are strikingly similar to Plutarch's historical narrative. Practically all the protagonists, the description of Sulla's personality, his self-designation as "Epaphroditus" (F, 250) and "the happiest of men" (F, 264), his appetite for food, drink, and women, and his friendship with jesters and actors, as well as specific scenes,[6] seem to be taken straight and often literally from Plutarch's account. Even the encounter with the beautiful woman at the gladiator's spectacle is described by Plutarch in words similar to those employed by Herzl. In Plutarch we read: "Passing along behind Sulla, she leaned on him with her hand." But whereas Plutarch's Sulla will eventually marry this lady of high birth and die only later from a gruesome illness, she becomes in Herzl's story the instrument of the trap laid by Sulla's enemies as well as his ironic escape from their murderous wrath. It is only there, at the end of Sulla's life, that Herzl's tale no longer coincides with Plutarch's account.

The striking similarities with Plutarch's *Life of Sylla* make Herzl's changes and additions particularly significant. At the plot level these consist essentially of the failed conspiracy and Sulla's happy death. How can these deviations from Plutarch's narrative be understood? Possibly, in introducing the dramatic irony of Sulla's ultimate escape from his rivals through his death in the bed of his enemy's mistress, Herzl does not merely let the dictator retreat into a serene privacy within which he will waste away toward an equally private death. Instead, he turns Sulla's very retreat from power into *a victory over his enemies,* and ultimately over the bloodshed committed in the name of power and glory, over "world history" itself.

In Herzl's tale Sulla is clearly both victor and carrier of the narrator's sympathies: like Sulla himself, the narrator enjoys the "wondrously mild night at the shore" (F, 264) and defies those who commit bloody crimes in the name of "saving the republic." The repetition of this phrase clearly unmasks it as a cheap and treacherous slogan, as nothing but a means to attain personal glory in posterity. What those who rush to kill Sulla for the sake of the republic really have in mind is "das Denkmal, das sie für diese Tat erwarteten" (F, 265) (the monument they expect in return for their deed), a monument to their own heroism and bravery. In Plutarch's account, the beautiful woman is called not Fannia, but Valeria, and she is not Caesar's mistress but the daughter of Messala and sister to Hortensius the Orator. But the name Herzl gives to the woman who turns out to be a trap for Sulla is not accidental: "Fannia" was the appellation of one of the sumptuary laws proposed by the consul C. Fannius in 161 BC in order to restrain inordinate expenses and limit the sums which were to be spent on feasts and entertainments for the sake of saving money for the public expenses and, one is led to believe, the heroic conquests of the republic.

A dialogue in an early scene literally taken from Plutarch's account suggests an alternative to the heroic ideal. Plutarch relates that Sulla, after his unexpected resignation of power, "not only declined to seek that office, but in the forum exposed his person publicly to the people, walking up and down as a private man" (F, 265). Similarly, in Herzl's story, Sulla, after his conversion, walks in the marketplace unarmed and unprotected. Valgus, an old centurion, approaches him and remarks that nothing, not even the fiercest of battles, required as much courage as this walk. But Valgus also teasingly remarks that Sulla is no longer a powerful man and reminds him that "Die Götter und insbesondere die Göttinnen lieben nur die Starken" (F, 250) (The gods, and especially the goddesses, only love the strong). Upon this, Sulla replies with a triumphant smile: "Woher weisst du das? Vielleicht fange ich erst jetzt an, ein Starker zu sein. . . ." (F, 250) (How do you know this? Maybe I'm only starting to be a strong one now). If Sulla's wisdom in holding that true strength resides not in weapons and armies but in the daring freedom to expose oneself unshielded and step into the marketplace as a private man is transported back into Herzl's vision, its truly utopian dimension is revealed. It suggests not only the virtue but also the success of what would today be called "unilateral disarmament."

It is in some ways ironic that Herzl's philosophical tale uses the foil of a historical episode and turns to "public history" to narrate a man's conversion from public to private life. The triumph of the private over public existence is thereby not treated as mere refuge or resignation, but is introduced *into* the very course of "world history" as an alternative and a critique of its values, which are dictated by power and glory. However, Herzl's tale should not be misread as a one-dimensional parable propagating the virtues of private happiness over public grandeur. The double-edged ending of the story reveals the tragic irony that Sulla's final escape—like the knowledge he gains of a happy death—occurs only in death itself.

Although Sulla escapes through his timely death, his relinquishing of power does not suffice to make his rivals believe that the battle is over. A true and ultimate escape from the games of power may not be attainable in life as it is. Possibly, only a redeemed time will have obliterated those forces, drives, and motives that murderously "save republics" and build monuments in their glory. But of that time Herzl's tale does not say more.

Däumerle and Bäumerle or the Future

The second "philosophical tale" Herzl selected for the *Feuilletons* carries the somewhat childish and humorous-sounding title "Däumerle and Bäumerle or the Future," *Däumerle* and *Bäumerle* meaning literally "little thumb and little tree." In spite of its resemblance to burlesque folk tales, it comes closest of all four stories to a traditional parable. The main protagonists, two contrasting friends strongly reminiscent of Don Quixote and Sancho Panza, are clearly recognizable archetypes and stand for opposite principles of behavior that could somewhat simplistically be termed "idealist" and "realist" or "visionary" and "practical." It is also the story that most obviously and directly refers to Herzl's project of a Jewish state, to the point that it has been reckoned among his "Zionist writings" (Bein 1942, 469). Alex Bein describes the tale as "a story about one who sees the future, builds his house out in nature and lives to see how the city grows toward him, while another, a coolly calculating man, understands too late that the one he laughed at for being unrealistic turns out to be the wiser of the two" (1942, 469). However, as in "Epaphroditus," the literary medium transporting the moralizing principle deflects its single-mindedness and introduces an ambiguity into the parable's "lesson," suggesting a self-reflexive uncertainty that is lacking in Herzl's more straightforward political writings.

Däumerle, the shorter of the two friends, is practical, realistic, and pragmatic, concerned with material goods, physical well-being, and the needs and necessities of the day, as opposed to tall and skinny Bäumerle, a dreamer and visionary, who constantly and unremittingly looks into the future. The tale unfolds as a retrospective narrative of how the idyllic suburb where the two friends are taking a walk at the beginning of the story came into being. When they are still young boys they set out to discover Africa, described as a dark continent, with nothing in their backpacks but a sausage and some glass pearls destined to conquer the "wild population" (F, 267) they would encounter. Their adventure is poorly planned, and they are forced to return when their provisions become depleted. Däumerle gives up on their idea but Bäumerle vows to try again. Against Bäumerle's advice, Däumerle marries a rich but increasingly unattractive woman, soon regrets it, and is scorned by Bäumerle for having been too shortsighted. One day Däumerle, the practical one, notices the foul smells in the city's narrow streets, which prompts Bäumerle, the visionary, to point to a place far away on the horizon. Excitedly, they drive off in a carriage to the outskirts of the city, where there are, at that time, nothing but empty fields. "Here," Bäumerle prophetically proclaims, "there will one day be villas surrounded by gardens . . . I call [these fields]: the future!" (F, 271–72). Däumerle is incredulous at first, but they manage to buy the fields from the owner. They try in vain to raise the means and mobilize the masses to leave the city and settle "out there." Bäumerle, the dreamer, dismisses the objections and mocker-ies of the crowd and pursues his dream, while his friend is soon discouraged and turns his back on their project. Eventually, they sell the fields except for one little corner where later Bäumerle builds a house for himself. He lives there in solitude until another loner joins him, then another one, until, we are told, the "enterprise stopped looking foolish" (F, 274). More and more houses shoot up outside the city, built by those who are yearning for more light and freedom, and soon the houses seem to flow toward Bäumerle's dwelling place. When, many years later, Däumerle, now an old man, visits his farsighted friend and sees the marvelous villas and gar-dens where once there had been only naked fields, he regrets his former disbelief in their project, admires what has been achieved there, and asks Bäumerle: "Tell me, where is the future now?" (F, 274). The dreamer replies by pointing his finger to empty fields far away on the horizon and says, "Over there!" (F, 275)

Herzl's tale reads like the story of a successful colonization and seems to em-brace wholeheartedly the visionary's farsightedness and endurance against all odds. After all, it is thanks to Bäumerle, and despite the resignation of his practi-cal friend and the all-too-realistic objections of those who at first refused to follow him, that the inhabitants of the dark and smelly city, clearly an image of the ghetto, now live in a paradisiacal place. Read in this way, "Bäumerle und Däumerle" would be nothing but a somewhat naive, propagandistic fable written to convince the skeptics and disbelievers. Its relevance for today would, at the most, consist in providing the simplest of proofs of Bäumerle's erroneous belief that the fields were indeed empty. However, the story reveals more.

The tension between the conflicting standards and assumptions referred to in the story is obviously a conflict Herzl experienced not only between himself and others, but also within his own thinking. Two diary entries written years before "Däumerle und Bäumerle" illustrate the persistence of this doubleness in very similar terms. On 18 June 1895 Herzl mentions an encounter with Emil Schiff, who warned him he would never be taken seriously and suggested alternative solutions to the "Jewish question":

Ebenda mit S . . . gewesen. Er hat mich "geheilt"—ich akzeptiere nämlich den negativen Teil seiner Bemerkungen, "dass ich mich lächerlich oder tragisch ma-chen werde." [. . .] Den negativen Teil akzeptiere ich—dadurch unterscheide ich mich von Don Quixote. Den positiven Teil (Gerede von Sozialismus, . . . usw.) lehne ich ab—dadurch unterscheide ich mich von Sancho Pansa. (T, 127)

Was here with S. He "cured" me—I now accept the negative part of his remarks, "that I will make myself ridiculous or tragic" [. . .] I accept the negative part and therewith distinguish myself from Don Quixote. The positive part (talk about Socialism, . . . etc.) I refuse—and therewith distinguish myself from Sancho Panza.

In a letter draft to Baron Hirsch following this entry Herzl repeats:

> Was wollen Sie? Ich möchte nicht wie Don Quixote aussehen. Aber die Lösungen: Ihre 20 000 Argentinier oder den Übertritt der Juden zum Sozialismus akzeptiere ich nicht. Denn ich bin auch kein Sancho Pansa. (T, 129)

> What do you want? I don't want to look like Don Quixote. But I don't accept the solution—your 20,000 Argentineans or the conversion of the Jews to Socialism— either. Because I'm no Sancho Panza either.

In these passages Herzl clearly situates himself *between* the dreamer and the pragmatic, while five years later, in his philosophical tale, Herzl seems to fully side with Bäumerle the dreamer. He appears to prophetically congratulate himself for his tenacity and to proudly confirm his own visionary insights against the pragmatic considerations put forth against his project by the likes of Däumerle. However, a closer look at several details in the story blurs the seemingly clear-cut evaluation of the opposition embodied by the two contrasting figures and reveals Herzl's self-mockery of the excesses in his own visionary pose.

As much as Bäumerle's vision and perseverance turn out to be successful, the story does not spare him a good dose of irony. This irony may turn out to be one of the tools for self-criticism that Herzl believed he should omit from his political writings, but could voice in his literary work. Several passages in the story humorously hint at the excesses of Bäumerle's idealism. The first expedition to Africa undertaken by the two friends fails because their provisions for the journey, "the sausage" (F, 267), are soon depleted. Bäumerle's conclusion that "next time they will take with them the glass pearls only" (F, 267), because they had been "too dependent on the sausage" (F, 267), is hardly to be taken as serious advice. Anyone wishing Bäumerle well can only hope that Däumerle will keep an eye on his friend when he sets out on his next journey. Similarly, some lines in the dialogues between the two friends reveal the excesses in Bäumerle's visionary focus on the future. Däumerle's marriage may turn out to be unhappy, but Bäumerle's objection to his friend's betrothal, namely that the prettiest girls get old and ugly and that one always has to see the old woman in the girl one marries and imagine the death mask that lurks behind every pretty face, eventually turns into a mockery of the one who is fixated on the future. The humorous wisdom expressed by the visionary that "one always marries one's mother-in-law" (F, 268), and his decision therefore to stay single, is not likely to be taken as a serious alternative to Däumerle's unhappy marriage.

Furthermore, it is significant that Däumerle is called a "typical thumblong Hans" (F, 266). A popular German tale called "Hans guck in die Luft"—a typical cautionary tale in the tradition of black pedagogy—demonstrates how the one looking "in the air," instead of seeing what lies immediately before him, is likely to fall into the water pit. In Herzl's story, however, this figure would correspond to Bäumerle, not Däumerle. A detail in the story makes an obvious reference to "Hans guck in die Luft." At one point, Bäumerle is challenged by his practical friend and defends the advantages of farsightedness: it is, he believes, a protection "against falling into the pit, as happened to a friend of mine who always hurriedly grabs the visible, immediate advantage" (F, 269). Herzl's not exactly logical or persuasive inversion of the popular tale indirectly invites an objection and introduces the opposite wisdom into the story: that the one who does not see what is immediately present may be the one to drown. It seems as if the story's attempt to demonstrate that visionary idealism is reasonable fails precisely where the heroic ideal clashes with the expectations and the atmosphere of the cautionary wisdom inherent in the story's literary genre and set-up. It is also noteworthy that Bäumerle's final success in settling out in the fields results not from a romantic expedition or an attempt to make the inhabitants of the city collectively move out there, but from the incomparably more realistic decision to buy a parcel of land for himself and build a house there, a modest one, as we are told later on in the story.

The most significant detail in the story, the one that links it most directly to Herzl's project of a Jewish state, lies in the "division of labor" between Däumerle's pragmatism and Bäumerle's visionary idealism. The origin of the eventually successful evacuation of the dark and crowded cities and the colonization of the empty fields does not so much lie with the visionary impetus itself. Instead, it is the shortsighted, sensible, and, one would guess, sensuous Däumerle who says the crucial sentence that precedes Bäumerle's ominous gaze toward the distant fields: "Don't you think that it stinks in these smelly streets?" (F, 269). Like Herzl's project of a Jewish state, Bäumerle's vision of a better future arises out of a search for an alternative to the miserable and dangerous living conditions in the present. But—and this is where the story makes a crucial comment on the legitimation of Bäumerle's colonization of the fields—is this still the case in the final scene of the story, when once again Bäumerle points in the direction of empty fields, designates the next spot to be conquered, and exclaims, "Over there!" (F, 275)? Bäumerle's gesture in reply to Däumerle's question as to where the future lies now is an echo of a diary entry from 30 September 1898 where Herzl writes: "I see a city suddenly rising from the plain, without mountain, river, or sea—without motive, so to speak. This is The Hague. A proof that willpower makes cities rise. If I point my finger at a spot, and say: Here shall be a city—a city will come into being there" (T, 674). Shlomo Avineri quotes this diary entry as a proof of Herzl's belief in the "sovereignty of human will" (1999, 4). The ending of the philosophical tale, however, reveals that the initial motivation to seek an alternative future—the smelly streets of the city—no longer applies and that they forgot that years ago they sold the fields. The two friends are now walking in the midst of beautiful villas and gardens. The pointed finger at the "future" has become a goal in itself. The story ends on Bäumerle's exclamation. No comments or explanations indicate whether Herzl intended to affirm or question the legitimacy of a colonization extending beyond the necessity to escape from the smelly streets, beyond the imperative to improve the living conditions of the city's—the ghetto's—inhabitants. An inconspicuous passage from Herzl's literary marginalia points to larger—and highly topical—

political issues. Could it be—but we have to take the literary dimension of the story seriously to see this—that the closing line of Herzl's tale presents us with the opposite, yet equally disconcerting, openness from what we see in the ending of "Epaphroditus"? Just as the Roman ruler's death cannot be taken as a lesson for a good life because it cannot be experienced in any *lived* present, so does Bäumerle's successful project of colonization eventually put itself into question: his looking far away onto the distant horizon risks going on, endlessly and forever, with no satisfaction, no present in sight.

The Left Bell

Like "Däumerle and Bäumerle," "The Left Bell" develops out of a retrospective narrative and tells the story of what at first seem to be the successful adventures of a man who left his hometown to seek his fortune elsewhere. After twenty years of absence Herr Wendelin returns to his town without telling anyone where he has been. One evening Wendelin overhears one of the rich and powerful members of the town's establishment confidently stating that all losers deserve their fate, that their failure is, in the end, always their own fault: "Capable men," he continues, "may occasionally have bad luck, but they will always manage somehow" (F, 278). When his nodding listeners agree, Wendelin decides to tell his story: how he had hard times at first until he landed in a seaport where a rich and mysterious man handed him an address and invited him to present himself there. This recommendation would open all the doors for him and get him a lucrative job, the stranger said. Wendelin followed his advice and found himself in front of a door with two bells belonging to two different companies; the man had not told him which was the right one. Without realizing the importance of the moment at the time, Wendelin pulled the right one, got the job, eventually became the owner of the prosperous business, married the daughter of his former boss, had children, and lived happily ever after. However, Wendelin insists that the left bell is part of his story as well. He came to know where pulling that other bell would have led him: the other company went bankrupt, and its owner's successor got married to an unfaithful woman and ended miserable and humiliated. When Wendelin finishes telling his story, one of his listeners asks whether things have really happened this way. Wendelin replies that he has told them his life as it was and as it could have been. "This," he adds, "is my response to your statement that a capable guy always succeeds. He only has to pull the right bell; then he will have been a capable guy. For the rest, ask my cousin if I spoke the truth" (F, 284). After Wendelin leaves, his cousin reveals that he has indeed spoken the truth, except for one detail: Wendelin had rung the left bell; he was the loser.

At first sight, the story's lesson seems so obvious and banal that one wonders why Herzl needed a whole narrative including the ironic twist at the end to illustrate it. The wisdom that success and failure are not a question of merit and fault, but that luck at the decisive moment is often all that counts, barely needs such elaborate demonstration. What is it then that makes of "The Left Bell" a "philosophical tale"? Undoubtedly, the moral of the story—the contingency of fate—clashes with the absolute belief in the "sovereignty of human will" usually associated with Herzl, and it certainly undermines the celebration of heroic action. Of course one could argue—and it would not be far-fetched to imagine—that Herzl wrote this story as a consolation for himself and as a justification to others in a time when he feared that despite all his efforts his project would come to nothing. The story would provide him with the excuse that he simply was not lucky, that his eventual failure would not be his fault. However, this autobiographical explanation does not answer questions that arise out of a reading of the story from a literary perspective: why the details, why the detours? Above all, why did Wendelin tell the story of the road he did *not* take, the life he did *not* live, rather than straightforwardly narrating his own adventure? This could be answered in a nutshell with one of Nietzsche's aphorisms from his *Fröhliche Wissenschaft:* "Kein Sieger glaubt an den Zufall" (1959, 209) (No winner believes in chance). The situation in which Wendelin's story is framed indicates that a tale told by a *nebbich,* a loser, would not do to demonstrate the contingency of fate to an assembly of rich and arrogant members of the town's elite, to men who have a stake in considering their own position to be a result of their own merits. The realization that things could be different, that self-confidence based on success is an illusion, must be driven home by one of their equals, by one who made it in the world. Had Wendelin told his story as the loser that he turns out to be, no one would have listened; his story would have been dismissed as the alibi of one who does not take responsibility for his failures. The story's final irony—that Wendelin lied about his own persona—participates in undoing the myth of meritorious success on which legends of individual glory rest.

A detail in the story gives additional weight to this demystification and sheds light on the role assigned to literature in the story. The figure who directs Wendelin to the door with the two bells seems to come straight out of a fairy tale. As if by magic, wherever Wendelin turns, he sees and hears the name of Wilhelm Wielemann; the boats, the finest palaces, everything that shines and glitters in the city is said to belong to him. The name of this admired self-made man is significant: *Wieleman,* in Dutch, means man of the wheel, the wheel of fortune that turns according to its own designs, disregarding all human faults and merits. When Wendelin actually encounters this mysterious figure, he turns out to be a little old man with shining eyes who uncannily seems to know Wendelin's innermost thoughts and secrets and who summons him to what, in fairy tales, is the hour and place where fate is decided. But there is more. Beyond these magical connotations, there is an explicit reference to a specific folktale: three times, the little old man is associated with the obscure word "Kannitverstan." It is the title of a popular tale written by the eighteenth-century Swiss author Johan Peter Hebel. In Hebel's story a poor young stranger comes to Amsterdam, where he marvels at the riches of the town. He does not speak the local language and when he inquires about the owner of all the sumptuous ships, houses, and gardens, the reply is always the same: "Kannitverstan" (F, 279), which, in Dutch, means "I cannot understand." As the young stranger is erroneously led to believe that all these riches belong to one man, his envy grows and he is increasingly dissatisfied with his own lot until he witnesses a burial and is told again that the man who is led to his grave is "Kannitverstan." This leads him to realize the transitoriness of worldly riches, and he happily enters the next pub and feasts on a piece of Limburger cheese, forever satisfied with the modest joys of life.

Hebel introduces his story with the popular wisdom that occasionally errors can lead to truth and insight, in this case the futility of grand ambitions and the primacy of simple, everyday pleasures. Kannitverstan, the rich and powerful owner of it all, does not exist; he is nothing but a misunderstanding, an illusion. However, "Kannitverstan" is also the title of a tale, an existing fiction like Wendelin's lies, the imagined successes he boasts about to the assembly of the rich and mighty in Herzl's story. In both cases, this "unreal" fiction leads to real insights, be they into the value of a piece of cheese or the element of chance in every life that redeems "losers" and dethrones heroes. In the end, it is suggested that Wendelin is victorious: after his performance, by which he tricked the town's elite into understanding their self-serving error that success is merit and that failure is self-incurred, he leaves the stage without even needing to witness his adversaries' defeat.

The Spectacles

The tension between distant vision and the immediate concerns of everyday life is formulated most explicitly in "Die Brille" (The Spectacles), the story that closes Herzl's collection of selected minor writings. "The Spectacles" is set up as a fictive letter written by Johannes, a forty-one-year-old, educated, and refined man, clearly the alter ego of Herzl himself, to his friend Franz, a former schoolmate. In this letter Johannes shares his recent experience of getting his first reading glasses and conveys to his friend the impact of this event as an inaugural moment of a new phase in his life. He writes how, on a recent day, he had to hold a letter at arm's length, how an ophthalmologist encouraged him to get reading glasses, and how this newly acquired instrument on his nose influences his social behavior and his outlook on life. This narrative is accompanied by nostalgic memories and philosophical musings about the transitoriness of time and the vanity of men. Johannes's loose reflections are held together by the metaphoric extension of the story's title: the reading glasses are both real, concrete spectacles and a signifier for the waning capacity to see things that are close by. This oscillation between literal and metaphoric meaning corresponds to the issue at stake in the story: both tangible object and symbol of a necessary adjustment of vision, the spectacles mediate between a concrete, "literal" reality on the one hand and a generalizable perception on the other. Farsightedness, Johannes's affliction and the natural condition of an ageing man's eyesight, is equated with the loss of interest in everyday matters and the simple things of life:

Das Geringe, das uns umgibt, schwindet im Werte. Nur das Grössere, Fernere sehen wir noch und immer weiter rückt dieser Kreis, bis wir endlich kein Interesse mehr am Gewöhnlichen des Lebens haben. (F, 289)

The simple things lose their value. We now only see what is great and distant and this circle recedes more and more into the distance until we are finally no longer interested in what is common in life.

This loss of touch with everyday things, however, is not described as an increase in visionary power. On the contrary, the story suggests that farsightedness without perception of the concrete particulars is a transition toward the "end of things" (F, 289). As in the story "Däumerle und Bäumerle," the exclusive focus on the distance eventually points toward death. The spectacles alluded to in the title are a corrective to this melancholic farsightedness and bring nearby reality back into view. However, the price of this correction is the loss of heroic stature: with some sadness, but ultimately with a newly gained wisdom, Johannes accepts his dwindling powers and recognizes the folly of those who continue to strive for glory. He overcomes his vanity, gives up his drive to conquer and his attractiveness as charismatic, powerful male, puts his glasses on his nose, and joins the elderly gentlemen in the club. There he reads "Weber's *Demokrit,* Machiavelli's *Florentine Stories,* Horace Walpole's *Letters*" (F, 290), all of them political writings, but Johannes admits to his friend that he has difficulties deciphering the small print of Weber's and Machiavelli's books. What he likes most are the passages in Walpole's writings where the English author talks as a private man and complains about the first signs of ageing.

Johannes tells his friend that he occasionally takes off his glasses; they are, he explains, not necessary for thinking. It is implied, however, that the thinking that can be done without spectacles produces nothing but chimeras such as those Johannes imagines as he watches a little white cloud change its shape in the sky. In a passage reminiscent of typical fin de siècle dream-imagery, he describes the cloud's changing shapes in which he discerns swarms of birds on San Marco, exotic caravans moving through the desert, and graceful swans seducing fairytale princes. At the end of the letter, these chimeras dissolve for good as Johannes, his glasses firmly on his nose, bids farewell to the cloud and to his friend, self-consciously signing, "Your far-sighted Johannes" (F, 295). In the letter's last paragraphs Johannes graciously and somewhat humbly accepts his fate while making it clear that farsightedness is, for him, no longer equated with prophetic vision. Instead it signifies a handicap, the loss of eyesight's capacity to adapt its focus.

A crucial passage in the story makes the link from the concrete weakening of Johannes's eyesight to a more general philosophical insight. After recommending that he get glasses, the ophthalmologist, an assistant of Hermann Ludwig Ferdinand von Helmholtz, the famous nineteenth-century scientist and founder of modern optics, quotes his former teacher:

> Wenn mir ein Optiker ein so mangelhaftes Instrument brächte, wie es das menschliche Auge ist, ich würde es ihm als unbrauchbar zurückgeben. [...] Und doch hat das menschliche Sehwerkzeug eine wunderbare Eigenschaft, nämlich die Akkomodation. Darunter verstehen wir seine Fähigkeit, sich für grössere und kleinere Entfernungen einzustellen. (F, 288)

> If an optician would create an instrument as fallible as the human eye, I would return it to him and tell him that it is useless. [. . .] However, the human tool of sight has a wonderful property, which is its capacity of accommodation. I mean its potential to adapt itself to greater and smaller distances.

From these words Johannes derives the general wisdom that life itself is one "accommodation" (F, 288), the capacity to adapt one's focus from far to near according to the circumstances. This insight is to be gained in old age, but an ageing man can put it into practice only when he resigns himself to wearing glasses that correct this farsightedness. The eye can remain flexible only when the pragmatic adaptation to contexts and situations prevails over the mourning about the loss of one's visionary "look."

Visionary farsightedness, however, is not denigrated altogether. Helmholtz's assistant tells Johannes about a legendary shoemaker from Breslau who had the rare gift of perfect eyesight. He could see the satellites of Jupiter with naked eyes, and, most remarkably, he nevertheless chose to remain a shoemaker, to stick to his last—"Er blieb bei seinem Leisten" (F, 289)—which alludes to the German saying "Schuster bleib bei deinem Leisten." But after reporting this anecdote, Johannes quickly adds that not everyone who stays a shoemaker sees the satellites of Jupiter (F, 288). To have the capacity of seeing the stars and yet to stay with common, nearby things is what Johannes—and obviously Herzl—most admires. His last philosophical tale ends on Johannes's tender farewell to his friend: "Lebe auch du wohl für heute, Franzisce" (F, 295). Johannes, the New Testament's prophet of apocalyptic and redemptive visions, greets Saint Francis, the humble lover of creation. It is with the simplicity of this farewell greeting, a literal "live well" (F, 289), that Herzl closes his book.

In some ways this story seems to point in a direction opposite from that of "Epaphroditus." While the old Sulla gives up power in an act of free will, energetically plunges into the joys and pleasures of life, and outwits his enemies and, ultimately, the scandal of death itself, Johannes, in "The Spectacles," gradually and nostalgically observes the dwindling of his former attractiveness and strength and quietly prepares for death. In "Epaphroditus," written when Herzl was two years younger, the soldier's and the statesman's struggle for victory and glory is still replaced by another, ultimately even grander battle. As Sulla dies his happy death, he not only wins over his adversaries but wins over the gods themselves. While Sulla's free choice to retreat from the public sphere and live life—and even death—to the lees can be seen as an act of resistance, even a victory, Johannes's freedom is restricted to an acceptance, an affirmation of the inevitable. However, both stories present alternatives to the heroic ideal. Sulla crosses the marketplace without protection, displaying even greater courage than on the battlefield, while farsighted Johannes puts on his glasses and learns about the greatness of "accommodation." Respectively pointing to sensuous fulfillment and to sobering wisdom, the two stories convey different modes of leaving ambitions of glory behind, but both Sulla and Johannes replace the striving for power with a possibly even more fundamental if not daring vision, one that is to be gained in maturity alone: leaving *Weltgeschichte* behind, they bring *Leben* into sight.

Herzl's Legacy

Herzl's late "philosophical tales" convey the change of focus occurring when youthful ideals of power, conquest, and success are replaced by the enjoyment of private life and the wisdom of maturity. The retrospective gaze of the two ageing protagonists Sulla and Johannes, the problematization of Bäumerle's self-serving pursuit of expansionist dreams devoid of pragmatic concerns, and Wendelin's demonstration of the dictates of chance undoing heroic conceit suggest that maturity entails a changing relationship to that which, in Yehuda Amichai's poetic scene evoked at the beginning of this chapter, is signified by the arch from the Roman period. In this scene, the man with the baskets of vegetables insists that he is "moving, he's moving," that human beings cannot be a reference for the monument of heroic triumphs because their distance to historical events is changing. That such a change over the course of time—and especially with approaching maturity—is not only an individual matter but a reality concerning entire nations is what Herzl may have had in mind when, in a diary entry from 20 July 1895, he looks ahead at how a "mature" Jewish state should eventually be governed:

> Die Monstra, die Ungeheuer sind notwendig für das Erschaffen, aber schädlich für das Bestehende—ob sie es nun durch Grösseres ersetzen oder in den Wahnsinn hinausbauen. So lassen können sie die Welt nicht, wie sie sie vorfanden; sie gingen daran zugrunde, wenn sie nicht etwas—Schlechtes oder Gutes, gleichviel!—zerstören könnten. [. . .] Das Bestehende, zu Erhaltende, darf nur von mittelmässigen Menschen regiert werden. Die Monstra verstehen die Vergangenheit, erraten die Zukunft—aber die Gegenwart [. . .] wollen sie eilig wegräumen. Es drängt sie ja, ihre Spuren zu hinterlassen. Sie haben Angst, sie könnten vorübergehen, ohne dass man merkt, sie seien dagewesen. Zur Regierung braucht man mittlere Menschen, weil *die* alle kleinen Bedürfnisse der Menschen: Essen, Trinken, Schlafen usw. verstehen. Die Monstra gehen über diese Bedürfnisse hinweg—bei sich wie bei anderen. (T, 139)

> The monsters [*Monstra*] are necessary in order to create, but harmful for that which exists [*das Bestehende*], whether they replace it by something greater or aggrandize it into madness. [. . .] That which exists, which is to be maintained, may only be ruled by mediocre men. The Monstra understand the past, they envision the future—but the present [. . .] they want to quickly eliminate. It is because they are driven to leave their mark. They fear that they could pass unnoticed. To govern, one needs common men, because they alone understand all

the simple human needs: eating, drinking, sleeping, etc. The monster disregards these needs—in himself and in others.

In what can be regarded as Herzl's most farsighted prophecy, one that goes beyond the mere creation of a Jewish state, he envisions what Israel will really have become: "ein Bestehendes," "zu Erhaltendes," something existing, something that needs to be taken care of and preserved. The vision that this existing state will eventually have to be governed by common men and not by heroes is inspired by a hope similar to the one expressed in Yehuda Amichai's poetic scene. Herzl's diary entry foreshadows Amichai's utopian dream that redemption will come when the arch of triumph is subordinated to the "simple human needs," when the monuments of heroism and glory lose their significance in the face of the man with baskets of fresh vegetables. In the light of Herzl's late philosophical tales, in which he revokes his earlier shift from *Leben* to *Weltgeschichte* and reinstates the primacy of simple, everyday existence, one could possibly modify the message of a post-Zionist pamphlet ending on the words "There is life *after* Zionism" (Segev 2001, 161). Rather, it appears that there is more life *in* Herzl's Zionist legacy than meets the eye.

Diverting the Lineage: Biblical Women in Else Lasker-Schüler's *Hebrew Ballads*

> We artists are God's darlings, the children of the Marias of all
> lands. We play with His sublime creations and rummage in
> His colorful morning and golden evening. But the bourgeois
> remains God's step-son, our reasonable brother, the killjoy.
> He cannot feel at ease with us, neither he nor his sister.
>
> —LASKER-SCHÜLER 1998, 166

Else Lasker-Schüler's lyrical representations of female biblical figures are part of a literary tradition that takes up the original Bible stories and brushes them against the grain in order to both evoke and question values that have, in one form or another, prevailed from biblical times until our own day. Most artistic renderings of biblical motifs in the Western tradition have endorsed or at least been favorably disposed toward the original values or the religious precepts they inspired. There are, however, others—even before modern times—that call the authority of these ideas into question. In her book *The Story of Eve* (1998), Pamela Norris shows how women writers from Hildegard of Bingen in the eleventh century to the romantic Mary Shelley to contemporary authors such as Angela Carter and Margaret Atwood have brushed the story of creation against the biblical grain in order to salvage the honor of Eve, the "mother of all things." Else Lasker-Schüler's contributions to this alternative version of the story of creation in poems such as *Eva* and *Evas Lied* are impressive examples of rebellious poetry by a female twentieth-century author. Her reworkings of other female figures from the Hebrew Bible, to be explored here, are no less disruptive.

Few books have been so unanimously accused of being patriarchal as the Hebrew Bible. The male supremacy embodied there is still evident in the work of the French-Jewish philosopher Emmanuel Levinas, who, thanks to the radicalism of his conceptions of alterity, is frequently counted among the master-thinkers of the later twentieth century. In his essay "Judaism and the Feminine" (1990), Levinas describes the biblical origin of the Jewish determination of the feminine:

> The characteristics of the Jewish woman can be fixed, thanks to charming feminine figures of the Old Testament. The wives of the patriarchs, Miriam and Deborah the prophetesses, Tamar [. . .], Naomi and Ruth the Moabite, Michal, daughter of Saul, Abigail [. . .], Shulamite, and a whole host of others, all play an active role in the attainment of the biblical purpose and are placed at the very pivot of Sacred History. (1990, 31)

Levinas emphasizes the difference between this role and other Oriental determinations of the feminine of the same period, in which women are assigned an entirely passive, subordinate position. But what, for Levinas, does this positive role consist of? We read on:

> Isaac would have been schooled in the violent games and laughter of his brother but for the painful decision of Sarah [to banish Hagar and her son Ishmael], Esau would have triumphed over Israel but for Rebecca's ruse [. . .], David, and the Prince of Justice [meaning the messiah] who one day was to be born of him, would not have been possible without Tamar's stubbornness, without Ruth the faithful [. . .]. All the switches along this difficult path, on which the train of messianic history risked being derailed a thousand times, have been supervised and controlled by women. (1990, 31)

As much as Levinas emphasizes the importance of this role of biblical women and of women in Judaism as guardians and helpers of a messianic history, he also marks its limits. In the last paragraph of his essay, Levinas makes it clear that the figure who is the focus of all the longing of the Jewish people is not female: "But the Biblical figure which haunts Israel on the paths of exile, the figure that it invokes at the end of the Sabbath, in the dusk where it will soon remain behind without help, the figure in whom is stored up for the Jews all the tenderness of the earth, the hand which caresses and rocks his children, is no longer feminine. Neither wife nor sister nor mother guides it. It is Elijah, who did not experience death, the most severe of the prophets, precursor of the Messiah" (1990, 38). In the biblical scheme there is, according to Levinas, nothing feminine about the herald of the Redeemer. In recent decades, however, Levinas's view of women as midwives in a history to whose ultimate fulfillment they do not actively contribute has been disputed by male and female, Jewish and non-Jewish commentators who do not accept this view of male supremacy in the Bible. Two approaches are available to these critics. They can either criticize the Bible for its misogynist conception of the feminine, or they can reinterpret the passages mentioned and extract aspects of the Bible narrative that refute Levinas's argument in order to find proofs of the equality or perhaps even the dominance of women in the Hebrew Bible.

Poets and writers have a further possibility open to them: they can rewrite the stories of the Bible. If literature is the medium that keeps alive the idea that things can be different than they are, then the literary reworking of Bible stories can not only alter views of the Book of Books but, by "usurping" its authority, also alter ancient ideas of how things are supposed to be.

Else Lasker-Schüler, Judaism, and the Bible

"And thou shalt be as Sarah, Rebecca, Rachel, and Leah": even if it is unlikely that Else Lasker-Schüler ever heard this blessing given to Jewish daughters, she nevertheless grew up in surroundings in which, despite assimilation, traditional role models were maintained. This may have had more to do with the middle-class nature of her parental milieu than with its traditional Jewish character, which in her case was rather limited. Her consciousness as a Jew was no doubt determined more by the anti-Semitism of her German environment, which eventually forced her into exile, than by her family's knowledge of the Bible. Nonetheless her consciousness as a Jew—in all its ambivalence—found expression precisely in relation to biblical stories and motifs. She felt closer to what she called the "wild Jews" she repeatedly evokes in her poetry than to the assimilated Jewish middle class she had come from. This aspect of her writings has been interpreted as the product of her fascination with the archaic and the exotic, and her remoteness from reality. Looking more closely, however, one can recognize here an inclination to anarchic rebellion against the repressive order of her own bourgeois environment and the imaginary creation of an "uncommon community" embracing the "children of the Marias of all lands," the poets and strangers, the outcasts, and all those who stand up against oppression by their "reasonable brother, the killjoy" and his female accomplices.

Perceptions of Lasker-Schüler as an "escapist" poet not much interested in political reality range from descriptions of her as a childishly naive dreamer to mystifications of her as a primeval priestess or a messianic figure of redemption. Her work is often categorized as decorative aestheticism or else seen as expressing an autocratic, pompous pathos. Until the 1970s the view prevailed that Lasker-Schüler's poetry was primarily a florid and mystically tinged condensation of religion, love, and art. Margarete Küppers, for example, sums up Lasker-Schüler's worldview as follows: "The pious in prayer, the lover in love, the artist in art break through the crust of the earthly and temporal world and experience paradise and eternity; piety, love and art are possible ways of redeeming the world, of reconciling God and the world and of turning the darkened world back into shining Eden."[1] Lasker-Schüler's extreme claim, however, hardly corresponds to these spiritualized, conciliatory, and orthodox approaches. In her poetry the possibility of redeeming the world through piety, love, and art is combined with a destructive dynamic and a mischievous irony in the shape of an often heretical and iconoclastic art. These are also characteristic features of her *Hebrew Ballads*[2] and other poems related to this cycle, in which she engages directly with the biblical tradition, and which at first sight appear almost devout and uncritical.

Lasker-Schüler's Biblical Figures and Their Reception

Along with the Oriental settings found throughout this work, references to biblical language and imagery form the most important background of Lasker-Schüler's poetry. References to the Bible pervade her hymns to God and His creation, frequently uniting ecstatic sensuality and religious flights of the imagination. The poems dealing with biblical characters are usually alternative versions of the original tales that take great liberties with traditional figures and events, often going so far as to add narrative elements, make metaphoric displacements, and carry out a complete reevaluation of the values propagated in the original text. Most of the early interpretations of these poems take little notice of the rebellious tenor of Lasker-Schüler's Bible references.[3] More recent commentators, interested in the gender issues raised by these adaptations, try to prove that in her biblical poems she identifies with male characters—such as the Joseph figure—in order to assert and empower herself.[4] These critics consequently overlook the quite independent function of the biblical women in Else Lasker-Schüler's poetry.

Most noteworthy in this respect is Dieter Bänsch, whose influential study *Else Lasker-Schüler: Zur Kritik eines etablierten Bildes* sees the relationship of the poet to biblical ideas in terms of the messianic promise of redemption typical of neo-Gnostic tendencies of the late nineteenth and early twentieth centuries, placing it among those "apocalyptic and chiliastic visions" and promises of salvation that fed the seductive violence of the Third Reich. According to Bänsch, Lasker-Schüler avoided confronting the political reality of her times and, in an incomparably "fantastic attempt at literary self-mythification" (1971, 211), regarded herself as the messiah. The most astonishing thing about Bänsch's conclusions is that he feels compelled to demonstrate the falseness of this attempt and to show that the poet was not this messiah at all. As proof he tries to point out inconsistencies in Lasker-Schüler's messianic self-stylization and finishes his indictment with the revealing comment, "The most conspicuous of these contradictions is of course that this messianic Joseph"—meaning Lasker-Schüler's self-projection into this figure—"nevertheless always remained a woman, even mother of a son" (1971, 211). Evidently, Bänsch's idea of the messiah, just like Levinas's, remains tied to a conventional Jewish-Christian tradition in which the Redeemer can be thought of only as masculine. Lasker-Schüler's anticipations of salvation do not always and explicitly have a female connotation, but her biblical adaptations show that her vision of redemption involves a radical questioning of this patriarchal conception and its correlates. She maps out a world in which a new age free of rulers emerges from the departure of the old ones. Lasker-Schüler's biblical women are the medium of this hope.

The Song of Songs: A Feminine Subtext

Lasker-Schüler's poetry consists largely of love poems. In them, melancholic recollections of past happiness, suffering in the absence of the loved one, and most of all the longing for reunion link the individual experience of love to ideas of collective redemption. Not only in this respect, but also formally, metaphorically, and in terms of motifs, the Song of Solomon is the subtext of a large part of Lasker-Schüler's poetry. This intertextual relationship is evident in stylistic elements—opaque metaphor, tonality of entreaty, phatic redundance—and in the basic situation of a pair of lovers duetting in praise of each other and embracing all things, plants, beasts, and landscapes, for their mutual celebration. One constant within these poems is a shifting between ecstatic union and the enforced and violent separation of the lovers, who cling to the yearning for a future restoration of their happiness.

The Song of Songs is grounded in a poetic process of the metaphoric intensification of sensual experience. The act of love is spiritualized through displacement and condensation of polyvalent symbols and images: "I have come into my garden, my sister, my bride; I have gathered my myrrh with my spice; I have eaten my honeycomb with my honey; I have drunk my wine with my milk. Eat, O friends; drink, yea, drink abundantly, O beloved" (Song of Songs 5:1). At the same time the lovers, through their exalted fascination with one another, sing the praises of the phenomena of the world:

> Thine ointments have a goodly fragrance;
> thy name is as ointment poured forth [. . .]
> (Song of Songs 1:3)

> My beloved is unto me as a gift of myrrh,
> that lieth betwixt my breasts.
> My beloved is unto me as a cluster of henna
> in the vineyards of En-gedi.
> Behold, thou art fair, my love; behold, thou art fair;
> thine eyes are as doves.
> (Song of Songs 1:13–15)

The many metaphors in the Song are originally intended to convey an inexpressible love. This love in turn becomes a metaphor for the poetic process of the reunification of what has been separated and hence becomes an eschatological vision of redemption. The poetic song, in which erotic pleasures and spiritual inspiration coincide, brings together the longing for a love fulfilled and the hope of a messianic age. Shulamite, the female protagonist of the Song of Songs, is simultaneously singer and the one who is sung about as a personification of the Bible itself. She is lover and beloved, who binds erotic desire and hymnic expression in a vision of messianic redemption. As described by Levinas (1990, 37), this text, unusual in the biblical context, was given a mystical reinterpretation in the rabbinical Midrash. Sensual love was understood in purely metaphoric terms and dissolved in the eschatological dimension: the erotic union of the lovers was entirely swallowed up by the pure symbol of the relationship between God and His people.

In her poem "Shulamite," Lasker-Schüler refers explicitly to the Song of Songs but combines sensual love and messianic anticipation in a way that does not admit a metaphoric dissolution of sensuality into pure spirituality.

Shulamite

O, from your sweet mouth
I learned too much of bliss!
Already I feel Gabriel's lips
Burning on my breast . . .
And the night-cloud drinks
My deep dream of cedars.
O, how your life beckons me!
And I dissolve
With blossoming heartbreak
And I drift away in the universe
Into time
To forever,
And my soul burns away in the evening colors
Of Jerusalem. (HB, 75)

With its title and its references to the Archangel Gabriel, to Jerusalem, and to the cedars growing there, a messianic vision of redemption emerges in this poem. However, this vision remains ambivalent. The poem begins with the recollection of a past experience of love and goes on to describe a process of self-dissolution, of a withdrawal from the reality of time and space, culminating in messianic Jerusalem. In the Bible, Gabriel is the archangel who delivers and interprets the Word of God. He announces to the prophet Daniel the time of the end, the defeat of Israel, and the destruction of Jerusalem, whereupon Daniel breaks into a song of atonement. As reward for Daniel's contrition, Gabriel appears to him again, "about the time of the evening offering," and proclaims the tidings of the future reconstruction of Jerusalem (Daniel 8 and 9). Lasker-Schüler's "Shulamite" can likewise be read as a song of atonement that is rewarded as evening falls, at the time of the end, with the announcement of approaching salvation.

The first two lines are already ambiguous: the "too much" of the pleasures experienced at the mouth of the lover could refer to possible regrets about lustful experiences of love, but could just as well be read as the hyperbole of excessive bliss or as mourning for the loss of such a state. The picture of Gabriel's lips and the metaphor of the drinking "night-cloud" in the following lines twice take up the motif of the mouth: step by step, the physical figure of the lover first addressed as "you" is replaced by an abstraction. Gabriel's burning lips, which at first replace the lover's mouth, are an expression both of passion and pain; then the "night-cloud" takes up the dream of redemption. However, at that point, the "night-cloud" also introduces a new darkness. In the middle of the poem this progression leads into a new invocation of the lover: "O, how your life beckons me!" The mouth of the lover has turned into the more abstract "life." The word "winkt" ("beckons" in the English translation), which can suggest both a greeting and a taking leave, embodies all the ambivalence with which the "I" of the poem faces this development. This duality becomes even stronger in the second half of the poem. The words "dissolve" (*vergehen*), "drift away" (*verwehen*), and "burn away" (*verglühen*) point to the sense of loss brought about by spiritual redemption: erotic love is forfeited along with the existence of the physical world. The heart blossoms and suffers at the same time. At Gabriel's kiss, it still bore traces of burning passion, but now when the world's evening falls, it burns up as a purely spiritual soul. The invocation of the messianic state of "worldlessness" (*Weltlosigkeit*) is accompanied throughout by a sense of loss and mourning. In contrast to the orthodox metaphoric sublimation of the Song of Songs, Lasker-Schüler marks the loss that accompanies the transformation from sensual experience of love to spiritual unification. In the poem, eroticism and spirituality are simultaneously analogous and opposed: Shulamite is not wholly absorbed into the image of a people yearning for God; she remains a lover caught between conflicting longings. Her song constitutes the keynote of Else Lasker-Schüler's adaptations of the biblical text.

The Foreign Maidservants

Despite the shift in emphasis, "Shulamite" stays relatively close to the original text, unlike other poems that introduce a female biblical figure. Its resistance to pure spirituality appears in a much more iconoclastic form in other poems of this cycle. A good example is "Jacob and Esau," which goes far beyond the gentle reluctance expressed in "Shulamite" and recasts the Bible story along with its scale of values.

Jacob and Esau

Rebecca's maidservant is a heavenly visitor,
The angel wears a frock of rose petals
And on her countenance, a star.

She always looks to the light,
And her gentle hands enfold
A repast out of lentils gold.

Jacob and Esau bloom in her presence
And do not quarrel over the sweet-cakes
That she kneads in her lap for their sustenance.

> The brother leaves the chase to the younger
> And his birthright for the maidservant's favor;
> And wildly flings the thicket over his shoulder. (HB, 61)

The poem refers to an episode in the first book of Moses in which the twin sons of Isaac and Rebecca, Jacob and Esau, contend for the right of the firstborn and the blessing of their father. Jacob, who "was a plain man, dwelling in tents," faces wild Esau, who "was a cunning hunter, a man of the field" (Genesis 25:27). In the Bible story, Jacob, the younger son, buys the right of the firstborn from his older brother Esau. Jacob is encouraged by his mother, Rebecca, who prefers him. Isaac's favorite is Esau, the hunter, but with Rebecca's crafty aid, which Levinas praises so highly in his discussion of biblical women, Jacob's plan succeeds: he becomes the successor to the patriarch and takes his place after Abraham and Isaac in the line of biblical forefathers. In her poem "Jacob and Esau," Lasker-Schüler invents an additional female figure, alters the central incident of the fraternal dispute, and subverts the traditional moral of the story. Through the figure of Rebecca's maid she declares her sympathy for the wild and sensual Esau, who at the cost of his patriarchal inheritance chooses Eros and freedom.

Rebecca's maid has been freely invented by Lasker-Schüler. This added "heavenly visitor" who has on her countenance the star of illumination, in Else Lasker-Schüler's poetry a symbol of poetic inspiration, is in the truest sense Rebecca's alter ego: an extraordinary female angel, who in this form calls into question the legitimacy of the action of the biblical Jacob. In the original text, it is Jacob who prepares the dish of lentils, exploiting the wild love of food and drink and sensuality of his brother Esau in order to appropriate for himself his brother's inheritance. In the poem it is the maidservant who prepares the lentils and the meal. Esau surrenders his privileges as firstborn to his younger brother and chooses "the maidservant's favor." This evidently consists not only of the "repast of lentils," but of a sexual favor as well.

Rebecca's little angel wears "a frock of rose *petals* (Rosenblätter)" and enfolds with "gentle hands" a *Gericht* (repast), a word which not by chance echoes *Gedicht* (poem). In the interplay of foreignness (*Fremdheit*), femininity, and poetry she becomes a (self-)projection of the poet Else Lasker-Schüler, who allows herself this liberty with the original text. Her message entails fundamental changes to biblical moral conceptions. She questions the legitimacy of the fraternal dispute and of the subsequent deceit, the preference for the domesticated Jacob over the wild vagabond Esau, and the female role as keeper of the spiritualized, orthodox line of the patriarchs. The triumph of Jacob in the brothers' dispute over the inheritance, over the favor of their father and preference in the patriarchal line of succession that the Bible represents as right and just, is canceled by the *Gericht/Gedicht* of the angel/poet (*Engelin/Dichterin*): both brothers "bloom in her presence," in their common lineage. Jacob and Esau "do not quarrel over the sweet-cakes," Esau "leaves the chase to the younger / And his birthright for the maidservant's favor." This generous, conciliatory renunciation is far removed from the biblical text: there Esau "cried with a great and exceeding bitter cry" and "hated Jacob [. . .] and said in his heart, the days of mourning for my father are at hand, then will I slay my brother Jacob" (Genesis 7:28). In the Bible story Esau's loss of the claim to the rights of the firstborn is implemented by the loss of the paternal blessing. When Esau tries to present his father with game he has killed in order to receive his father's blessing, he finds that Jacob has preceded him. In spite of Isaac's initial preference for his wild son Esau, the Bible story in the end, with the help of Rebecca, comes to a "proper" conclusion: to Esau's fury, the civilized Jacob becomes the legitimate successor in the patriarchal line. In Lasker-Schüler's poem Esau abandons the "chase" to the younger brother, an ironic reversal since hunting is actually his domain. This rewording underlines that it is really Jacob, the brother praised in the Bible, who has taken something by force. Esau, on the other hand, has preferred the "favor" of the poetic and erotic pleasures promised by the invented maid to the inheritance of property and the promise of power. "And wildly flings the thicket over his shoulder": according to Genesis 25:25, Esau was covered in hair as by a "garment." At the end of the poem his wild covering of hair seems to merge with the undergrowth of the woods into whose thickets he disappears, perhaps accompanied by the heavenly visitor in the dress of rose petals. Above them shines Lasker-Schüler's star.

The poem "Hagar and Ishmael" also presents an alternative reading of the biblical text, one that sets itself in opposition to the patriarchal line of succession and the woman who collaborates with it. If Lasker-Schüler, in the guise of Rebecca's foreign maidservant, follows Esau into the thicket of the wilderness, then here she accompanies Ishmael—who in the Bible is called "a wild man" (Genesis 21:20) and who, like Esau, is "an archer" (Genesis 21:20)—and his mother Hagar, the Egyptian maid of Abraham's wife Sarah, into the desert. In the Bible narrative Ishmael and his mother are cast out by Abraham at the behest of Sarah, the original Jewish mother: "Wherefore she said unto Abraham, cast out this bondswoman and her son: for the son of this bondswoman shall not be heir with my son" (Genesis 21:10). Levinas considers Sarah's "harsh decision" that contributes to the orthodox course of biblical history to be a model of Jewish femininity. Lasker-Schüler, on the other hand, grieves for the fate of Ishmael and his mother and indicts those who have expelled them.

Hagar and Ishmael

With shells played Abraham's young sons,
floating their little vessels of mother-of-pearl,
then Isaac, anxious, leaned on Ishmael.

And full of sadness sang the two black swans
such somber melodies around their colored world
and Hagar disowned, swiftly stole her son away.

Into his little tears she shed her larger tear,
and their hearts murmured like the holy well
and hurried faster even than the ostrich birds.

The sun blazed on the glaring desert plain
and Hagar and her boy sank down into the yellow fur,
into the sand they dug their Negro teeth so white.

(Translated by Esther Kinsky for this book)

As in "Jacob and Esau," the relationship between the young brothers is initially peaceful. It is only the decision of the arch-father Abraham—behind which, according to the Bible, lies Sarah's demand—that separates the two and drives Ishmael and his mother into the desert. That Isaac "leaned on Ishmael" underlines that the rupture between Abraham's sons does not result from a dispute between them, but is the fault of the father figure and his female ally. It is not by chance that the boys are playing with vessels of *mother*-of-pearl (*Perlmutter*). Lasker-Schüler does not mention the involvement of Sarah, but with this word she nevertheless draws attention to the mother's role. In this context, however, mother-of-pearl, shimmering in all colors, takes on another meaning in the subsequent verses: carried through to the end of the poem is a dichotomy between color on the one hand and black-and-white on the other. The world in which the half-brothers play before the Egyptian maid and her son are expelled is described as colorful, and it is this colorful world that they lose through their forcible separation. The grieving, separated boys become "black swans," and the poem ends with a contrast of black and white. Because of the expulsion of the two foreigners, a world has been lost in which heterogeneous elements can exist together in a colorful and playful way. Lasker-Schüler hallows the unjustly expelled pair: their flight is compared to the running of ostriches, which were sacred creatures in Ancient Egypt. She calls the tears of the banished a holy well. This sadness replaces the flowing waters on which the shimmering boats could float before the cruel decision was made to part the two unequal brothers.

In "Jacob and Esau" Lasker-Schüler honors the foreign maidservant, juxtaposing her with the conformist biblical Rebecca, who aids and abets the future patriarch Jacob. In "Hagar and Ishmael" the poet sides with the Egyptian slave Hagar, who in the Bible story was driven out by the devout Sarah. Levinas puts it this way: "Without Sarah's harsh decision, Isaac would have been carried away by the wild games and laughter of his brother" (1990, 31). Lasker-Schüler's poem celebrates these games and this laughter. Even the ending, which describes the hardship of the banished foreigners who do not just metaphorically have to bite the sand, carries a note of sensuality. The "yellow fur" of the desert and the "Negro teeth so white" give an impression of wild strength, which the obsessively xenophobic and domesticating guardians of the orthodox succession should not be able to (mis-) appropriate with impunity.

Female Harbingers of the Messiah

In the biblical tradition, Ruth of Moab is the epitome of the "good stranger." After the deaths of their respective husbands, Ruth, though not an Israelite, refuses to return to her Moabite tribe and instead follows her mother-in-law Naomi back to Bethlehem. There, at Naomi's bidding, she seduces a relative of her deceased husband, the respected landowner Boaz, in order to feed herself and Naomi. As the end of the book of Ruth announces, King David will descend from the family line founded by Ruth and Boaz, as will one day the messiah.

Lasker-Schüler devotes two poems to this story, "Ruth" and "Boaz." Both are love poems, describing the meeting of the couple, to which the poet adds an implicit undertone of erotic wildness.

Boaz

Ruth searches everywhere
For golden cornflowers,
Passing by the grainkeepers' huts—

Bringing sweet storm
And glittering games
To Boaz's heart,

Which sways so high
In his corngarden
Toward the fair corncutter. (HB, 73)

In the rabbinical tradition Ruth was celebrated for rescuing the inheritance of the deceased husbands. By her seduction of Boaz, a relative of those men, she makes it possible to buy back the land that would otherwise have fallen into the hands of strangers, so becoming a heroine of Israel.

In the first lines of the poem Ruth looks not for useful, nourishing wheat, but for poetic cornflowers; her gathering leads her not *to*, but *past* "the grainkeepers' huts," the settled population. Unlike them, she is not seeking sustenance and security, but the stormy play of passion that she arouses in the heart of the wealthy landowner. As the transformation of his fertile fields into gardens demonstrates, she succeeds in her aim. That it is this seduced landlord and the female stranger unleashing a storm in his domesticated body and soul, who will engender the messiah, is proof of Lasker-Schüler's unorthodox conception of redemption.

The poem "Abigail," written a few years later, also sings the praises of a female stranger:

Abigail

She strode from Melech's house in her shepherdess's robe
Toward her young dromedary herds.

In noble race with the wild stallions
She drove the silver-goats out to graze,
Until the amethysts of evening were strung around the globe.
King Saul feared for his daughter.

She did not let her straying animals
Fall prey to the wilderness of hungry jackals,
Her arm, bloodied, bore their teethmarks;
She rescued her young goat from the lioness's jaw.
—The blind seer prophesied it every time . . .
The grasses trembled in the valley of Judea.

While, in her father's lap, little Abigail slept,
Over Judea Israel's lord listened
For the hostile Hittites.
The very scarabaeus of his crown decayed—
But the moon, still true, watched over Melech's domain,
And his warriors made ready with bow and arrow.

Until the Almighty blew out the golden shepherd's flame.
"Father Abraham" . . . explained Melech to his child,
"Shone virtuous in his eternal light."
Even his long-awaited star gleamed clear and white;
One could still see it sparkle in the wind:
"Once his father bound it, a little paschal lamb,
At the bidding of his Lord."

When in the fields the young rice blossomed,
Saul closed his mighty Jewish eyes,
And his Abigail came upon an angel in the pasture,
Who proclaimed: "Jehovah blew out the soul of your father." (HB, 71)[5]

Abigail is the wise and beautiful wife of Nabal, the man of Carmel, who in the first book of Samuel refuses to give David hospitality even though David has sent his men to protect Nabal's shepherds. When Abigail learns of her husband's ingratitude and of David's need of supplies, she brings him and his men wine, bread, and meat and persuades David not to punish Nabal. She thereby defies both Nabal's hostility to foreigners and David's desire for revenge (1 Samuel 25). Lasker-Schüler is using this incident as both a critique of the biblical founding fathers and an expression of hope for a new age. Retained in the poem is the celebration of Abigail, who was admired in the Haggadic tradition for her generosity, beauty, and wisdom, but also for her prophetic foresight. Lasker-Schüler, however, adds further attributes to Abigail's description, allowing her to appear as a wild maiden: in the first stanza she leaves her father's house and the regimented town to go into the wilderness and play in exuberant freedom with her untamed desert animals until her father summons her home. Abigail has to interrupt her games when the stars appear in the sky, "the amethysts of evening." Amethysts are violet and purple, hardly realistic colors for stars; perhaps the function of this metaphor is related to the meaning of the word in antiquity: in Ancient Greek "amethyst" means "averting intoxication." Together with her father the heavenly bodies put an end to Abigail's euphoric freedom.

The plot of the poem consists of a collage of at least three narratives. The first is drawn from Abigail's saving of David from Nabal, which is recognizable in poeticized form in the second stanza. The second strand—mainly the third stanza—refers to King Saul's defeat and death at the hands of the Hittites. The third narrative strand refers to the episode of Abraham's sacrifice of Isaac, which Saul relates to his daughter[6] in the fourth stanza.

The motif linking the latter two stories, which Lasker-Schüler has added to the biblical Abigail episode, is that of the father figure. In the first stanza, it is the father who calls his wild daughter back to the order of house and town. It is also the father who, in the fourth stanza, tells her about and praises the readiness of the patriarch Abraham to sacrifice his son Isaac. The words of the royal father are in quotation marks; the poem itself, by contrast, dramatically expresses the memory of the son Isaac and takes up a position both against Saul, the father-narrator who praises Abraham's attitude, and against the patriarch himself, who "at the bidding of his Lord" was prepared to sacrifice his son as "a little paschal lamb."[7]

The innocent "little paschal lamb" links this episode to Abigail, who, unlike the patriarch Abraham, *plays* with the silver-goats and rescues the young goat from the lioness. She does not expose the "straying animals" to the dangers of the desert. Her kindness toward strangers contrasts with Abraham's expulsion of Ishmael and Hagar and implicitly echoes the critique of the God-fearing subservience of the patriarch. So all the father figures, associated with the gold of might, are amalgamated and are now confronted by all that is silver or white, young and innocent: the goats, the moon, the star of Isaac, and the little paschal lamb, and perhaps even the "young rice," which in the first line of the last stanza promises renewal. When in the final lines the father's "mighty Jewish eyes" close, his death is not only a loss: it is announced to Abigail by an angel in the meadow. So despite the father's death, the New Testament motif of the proclamation of the Savior's birth, which was already prefigured in the "little paschal lamb," concludes the poem with a joyful message, with the prospect of an age in which the mighty fathers will have abdicated, allowing the world to become a place in which the wild girl can carry on her games undisturbed and no innocent creature is sacrificed.

This motif can also be found in other poems of the *Hebrew Ballads*. "Moses and Joshua" deals with the transfer of power from the old Moses to the young "wild Jew Joshua," whom the maidens of the Jewish people call their brother. In this ballad, Lasker-Schüler recasts the biblical description of Moses' death. Recalling Saul's tired "Jewish eyes," the poem speaks of Moses' "old dying eye," of his "tired lion soul" (HB, 67). The Bible, on the other hand, says: "And Moses was an hundred and twenty years old when he died: his eye was not dim, nor his natural force abated" (Deuteronomy 34:7). In contrast to the biblical narrative in which Moses only reluctantly makes way for the younger Joshua, Lasker-Schüler, as in "Abigail," evokes the triumph of a new and young, impetuous and non-authoritarian age, which succeeds the old order of the mighty but now weary fathers. The alliance of a poetry-writing, female biblical figure with youth and youthfulness also characterizes the poem "Esther." In Lasker-Schüler's reworking of the book that bears this name, Esther, who was able to save the Jews living in the empire of the Persian ruler Ahasuerus, is a poet. At night, according to the poem, she rests "with a Psalm." In the last lines of the poem the young Jews—"Israel's children"—"compose hymns to their sister." They carve these songs "into the pillars of the antechamber." In the biblical tradition this world is described as an antechamber of a redeemed world still to come. To Lasker-Schüler this "messianic spark" (Walter Benjamin) stands under the sign of a youthful poetry inspired by women, who become the central pillar of the hope of a new age. "Im Anfang" (In the Beginning), the last poem of *Hebrew Ballads* (1996, 167), speaks in playful, humorous lines of a time in which God was still a "young father." The present, however, requires redemption because the authoritarian father figure and youth are incompatible. In Lasker-Schüler's Bible poems this central motif of literary modernism is marked by both female and youthful rebellion. Lasker-Schüler lends her messianic vision of redemption a dimension that is very much of this world: she opposes the patriarchs and paterfamilias of all lands and times, the men of the Bible and their devout wives, as well as the "step-sons of God," the all-too-reasonable bourgeois and their submissive sisters of her own time.

Lasker-Schüler's models are not Sarah, Rebecca, Rachel, and Leah, these founding mothers of orthodox tradition, but the sensual poets, wild and free women from foreign nations: Ruth and Abigail, Hagar and Rebecca's maid. They are the true companions of Shulamite; their object of longing may be called Jerusalem, but Lasker-Schüler's idea of it is not to be found in the Book of Books.[8] In her Jerusalem the young brothers do not quarrel about the heritage of the fathers, because as long as the latter are willing to sacrifice and banish to the desert the foreigners and the wild at heart, the young and the poets, then other hopes are needed. These are, for Lasker-Schüler, only partly to be found in the Bible. The missing rest derives from a poetic, wild, and feminine imagination and her dreams of another possible community, another consciousness, another sensibility.

Saving Confusions:
Else Lasker-Schüler's Poetics of Redemption

The repeated attempts to impose a fixed identity on Else Lasker-Schüler, that master of performance, masquerade, and metamorphosis, are among the more paradoxical aspects of the reception of twentieth-century German-Jewish literature. Although Lasker-Schüler was mostly regarded as a poet of exotic dreams and playful fantasies who lived and wrote in a world out of time and far removed from reality, debates nevertheless flared up time and again as to whether she should be considered a German or a Jewish writer. This question was still an issue when, in the 1980s and early 1990s, literary studies had already largely turned their attention to intercultural and transcultural phenomena and, within German-Jewish literature, to the contentious hyphen between these two denominations. As late as 1993 there still was a discussion over whether she should be regarded as a true "representative of German 'Geist,' sent into exile"[1] or as a "conscious representative of her Jewish people."[2] One aspect of this discussion concerns the Oriental motifs in her work.

In 1955 Karl-Joseph Höltgen explicitly linked Lasker-Schüler's recourse to Oriental imagery to her Jewish identity and described it as an "unconscious unfolding" of her "ancient [Jewish] inheritance" (1955, 65): "Else Lasker-Schüler," according to Höltgen, "by no means imitates forms of oriental poetry, but, rather, draws on the same essential, oriental spirit from which such forms emerged" (1955, 39). This assessment fails to recognize the extent to which the Orient is deployed in Lasker-Schüler's writing as a means of artistic *Verfremdung* (defamiliarization) aimed at raising a critical awareness of existing conditions in her own time and place. Her Oriental masquerades contribute to a liberating blurring of precisely the categories of communal or collective belonging so often stressed both in her post-war reception and in more recent studies focusing on her Jewish roots. This subversive game occurs paradigmatically in Lasker-Schüler's 1907 poetic prose work *Die Nächte Tino von Bagdads*[3] (The Nights of Tino from Baghdad), of which the story "Der Grossmogul von Philippopel" (N, 48–57) (The Grand Mogul of Philippopel) is a powerful example.

The Nights of Tino from Baghdad

For a long time there was a consensus that Lasker-Schüler's prose was inferior to her poetry; it was rarely examined closely and often dismissed as belonging to the "debris of [her] failed efforts" (Kraft in Bänsch 1971, 43). Friedhelm Kemp writes that "most of the prose books," and he explicitly mentions *The Nights of Tino from Baghdad,* "have become unreadable" (in Bänsch 1971, 230). Werner Kraft observes "that artistically this prose is not of the quality of the poetry" (1951, 15). Höltgen, one of the first interpreters of her poetic oeuvre, states that the prose books are "only of historical or biographical interest" and maintains that one can "dispense with a detailed analysis" (1955, 3). He describes *The Nights of Tino from Baghdad* as "stories of trivial content" (1955, 26). That these judgments are based more on the expectations of the various critics than on considered aesthetic criteria is shown by the remark in an early dissertation on Lasker-Schüler by Fanni Goldstein that one could certainly "write a commentary on *The Nights* as if it were Faust," but that such a commentary was "*unnecessary* for literary studies" (1936, 12, emphasis added). However, what is considered "necessary" is historically determined and already implies an interpretation: if the post–Second World War period "needed" the conservative immortalization of the Jewish-German poet as a conciliatory figure and the early 1970s the unmasking of this legend, then contemporary discourses on the potential of literature to interrogate cultural barriers—not least between the West and the Orient—prompt a renewed discussion of Lasker-Schüler's work.[4] This perspective makes it possible to demonstrate that it is precisely Lasker-Schüler's prose, in particular *The Nights of Tino from Baghdad,* that justifies her topicality and her present "necessity."

The Nights of Tino from Baghdad, published in 1907 by the Axel Juncker publishing house, was, after *Peter Hille Buch* (1906), Lasker-Schüler's second prose work, and it represents a significant moment in her development. The period in which the stories in this book were written is also the time of her divorce from her first husband, the Jewish doctor Berthold Lasker, shortly after the birth of her child, of her marriage to Herwarth Walden, and of the separation from her bourgeois Jewish milieu. In this sense the book can be regarded as the veiled documentation of a triple emancipation—social, emotional, and artistic.[5] Through the persona of an Arabian princess, Tino, Lasker-Schüler presents a conception of poetic calling that articulates a rebellion against the power of patriarchal instances and their discourses.

Critics almost unanimously declare Lasker-Schüler to be "unpolitical," if they do not, like Bänsch, consign her to the camp of proto-fascist mythologists, or see her work in terms of a negative dialectic as a legitimate "flight from the world" and the poet as a dissident precisely where she avoids confrontation with political reality. An exception is Wieland Herzfelde, who knew Lasker-Schüler well in the years around World War I. According to him, Lasker-Schüler's self-declaration as "Prince of Thebes," her most famous persona,

> was the product of a truly democratic impulse. This uplifting impersonation was her way of rebelling against the ruling "Monarchy by God's Grace" [. . .] The elevation of the artist as self-ruler which she performed was a revolt against the spirit of subservience, against the division of society and of races into superhumans and subhumans, against the degradation not only of artists and poets, but no less of the "common people." (Herzfelde 1969, in Bauschinger 1980, 103)

Sigrid Bauschinger comments: "It does seem rather improbable, that [Lasker-Schüler] [. . .] wanted to protest against the Hohenzollern monarchy with the figure of the Prince of Thebes. Rarely would a protest have passed as entirely unnoticed as this one. There is not a word in all of her work that could be drawn on to support this argument" (1980, 103). It needs only a little imagination, however, to find Herzfelde's thesis confirmed in *The Nights.* It is also in this context that the Oriental background of the stories takes on a function that goes far beyond the purely ornamental. It becomes evident in "The Grand Mogul of Philippopel," one of the artistically more impressive stories of *The Nights,* that there is to be found neither the unfolding of an "unconscious Jewish inheritance" nor a German Orientalism with self-mystificatory intent, but a modernist mode of writing that takes the idea of defamiliarization seriously and whose effect is linked to the undermining and dissolution of established boundaries that could be observed in Lasker-Schüler's *Hebrew Ballads.*

"The Grand Mogul of Philippopel," one of the last and longest stories in the book, begins like a joke:

> The Grand Mogul of Philippopel is sitting in the garden of the Imperial Palace in the City of the Sultan; there comes a strange insect from the West and stings him on the tip of his tongue. He is, indeed, in the habit of letting it rest on his lower lip while he's thinking. And although the doctors attach no further importance to the mishap, it nevertheless comes to pass that the exalted lord imagines that he is no longer able to speak. (N, 48)

The story opens with an incident that is as banal as it is arbitrary and expands into a bizarre political and poetological parable. The principal characters in this fantastic story are the Grand Mogul, Minister of the Sultan, and the woman poet Tino, who is in love with Hassan and who tells the tale in the first person. The complicated content needs to be briefly summarized: the Grand Mogul, who believes that as a result of an insect sting he is no longer able to speak and who is urgently needed for the state affairs of the threatened empire, is to be healed by the poet after the efforts of the doctors and priests, the wise men, and the guards have proved futile. She is to find the legendary magic word that will restore the minister's speech and save the country. The "wonder-working lips" of the poet and her erotic love play do indeed cause the Grand Mogul to speak again, but in a language only Tino understands. She therefore becomes the official mouthpiece of the minister and is acknowledged by the Sultan and his entourage. At the very moment when the change overtakes the Grand Mogul, with whom the poet now appears to be living in a curious symbiosis, the poet herself, so it is said, also loses her own language. In reality, however, she is thinking about Hassan, the addressee of her "lost" language—a situation that echoes the motif of a secret, forbidden love that must "remain silent," and runs through the whole book.

Meanwhile, Tino stays at her post and transmits the expert opinions of the Grand Mogul, in a language, however, that is neither his—the official language of power and authority—nor hers—the hymnic language of her true love: instead it consists of *distortions* of the minister's decisions. The decrees that result from Tino's willful misrepresentations of the ruler's intentions are successful: Tino puts the Grand Mogul's enemies to flight and brings prosperity to the land. She introduces the duty-free import of "spices of foreign lands," invents new, nonviolent weapons, and changes "the death sentence on the pack of stray dogs" pronounced by the Grand Mogul into an instruction to build palaces for them. If in an earlier story the poet complains that she is not admitted into the palace, then here she temporarily wins recognition, at least as long as she is legitimated by the authority of a powerful man and appears to speak in his name. She exploits this situation with subversive intent to achieve political and social changes. But she gets no real pleasure from her success, because Hassan, her lover, has disappeared. Her work at the Imperial Diet (*Reichstagsgebäude*) is a welcome distraction, one which, however, is brought to an abrupt end: her deception is discovered in the documents of the Imperial Book and she is driven out of the palace in disgrace. Hassan does not acknowledge her and mocks her. She now wanders through the night as a solitary accompanied by a donkey: "And in the evening we lie under the big face of the moon, my donkey and I, and I read my fate, the engraved pictures of his shaggy hide!" (N, 57).

Like the other prose pieces in the book, "The Grand Mogul of Philippopel" is an extravagant story with autobiographical undertones. It is a disguised reflection on the role and fate of the writer in a philistine society, with clear allusions to the Wilhelmine Empire. The representatives of the country meet in the "Reichstagsgebäude" (Imperial Diet), and the Balkans are in danger of being swallowed up. In the story, however, the "Balkans" are the Empire and the "Reichstagsgebäude" unmistakably evokes Berlin. Like the whole story, this is evidently a transposition to the Orient of the circumstances of the German Reich. The duties "on spices of foreign lands" is an allusion to its protectionist economic policies and, more generally, to the exclusion of foreign influences of every kind—possibly an additional pointer to Lasker-Schüler's understanding of her Oriental imagery as resistance to the chauvinism and uniformity sought by official Wilhelmine cultural policy.

It is not by chance that the creature upsetting the order of the empire is a "strange," literally a *foreign* insect that comes from the Occident, "from the West": seen from the Orient, it is thus the West that is foreign. This inversion, in which the West is the disturbing exotic force, one with which the (Western) reader finds herself identifying, makes the latter aware of the exclusion of the foreign by way of a reversal of the habitual situation. The Grand Mogul's "death sentence on the pack of stray dogs," which the poet falsifies and transforms into a blessing, suggests a condemnation of traveling people, vagabonds and artists, clowns and bohemians. "The inhabitants of the Balkans no longer doubt in the least that blue blood flows through the veins of the shabby animals. The canine aristocrats living in misery become fashionable, rich harem ladies buy unkempt canine princesses for a thousand piasters as lapdogs" (N, 55). In a fairy tale–like utopia demonstrating the effect of artists on the conditions of cultural policy, palaces are built for the impoverished stray artists/dogs thanks to the intervention of the poet. At the same time these lines contain a reference to the danger of the incorporation and domestication of the subversive influence of these "stray" artists ("herrenlos," literally "masterless"): they must beware of becoming bribable and so losing their independence, of becoming "fashionable" and turning into "lapdogs of the philistine ladies."[6]

The poet Tino, we are told, loses her "own" language as she misrepresents the decisions of the minister; when she finds it again, she is simultaneously exposed. The language she recovers—that is, the language of the story itself—unites three elements: it is a poetic language (she speaks "only in verses now"), it tells of a forbidden love ("Oh Hassan, marvelous Hassan"), and it is—as substratum of the linguistic distortion of the powerful—the medium of those expelled from the marketplace, those who represent a threat to the political, social, and cultural order of the empire. After the discovery of the deception Tino is driven out of the city. She has used feminine wiles to seduce the minister, and now her "long locks are cut off," and she roams around poor and lonely, a woman in shabby men's clothing, a drifting poet—no lapdog for fine ladies.

In the concluding scene of "The Grand Mogul of Philippopel" a biblical reference is superimposed on the oriental background that, while evoking Jewish scriptures, neither produces these "unconsciously" from her Oriental-Jewish "blood" and "spiritual inheritance" (Höltgen 1955, 65) nor misuses them for purposes of self-mystification, but transposes them into a modernist poetics. The final image of the story, where the outcast wanders through the desert, suggests a messianic figure whose interpreting of the oracles on the donkey's hide reinforces the impression that Lasker-Schüler has incorporated elements of the biblical story of Balaam. Balaam, the foreign soothsayer, is appointed by the Moabite king Balak to curse the people of Israel. Balaam sets out on his donkey, but turns the curse he was charged with into a blessing and so saves the Israelites. To the fury of his enemies his prophecies come true and change the course of history. According to some traditions Balaam is a herald of the messiah. Two further details confirm this link. In "Der Magier" (The Magician), the prose text preceding "The Grand Mogul of Philippopel," the father figure bears the name "Bor Ab Baloch." The father of the biblical Balaam is called "Beor," "Ab" means father, and "Baloch" may refer to Balak, who commissioned Balaam.[7] In "The Magician," Bor Ab Baloch is the father of Tino's weak lover, who abandons her. It may be concluded from "The Grand Mogul of Philippopel" that here, after Tino's lover, who in this story is called Hassan, has disappeared, Tino, the alter ego of Lasker-Schüler, assumes Balaam's inheritance as prophetic and messianic figure instead of the legitimate but unworthy son. Transferred to the level of Lasker-Schüler's poetics, this motif recapitulates the model running through *The Nights* of a self-assertion of the female poet who opposes the old order of the strong fathers and takes the place of the unreliable inheritor who has been judged too weak. She achieves this through the effect of defamiliarization, distortion, and confusion created by her poetic language.

That Lasker-Schüler was at least aware of the Balaam legend and equated the function of the biblical interpreter with redemption through confusion—in the story a liberating distortion—is evident from the correspondences between her 1902 poem "Weltflucht" (1996, 234) (Flight from the World) and the poem "Elbanaff" (1996, 520–21), which according to Lasker-Schüler herself represents the "translation" of the former poem into a "mystical Asiatic language."[8]

In "Elbanaff," the mystical-Asiatic version of her poem "Weltflucht," only individual semantic particles are comprehensible, and the eighth and ninth lines read "Anahu jatelahu / Wanu *bilahum*"—in the German "translation" the corresponding lines are *"Wirrwarr* endend! / [. . .] *verwirrend"* (Ending the tangle / confusing): "bilahum" accordingly stands for "confusing." "Anahu" contains the Greek root *ana*, which in words such as *anagram* and *anastrophe* stands for "rearrangement, transformation, reordering": thus "Anahu jatelahu" indicates "ending the tangle," that is, ending confusion, through—confusion? This correlation also reflects the actions of the poet *in* the story—her distortion of the decrees of those in power—and the confusing shape of the story itself.

On both levels, confusion/distortion is granted a liberating and redeeming function: the story's distortion of the language of the rulers by the poet leads temporarily to a new order, to a utopian state of affairs, in which borders are opened, enemies retreat, and artists move into the palaces. There is a correspondence to this distortion in the narrative mode of the text: its estrangement of linguistic and narrative conventions aims at a similar liberation. The undistorted—that is, "realistic"—mode of representation is equated with the form of communication used by the rulers. Tino/Lasker-Schüler is the poetic rebel who threatens their power by infiltrating and "corrupting" their medium of expression. The modernist poetics sketched out here confers a revolutionary function on the effect of experimental modes of writing.

Weltflucht

Ich will in das Grenzenlose
Zu mir zurück,
Schon blüht die Herbstzeitlose
Meiner Seele,
Vielleicht ists schon zu spät zurück,
O, ich sterbe unter euch!
Da ihr mich erstickt mit euch.
Fäden möchte ich um mich ziehen
Wirrwarr endend!
Beirrend,
Euch *verwirrend*,
Zu entfliehn
Meinwärts.

Elbanaff

Min salihihi wali kinahu
Rahi hatiman
fi is bahi lahi fassun—
Min hagas assama anadir,
Wakan liachid abtal,
Latina almu lijádina binassre.
Wa min tab ihi
Anahu jatelahu
Wanu *bilahum.*
Assama ja saruh
fi es supi *bila* uni
El fidda alba hire
Wa wisuri—elbanaff!

Flight from the world

I will go back into the endlessness
Back to myself,
The autumn saffron of my soul already
in bloom,
maybe it is too late already to go back,
Oh, I am dying among you!
As you suffocate me with yourself.
I want to spin threads around myself
Ending the tangle,
Leading astray,
Confusing you,
To take flight
Mywards. (Emphasis added)

(TRANSLATED BY ESTHER KINSKY FOR THIS BOOK)

The "confusing" stylistic features of the story are manifold: the opaque allegory; the muddling of time and space; the jumbling of Occident and Orient with the "Reichstagsgebäude" in the capital of the Sultan and the "Negro and Occidental laborers" as the builders of the dog palaces; the elements of a childish, a-syntactical, or dialect-like use of language ("wir können uns nicht heiraten"—we can't marry ourselves; "streiten sich einander"—argue one another; "dem Gespräch, [. . .] was wir führen"—the conversation [. . .] what we have); but above all the continuous irony and the various elements of the fantastic. The liberating function of the distortion holds good equally for the poet Tino *in* the story as for Lasker-Schüler's readers. Expelled because of her misrepresentation of official language, she evades the fate of the canine aristocrats in their palaces, of being sold as a "lap toy." She makes fun of the philistines' use of art and conveys the vision of redemption through art.

Redemption in "The Grand Mogul of Philippopel" is located at the level of language: it is not by chance that the starting point of the story is the patriarch's loss of the power of speech. He is evidently suffering from a "linguistic crisis" produced by the sting of a foreign insect, feeling alienated from language. In its estrangement it is no longer at his disposal, is no longer at his command. The poet, too, was robbed of her speech—but she, it is said, loses only *her* language. He is presented as a hypochondriac, a *malade imaginaire*—perhaps a caricature Lasker-Schüler draws here of literary contemporaries suffering from the crisis of language (*Sprachkrise*).[9] *She* by contrast has magical poetic power and speaks in a "foreign," an alien language. Unlike the minister, who refuses "to make himself understood in any other way," the poet certainly does find alternative means of expression—that is, by way of an inauthentic (*uneigentlich*—not her own) language, of distortion and estrangement. The speech-sickness of the Grand Mogul is confronted with the usurpation of his words by the poet with the aim of both social criticism and linguistic creativity. Her role corresponds to that of the trickster as an agent of cultural rejuvenation who lends language new life. In the "false" transmission of the words of the Grand Mogul, she acts as the joker who undermines the rules. The trickster is, by definition, a double thief, endowed with magical powers, "who steals things, but who also, thanks to his mimetic talent, infiltrates himself into all things" (Lenk 1983, 45). The poet "steals" the words of the Grand Mogul with female cunning; her magical power—her gift of finding the magic word, the spell that liberates—consists in her ability to steal herself into the language of the rulers. There she does not speak her *own* language, but in her function as transforming medium—in the "inauthenticity" of her expression, characteristic of literature—she effects changes in reality. She replaces the words of those who are in power with a language that is not her own (*eigen*), that is neither "authentic" (*eigentlich*) nor her "property" (*Eigentum*), a language that neither belongs to her nor grants belonging. The end of the story associates this rejection of a fixed place, a finished figure, and a defined identity with the role of the trickster just as much as it does with the Oriental wanderer in the desert, the expelled Jew, or the outcast Redeemer: straying and causing confusion (*irrend und verwirrend*), the trickster "wanders further, ever further, aimlessly across the earth" (Lenk 1983, 55). Like the trickster, like Tino, Lasker-Schüler steals into the various traditions and identities, incorporating them into her poetic imagination and carrying them further.

PART THREE

COMMUNITIES OF FATE

A Counter-Prayer:
Paul Celan's "In Front of a Candle"

Any attempt to situate Paul Celan and his work in relation to Judaism and the Jews is confronted with the controversies that accompanied his rise to fame as the most important post-war poet writing in the German language. Even prior to asking how "Jewish" Celan's poems are, critics disagreed about the concreteness of their signification—the literalness of their references, the specific historicity of their dates, the identity of their addressee (Gadamer 1973). These controversies arose even in Celan's lifetime and were, at least partly, generated by often polysemic or seemingly contradictory statements made by Celan himself. While no one contests the impact of his Jewish origins and fate and the importance he attached to several Jewish precursors or fellow poets, or the presence of Jewish topics and motifs in his poetry, critics disagreed about "what it means to identify Celan as a Jewish poet" (Ivanovic 1999), and about the specific relationship Celan entertained with "the Jews" as a community or, by extension, with communities altogether. The elucidation of this relationship is complicated by Celan's own warning against "forcing his poems into the confines of Judaism or the fate of the Jews" (Meinecke in Ivanovic 1999) on the one hand, and on the other, by the famous epigraph "vse poety zhidy" (All poets are Jews), that introduces his poem "Und mit dem Buch aus Tarussa" (2003, 164)[1] ("And with the Book from Tarussa"). This epigraph, a variation on a verse by Marina Tsvetayeva (Ivanovic 1999), has itself given rise to multiple conflicting interpretations.

For some, the epigraph's fusion of poet and Jew proved that Celan regarded Jewishness as essentially a metaphor for a sensibility originating in subjugation, exile, and oppression and applicable to all poets independent of their origin or history, because they are inherently outsiders to mainstream society. Others read the epigraph as an affirmation and consolidation of Celan's identity as a Jewish poet or—in a more disparaging mode—as a poetic "caretaker of Jewish collective suffering" (in Ivanovic 1999). The French critic Henri Meschonnic, who accuses Celan's first French translators of disregarding the poet's Jewish origins, of universalizing the specific experiences voiced in his poems, and of concomitantly transforming "a historical into a metaphysical suffering" (1973, 383), insists that the epigraph meant to convey his commitment to the tortured Jewish community. In explaining the function of Celan's frequent biblical references, Meschonnic writes: "[In his biblical allusions] Celan makes himself be one with those, his own [people], whose suffering he cannot bear; he thus marks a *we* [. . .]. It is this *we* that Marina Tsvetayeva's verse renders boundless" (1973, 377) ("Celan prend [dans les allusions bibliques] surtout de faire un avec ceux, les siens, dont il ne supporte pas la souffrance. Il y prend donc un *nous* [. . .]. C'est ce *nous* que le vers mis en épigraphe, de Marina Tsvetajeva, rend sans frontières"). For Meschonnic, universalist readings of Celan's verses imply a denial of the poet's "rootedness in a cultural elsewhere" (1973, 386).

For Jean Bollack, who knew the poet personally and who became one of the major readers of Celan in France, Meschonnic does not go far enough in his critique of universalist interpretations of Celan because he neglects to mention the insult implied in the Russian *zidy* quoted by Celan from Tsvetayeva: "Meschonnic," Bollack writes, "erroneously believed that the epigraph undoes the boundaries of the 'we,' although he elsewhere [correctly] emphasizes the Jewish specifics [in his poetry]. This is hard to understand. Does the quote, with this positive connotation of the word Jew [instead of the Russian slur *zidy,* which Celan actually uses], transfer Celan's experience to all poets? These would then be compelled to become Jews like himself. This does not make sense" (2000, 201). Likewise, Bollack rejects the interpretation of the epigraph by Jacques Derrida, who, in *Schibboleth pour Paul Celan,* writes:

> The wound, the experience of reading itself, is universal [. . .]. To say that "all poets are Jews" is a statement that marks *and* crosses out the marks of a circumcision. It is metaphorical. All those who inhabit language as poets are Jews, but in a metaphorical sense. And therefore the one who, speaking as a poet and using a metaphor, no longer presents himself literally as a Jew.

> La blessure, expérience même de la lecture, est universelle [. . .]. Dire que 'tous les poètes sont des Juifs', voilà une proposition qui marque *et* annule les marques d'une circoncision. Elle est tropique. Tous ceux qui habitent la langue en poètes sont des juifs, mais en un sens tropique. Et celui qui le dit, par conséquent, parlant en poète et selon un trope, ne se présente plus littéralement comme un juif. (Derrida 1986, 98–105)

After noting that "Celan strictly avoided metaphors," Bollack explains that "Derrida transferred the community to the structure of language" and comments sarcastically: "They all should be Jews, as poets are Jews. They are all exiled, even the Jews. Everyone a Celan" (2000, 201).

These controversies perhaps reveal more about these writers than about Celan, and determining how Celan's epigraph "All poets are Jews" is to be understood requires a closer look at its source. It is worth noting that the epigraph is already a variation on Tsvetayeva's original verse: "Poety—zhidy!" (Ivanovic 1999) (Poets are Jews). In a lucid reconstruction of the epigraph's origins Christina Ivanovic quotes the original verse by Tsvetayeva in its context, a poem entitled "Poem of the End," which was written on the occasion of a last walk with a lover that led them past the Prague ghetto and which includes the lines:

Ghetto of the chosen-ones!	(Getto izbrannich estv!
Wall and ditch.	Val i rov.
Expect no mercy!	Poshchady ne zhdi!
In this most Christian of all worlds,	V som khristianeishem iz mirov
The poets are Jews!	Poety—zhidy!)

Tsvetayeva, a non-Jewish poet, expresses her solidarity with the Jews on the other side of the ghetto's fence. Celan's response, on the one hand, is to honor this gesture by his fellow poet by extending his own identity as a Jewish poet to *all* poets. This community created across religious, ethnic, or cultural divides is undone by critics who want to enclose him strictly in Jewish folds. At the same time, however, Celan's variation on Tsvetayeva's verse implicitly calls the gesture of the poet—including Tsvetayeva's poetic expression of solidarity with those on the other side of the ghetto wall and, by extension, the one of his own epigraph itself—"Jewish." This paradoxical attitude and its ramifications can inform a reading of poems by Celan that display a similar attitude to alliances based on a pre-established consensus and the adherence to common beliefs and traditions.

Celan's poem "Vor einer Kerze" (In Front of a Candle)[2] is a commemoration of the dead that transforms a collective ritual into a radically private poetic act. Between dialogue and meditation, between prayer and blasphemy, between quotation and secret language there develops a poetic ritual of *Beschwörung*—conjuration—in all the dimensions and meanings of the word: as oath (*Schwur*), as entreaty, as mystical spell.[3] Between hope and despair, between success and failure, in the kindling of memory the poem probes the possibilities and the scope of the poetic word as transformation of language into event. This intermediate position is related to the title of the volume from which the poem is taken. "In Front of a Candle" is to be found in *Von Schwelle zu Schwelle* (From Threshold to Threshold),

Vor einer Kerze

Aus getriebenem Golde, so
wie du's mir anbefahlst, Mutter,
formt ich den Leuchter, daraus

sie empor mir dunkelt inmitten
splitternder Stunden:
deines
Totseins Tochter.

Schlank von Gestalt,
ein schmaler, mandeläugiger Schatten
Mund und Geschlecht
umtanzt von Schlummergetier,

entschwebt sie dem klaffenden Golde,
steigt sie hinan
zum Scheitel des Jetzt.

Mit nachtverhangnen
Lippen
sprech ich den Segen:

Im Namen der Drei,
die einander befehden, bis
der Himmel hinabtaucht ins Grab
    der Gefühle,
im Namen der drei, deren Ringe
am Finger mir glänzen, sooft
ich den Bäumen im Abgrund das
    Haar lös,
Auf daß die Tiefe durchrauscht
    sei von reicherer Flut—,
Im Namen des ersten der Drei,
der aufschrie,
als es zu leben galt dort, wo vor ihm
    sein Wort schon gewesen
im Namen des zweiten, der zusah
    und weinte,

In Front of a Candle

Of chased gold, as
you instructed me, Mother,
I shaped the candlestick from
    which
she darkens up for me in the midst
of splintering hours:
your
being dead's daughter.

Slender in build,
a narrow, almond-eyed shade,
her mouth and her sex
surrounded by slumber beasts,
    dancing,
she drifts up from the gaping gold,
she ascends
to the crown of the Now.

With lips draped
by night
I speak the blessing:

In the name of the three who war
among themselves until heaven dips
down into the grave of feelings,

in the name of the three whose
rings glint on my finger whenever
I loosen the hair of the trees in the
    chasm,
so that richer torrents may
    rush through the deeps—,
in the name of the first of the three,
who cried out
when called upon to live where his
    word had been before him,
in the name of the second who
    looked on and wept,

im Namen des dritten, der weiße	in the name of the third, who piles up
Steine häuft in der Mitte,—	white stones in the centre,—
Sprech ich dich frei	I pronounce you free
vom Amen, das uns übertäubt,	of the amen that drowns our voices,
vom eisigen Licht, das es säumt,	of the icy light on its edges
da, wo es turmhoch ins Meer tritt	where, high as a tower, it enters the sea
da, wo die graue, die Taube	where the grey one, the dove
aufpickt die Namen	pecks up the names
diesseits und jenseits des Sterbens:	on this and the other side of dying:
Du bleibst, du bleibst, du bleibst	you remain, you remain, you remain
Einer Toten Kind,	a dead woman's child,
geweiht dem Nein meiner Sehnsucht	to the No of my longing consecrated,
vermählt einer Schrunde der Zeit,	wedded to a fissure in time
vor die mich das Mutterwort führte,	to which I was led by a mother's word
auf daß ein einziges Mal	so that once only
erzittre die Hand,	a tremor should pass through the hand
die je und je mir ans Herz greift!	that again and again reaches out for my heart!
(CG, 73–74)	(2002, 55)

in the section "Mit wechselndem Schlüssel" (With a Changing Key). Both titles are evidently concerned with the attempt to enter a place to which access is denied.

From Threshold to Threshold suggests someone who is standing at the door, who is "outside," homeless, wandering, seeking refuge. At the same time, these words recall the episode in the Passover story in which the angel of death passes from "threshold to threshold" and spares only those who have fastened the sign of the covenant with God to their door post. Contemplating the Third Reich's "angels of death," who brought destruction "from threshold to threshold" of Jewish houses, Celan retraces their path and searches for the entrance to the realm of the dead. This archaic theme of myth, religion, and literature finds in these lines its individual, poetic expression. "With a Changing Key" suggests the diversity of traditional forms and means of the conjuration of the dead that is alluded to in the poem "In Front of a Candle." The necessity of "changing" the key also conveys the inadequacy of traditional conventions of remembering the dead; these conventional rituals are alternately invoked and, through their estrangement in the poetic word, "exchanged": it is in this gesture that the individual space of the poem unfolds.

From Threshold to Threshold and "With a Changing Key" can also be understood as "reading instructions." *From Threshold to Threshold* describes a path, a movement, a wandering, and implicitly also a desire to be admitted to perception and knowledge, to the experience evoked in the poem. The threshold is a liminal place that offers neither shelter nor certainty. Rather, it brings to mind a knocking on the door, a sounding, a searching for possible openings that would lead into a place of concealment, into the secret of the poem. This metaphor is pursued in the title "With a Changing Key," which points to the encoded character of Celan's language as well as to the inadequacy of a single "code" in deciphering the poems. In describing Celan's poetry there is often reference to his "cipher language" (*Chiffrensprache*). Unlike the collective, generally accessible symbol, the cipher can be understood only in relation to the specific—that is, individual—context. For the reader the "changing of the key" means, on the one hand, paying attention to references and allusions to various collective traditions and, on the other, the necessity of unraveling the meaning of the words each time anew.

The resistance confronting the reader in the hermeticism of the poem parallels the individual refusal that Celan, in his poetry, offers to what is worn-out and misused in language. In the poem "In Front of a Candle" this "counterword" (*Gegenwort*) to the habitual use of words has not only implicit but also thematic and programmatic dimensions. Bernd Witte's explanation is particularly applicable to "In Front of a Candle": "The hermetic poem challenges the reader to [. . .] meditate in language [. . .] Seen in this way, poetry becomes through its form, as Celan himself remarks, an instrument of meditation" (1981, 145). Witte is alluding to Celan's famous words in the "Meridian" speech he gave on receiving the Georg Büchner Prize: "The attentiveness a poem attempts to devote to all it encounters, with its sharper sense of detail, outline, structure, color, but also of 'quiverings' and 'allusions,' all of that is, I believe, no achievement of the eye daily competing with constantly more perfect instruments. Rather, it is a concentration that stays mindful of all our data. 'Attentiveness'—allow me here to quote a saying by Malebranche from Walter Benjamin's Kafka-essay—'Attentiveness is the natural prayer of the soul'" (Celan 1983, 3:198).[4]

The title of the poem "In Front of a Candle" evokes meditation and prayer. The candle is the traditional means and symbol of remembrance of the dead. The transcendental tendency of its verticality, the unity of material candle and "spiritual" light, suggest the linking of earth and heaven. From church and churchyard candles to the Jewish memorial candles lit on the anniversary of a parent's death, the Sabbath candles, and the menorah, the seven-branched candelabrum of the Great Temple, from the rites of occultism to the "nocturnal beam of light" of the romantic literary tradition, the candle enjoins meditation, radiates magical fascination, and inspires poets. In *La Flamme d'une chandelle* Gaston Bachelard meditates on the ritual, magical, and poetic power of the candle and unites these dimensions, as in Celan's poem, under the sign of memory: "In front of a candle, as soon as one dreams, what one sees is nothing compared to what one imagines [. . .] Images and memories conjoin. The dreamer in front of the flame unites what he sees with what he has seen. He knows the fusion of imagination and memory" (1984, 17). With the title "In Front of a Candle," therefore, Celan starts with a collective sign creating a conventional space of anticipation, which, however, he leads into one's "innermost straits" (*eigenste Enge*), in which the poetic word is "set free" (CGW, 3:200). This transformation from common symbol to a private poetic act suggesting a liberation from communal consensus is both reflected upon in the content of the poem and enacted in each of its lines.

The poem has four parts: two stanzas of seven verses each, a short stanza of three verses, and a long section indented toward the middle of the page. In terms of content the poem is divisible into two parts. The first pair of sections, which can still be described as stanzas in the traditional sense, oscillate between description and invocation. After a brief "notice" there follows the "blessing" spoken in front of the candle that has been "shaped" in the first part. In changing speech acts, the poem aims for the magical and living word, which it simultaneously itself seeks to embody.

> Of chased gold, as
> you instructed me, Mother,
> I shaped the candlestick [. . .]

The poem starts out in old-fashioned, almost biblical language. In Exodus we read: "And thou shalt make a candlestick of pure gold: of beaten work shall the candlestick be made: his shaft and his branches, his bowls, his knops, and his flowers, shall be of the same" (Exodus 25:31). And further: "And he made the candlestick of pure gold: of beaten work made he the candlestick [. . .] And he made his seven lamps, and his snuffers, and his snuff dishes, of pure gold" (Exodus 37:17–23). The menorah, the biblical candelabrum, bearer of the "eternal light" destroyed with the Great Temple of Jerusalem, has seven lamps, seven branches; the first stanza of the poem also has seven lines. In the middle of the stanza (that is, at the end of its fourth line), there is also the word *inmitten*—"in the midst." From the beginning there is a quasi-mimetic correlation between the candlestick or candle and the poem.

In this context the multiple meanings of the word *getrieben*—beaten, chased, driven—lay down the perspective of the poem. "Chased" means "shaped by blows" and signifies, with reference to the goldsmith's work, the working of a precious metal. It can refer to the poet, to Celan's understanding of himself, who regards his verses as language shaped "by blows," marked by the traces of his own fate.

Hence, *getrieben* (chased) here is also a reminder of "hunted," of "chased or driven out." The creative urge of the poet likewise finds an echo here. Paradoxically, but also of significance to Celan, *getrieben* additionally calls to mind the sprouting, the *forcing* of plants, of fruit: the poetic gold as fruit of the poet's seeking and creating. The origin of the poem and of Celan's work altogether is constituted in the conjunction of these meanings.

In the first line the relationship between the golden candlestick and the language of poetry is emphasized by the enjambment undermining the traditional tone: "Aus getriebenem Golde, *so*" ("Of chased gold, *as*"; emphasis added). "As," that is, *just as* it happens here, the candlestick was formed in words, in language, in the poem. There is a similar performative dynamic in the third line: "formt ich den Leuchter, *daraus*"—"I shaped the candlestick *from which*." Because of the retroactive effect of the pause after "daraus"/"from which," there is the suggestion that the candlestick was also formed "daraus"—that is, from words.

In the transition between the first and the second line there also occurs, in terms of content, the first break with the Jewish tradition: God's original commandment to the people, to collectively shape the candlestick (or candelabrum), becomes the personal instruction of the mother to an individual "I." If in Celan the "mother," as elsewhere in his work, also refers in a much wider sense to what was lost, what was killed and destroyed in the Holocaust, then here the remembering, in contrast to religious ritual, occurs in the naming of a personal loss and a private relationship. In "I shaped the candlestick" it is not the paternal word of the Bible that was obeyed but "the word of the mother." In Proverbs we read: "My son, hear the instruction of thy father, and forsake not the law of thy mother. [. . .] For the commandment is a lamp and the law is a light [. . .]" (Proverbs 1:8; 6:23). By addressing only the mother Celan implicitly negates the paternal instance—that of "God the Father."

After the first three lines have specified the lowest part of the candle, the candlestick, now the candle itself appears:

> [. . .] from which
> she darkens up for me in the midst
> of splintering hours:
> your
> being dead's daughter.

In the verticality of the movement, through the chosen word *empor* (up) and through the elevated, antiquated word order, the desire of "drawing up" the past becomes evident. The candle "darkens up," disappointing expectations of light and clarity associated with candles. This creates, as with Novalis's "black-burning lamp" (1985, 146), an uncanny atmosphere opposed to the everyday and the familiar. This oxymoron underlines the darkness of the candle, the "dark" and therefore only faint memory, whose shadowiness is what must be overcome, but also the somber sorrow accompanying this memory.

The darkness, however, also refers to Celan's own language. He explains: "Remembering what is most somber, surrounded by what is most questionable, even if the tradition in which it stands is recalled, it [German poetry] can no longer speak the language which some willing ears still seem to expect of it. [. . .] It is [now] a 'greyer' language" (CGW, 3:167). Darkness also designates the difficulty of Celan's poetry itself. Through this linking of dark, hermetic language and the somber poetic work of mourning, the collective symbol of the candle is turned into the private cipher of Celan's commemoration.

In the lines "in the midst / of splintering hours," the temporal and spatial dimensions are drawn together. In the pictorial representation of the Now as "splintering hours," as in the transition from the past tense in "I shaped" to the present tense in "she darkens," the past is made tangible and brought up to the present. The "splintering hours" of this remembrance of the dead stand in contrast to the official Jewish prayer for the dead: "In front of you, God, I remember my departed—in childlike love. May you, too, remember them at a *blessed hour*."[5]

The homophony in *Mutter* (mother), *inmitten* (in the midst) and *splitternder* (splintering) is noticeable:

> wie du's mir anbefahlst, *Mutter,*
> formt ich den Leuchter, daraus
> sie empor mir dunkelt *inmitten*
> *splitternder* Stunden:

Step-by-step an implicit relationship is established between these words. The first two words, *Mutter* and *inmitten,* emphasize the central place of the mother as "middle," as thematically and existentially central to Celan. The alliteration in the second and the third words evokes the splintering and breaking-up of this middle, suggesting the dissolution of any centralized world view. Returning to the first of the three words, "mother" refers to the cause of this shattering of the center. With the "being dead" of the mother (*Mutter*) the center is marked by an absence and the only "middle" (*inmitten*) remaining is the splintering (Zer*splitter*ung) itself. As sole orientation there remains only the remembrance of those absent, the memory of "your being dead's daughter."

As the *Docht* (wick)—which in the last line of this stanza appears to echo in the sounds *Tot* (dead) and *Tocht(er)* (daughter)—is in the middle of the candle, so does "daughter," the "fruit" of the mother's being dead, become the central thread of the poem. The word *Totsein* (being dead), in contrast to *Tot* (dead), conjures up a visualization of the mother by pointing not so much to a past occurrence as to a present state. Memory, this "daughter" of the maternal "being dead," is also the "sister" repeatedly appealed to in Celan's poems, the ally for whose survival his poetry is accountable. Here, too, the traditional designation of the Jewish people as "daughters of Zion" (Ecclesiastes) is turned into a personal reference. In *Celan und die Mystiker,* Joachim Schulze brings out the complex relationship between the cabbalistic conception of the "eternal-feminine" and the "shechinah," the divine light, and mentions the "sexual union with the 'sister' corresponding to the 'shechinah'" (1976, 47). The shechinah is also symbolized by the middle candle of the menorah: "The wick stands for the main 'Sefirah' (vessel), equated with the 'shechinah.'"[6]

This first stanza begins to sketch out the central tension of the poem, which arises from the intersection between ritualized, collective, and conventional commemoration of the dead on the one hand and personal, private remembrance on the other. The second stanza now "lights" the flame.

> Slender in build,
> a narrow, almond-eyed shade,
> her mouth and her sex
> surrounded by slumber beasts, dancing[.]

The representation of the candle merges with a female figure already heralded in the first line: by way of "being dead's daughter," by way of memory, these (likewise seven) lines summon up the vision of the mother out of the flame of remembrance. The "she," the "slender," "narrow" figure, which refers simultaneously to the candle and to the mother figure invoked from the past, is conjured up in the verticality of her rising upward from the realm of the dead, perhaps also from Goethe's "realm of mothers" (*Reich der Mütter*). Like the dark memory, "slender" and "narrow" are also to be understood as the meagerness, which must be overcome, of the actual, pictorial imagination of the remembering eye. The "almond-eyed shade" corresponds on the figurative level first of all to the form of the flame. This metaphor, too, simultaneously transforms the traditional into a private reference. In Exodus we read again: "And thou shalt make a candlestick of pure gold: of beaten work [. . .]. Three bowls made like unto almonds, with a knop and a flower in one branch; and three bowls made like almonds in the other branch, with a knop and a flower: so in the six branches that come out of the candlestick" (Exodus 25:31; 25:33). The "almond-eyed shade" is reminiscent of Celan's cipher of the "almond" as sign of the Jewish eye, as, for example, in the poem "Andenken" (Remembrance): "das Mandelauge des Toten" (the dead's almond eye) (Celan 2001, 67). In "Zwiegestalt" (Two-Time Figure) the first line is "Lass dein Aug in der Kammer sein eine Kerze" (CG, 67) ("Let thine eye be a candle in the chamber"). In front of a candle the flame becomes a possibility of looking the one who is departed, deceased, "in the eye," "face to face." The flame, however, is not only a provider of light, but also a shadow, a "shade," which now holds only the dark outlines of the realm of the dead, of the "shades." In the next line "shade" now also refers to "mouth and sex." In the ambiguity of these two words the metaphor further suggests the two levels—the collective and the individual—that are fused here: it develops out of the image of the opening of the candlestick and of the rising candle and follows, on the one hand, the private, erotic association of the female figure, and on the other—in the meaning of "mouth" (or tongue) as language and *Geschlecht* as lineage—a public dimension as well. At the same time this line, in underlining the erotic correspondence of "mouth" and "sex," points to the bond between language and origin so central to Celan's poetry.[7]

The dancing "slumber beasts" sketch at the pictorial level the flickering shadows thrown by the light of the flame. The erotic image of the female figure and beasts dancing around it also calls to mind the idea of a ritual dance of invocation. At the reflexive level the combination "slumber beasts" (*Schlummergetier*) contains something at once narcotic and threatening: the beasts of slumber, of sleep, of forgetting, threaten the unity of language and origin, of language and past, of language and memory. In the middle of these beasts the flame of remembrance is now summoned in order to counter this threat. There

> she drifts up from the gaping gold,
> she ascends
> to the crown of the Now.

The flame of the candle rises from the golden shaft of the candlestick. Its "spirit" is conjured up, is snatched from the "gaping" deep, the abyss of the past, the threatening jaws of the "slumber beasts," and called into the present. The already-suggested association with the Faustian "realm of the mothers" is also underlined through the transcending motion of the female figure that "drifts up," "ascends." However, unlike in Goethe, where the "eternal-feminine [. . .] draws us up" from the transience of the Now into the true, heavenly eternity, the upward striving direction of Celan's words points to an overcoming of the infinite "being dead" into a living "Now." No "Come, rise up to higher spheres" (Goethe) is proclaimed here; there is no kingdom of heaven to be attained. Through remembrance, the dead woman is to be called back out of the abyss of the past and of forgetting into the moment of life. In this movement the "Now" of the "crown" is the highest point of an arc, of the arc drawn between the past and the present of the poem. The crown (in the sense of the crown of the head) is also a dividing point, marking a border, a threshold, and above all an empty space. The crown in itself describes and contains nothing, is only a function. In this quality of the Now, the present moment is determined entirely by what is past.

An incantatory music runs through the lines of this first part of the poem. After the dignified, liturgical tone of the first lines, particularly emphasized by the accumulations of "o" sounds in the German original, there is, from *splitternder Stunden*, ("splintering hours") in the alternation of "s," "t," and "sch" (*splitternder, Stunden, deines, Totseins, Tochter*) the hissing of a candle burning down. In the second verse (of the German) the repeated "a" conveys "elevated" prayer (*Schlank, Gestalt, schmaler, mandeläugiger Schatten . . .*), but the stanza is above all dominated by the "sch" sound that occurs at least once in every line. Calling for the silence of meditation and of concentration, it is a preparation for the "blessing" that follows.

The candlestick has been "shaped," the candle "lit"; the speech act changes. In the three lines of the next stanza the "blessing" is announced:

> With lips draped
> by night
> I speak the blessing:

After the almost blasphemous estrangement of the ritual remembrance of the dead through erotic suggestions (of a kind that are certainly encountered in mystical texts, but not in the liturgy, in a blessing), in these lines the "I" returns to the traditional and conventional starting point and there draws breath for renewed, personal speech. In the Jewish rite the lighting of the candles (both the Sabbath candles and the memorial candles) is followed by a prescribed blessing which, like most Jewish prayers, is spoken silently, but is nevertheless articulated with the lips. The composite word *nachtverhangen* ("draped / by night") is reminiscent of the romantic theme of the "veil of night," which simultaneously conceals and reveals. These references to religious and literary traditions are followed by mysterious and polyvalent metaphors, allusions, and estranged quotations that shatter the legitimacy of communal speech.

The "blessing" itself consists of a single, long sentence, to be "spoken" in one breath, whose climax is the main clause in the middle: "I pronounce you free." The first part of this blessing consists of a list, which sounds like a taking stock, like a string of appeals interspersed with references. From the line beginning with "In the name of," which is repeated five times, one can read the search for a point of reference, for an instance that can still be appealed to, in whose name it is still possible to speak. This first part can be further subdivided: up to the first dash ("torrents may rush through the deeps—") the formulaic "In the name of the three" occurs twice; after that we have "in the name of the first of the three, [. . .] of the second, [. . .] of the third." What names are these?

At first glance, the wording immediately calls to mind the structure of the Christian blessing: "In nomine patri . . .": "In the name of the Almighty Father, who created you; in the name of Jesus Christ, the Son of the Living God, who suffered for you; in the name of the Holy Ghost . . ." It is from this reading of the "three" that Joachim Schulze and Jerry Glenn develop their interpretation of these lines (Schulze 1976, 97; Glenn 1973, 82). Glenn sums up the key points of his reading like this: "The speaker in the poem is situated in front of a candle—an important object in Jewish ritual—located in a candelabrum which he formed according to the mother's instructions [. . .]. The Trinity of the Christian prayer is irreverently introduced in this Jewish prayer in the process of absolving the thou of the amen" (1973, 82). The poem is undoubtedly alluding to the Trinity; as an exclusive interpretation, however, it leads Glenn to draw one-sided conclusions, a reductionist deciphering and a simplifying resolution of the deliberate hermeticism and complication of these lines. Glenn sees a "break" arising from the intersection of two different, yet in themselves homogeneous, "intact" traditions. He fails to see that these traditional references are in themselves being broken, that an internal rupturing, not only of these two monoliths, the Jewish and the Christian, but also of the literary tradition, is taking place here. The disparate elements of these lines are evidence of the need to read them "with a changing key" and to keep this gesture itself in mind.

Particularly noticeable here is the juxtaposition of allusions and quotations, that is, of a familiar field of signs and symbols that is disrupted by unusual inversions, oxymora, and estrangements.

> In the name of the three
> who war among themselves until
> heaven dips down into the grave of feelings,

If "the three" refers to the unity of the Trinity, this meaning is shaken apart in the second line in an image that appears apocalyptic. The elementary prerequisite of the Christian creed, its center, fragments until its world tumbles in the plunging down of heaven. At the same time, with the word "grave," the dead are invoked, the dead the poem remembers. In the image of heaven dipping down, these lines intimate a heavenly unity (now no longer necessarily understood as Christian) in the face of this grave, these graves.

> in the name of the three whose rings
> glint on my finger whenever
> I loosen the hair of the trees in the chasm,
> so that richer torrents may rush through the deeps,

These lines initially suggest a number of literary allusions, whose relationship sketches an act of tender bending down which, however, as a surrealistic image, escapes a direct grasp. The gesture is an echo of the dipping-down heaven, although this movement is now performed by the speaking subject. The religious references open a place for the poetic words of commemoration that originate no longer in "heaven," with the poet serving as a mere mouthpiece, but in the "I" of the poem. The "three rings" remind one of Gotthold Ephaim Lessing's parable in *Nathan the Wise* (1779), where the three religions are the three sons of a single father—that is, derive from an original unity—but all three, because of their feuds, betray the father's legacy. In Celan's poem, the speaker of the blessing with the three rings on his finger points into the abyss, points to the graves, to the dead, as confirmation of the wisdom of the parable but also as a lament over the failure of enlightened literature and thought. On the trees in the abyss, on the dead trees of life, is bestowed the gesture of a lover: "whenever / I loosen the hair of the trees in the chasm, / so that richer torrents may rush through the deeps." The lines echo the romantic-poetic association of the hair of the beloved with the stream of a river. The water of tears is conjured up in the "richer torrents" of the German literary tradition. So far, in these verses, the Christian and the literary tradition are reminded of the abyss of graves. From there, the poem moves toward a description of each one of the three instances of authority invoked in the previous verses:

> in the name of the first of the three,
> who cried out,
> when called upon to live where his word had been before him,
> in the name of the second who looked on and wept,
> in the name of the third, who piles up
> white stones in the centre,—

This is how Glenn reads these lines:

> The attributes of the three persons of the Trinity are given metaphorically in vocabulary typical of Celan. The Holy Spirit, the inspiration and divine source of the Word of God, is described as the one who piles up stones, suggesting verbal communication. The attributes of Jesus, watching and weeping, are reminiscent of his passion and his prediction of the destruction of Jerusalem. The attribute of God the Father mentioned here is an allusion to John 1: "In the beginning was the Word . . . and the Word was God." (1973, 82)

Without excluding Glenn's interpretation (which differs only insignificantly from that of Joachim Schulze), the lines can also be understood in another way. Just as the Christian ritual again and again appeals to the "three" of the Trinity, the Jewish prayer repeatedly names the three patriarchs of the biblical tradition: "In the name of Abraham, Isaac and Jacob [. . .]." Then "the first of the three" refers to Abraham, whom God instructed to live "where his word had been before him": "Now the Lord had said unto Abram, Get thee out of thy country, and from thy kindred, and from thy father's house, unto a land that I will show thee" (Genesis 12:1). It is a particular land, hallowed by God, who "was there" before Abraham's arrival. In the Bible story, however, Abraham did not, as in these verses, "cry out," but obeyed God without resistance.

With "in the name of the second who looked on and wept" the reference is to Isaac (the "laughing one"), who "looked on" at his own sacrifice by his father's hand and did not weep. He submitted to God's commandment and "laughingly" bore witness to his joyful consent. In both cases, therefore, there is in Celan's poem an estrangement of the traditional Bible story: here the forefathers are no longer submissive figures, but articulate their resistance. Where this protest, in contrast to the Bible story, is expressed, a poetological dimension can be read from it. The one who "cried out [. . .] where his word had been before him" is also the poet Celan; his poems are a "cry" of protest; he is also the one who "looked on and wept"; his poems are "petrified tears."

"In the name of the third, who piles up / white stones in the centre,—": in the Bible this is said several times, in a variety of ways, of Jacob, the third patriarch: "And Jacob [. . .] took the stone [. . .] and set it up for a pillar" (Genesis 28:18; see also 31:13; 35:14). Jacob erected the last of these pillars at the grave of his wife Rachel (Genesis 35:20), as a sign of eternal remembrance. Of this memorial Rabbi Eliezer says, "This stone is called 'Even Sh'tiah,' stone dressed upright, from the Hebrew verb 'placing.' It indicates the nexus of the world" (Munk 1976, 295). To Jacob, the heaping up of the stones is the determination of the middle of the earth under the sign of remembrance. The self-referentiality of these verses is underlined by the present tense of the word "häuft" ("piles up"). Celan understands his own poems, as can be seen from the recurring figures of speech and symbols relating to the petrifaction of the poetic word, as memorial stones.

This reading of the lines does not necessarily contradict the reading of Glenn and Schulze. Neither approach can entirely explain every detail and make the references homogeneous. It is precisely through the interchangeability of these references that their claim to authority is challenged. This first part of the "blessing" appears as a confusing, tangled poetic complex. Allusions to and apparent quotations from the Christian, literary, and Jewish traditions are juxtaposed and mixed. They appear to be a conscious "medley" creating a referential chaos. The claim of these traditions to authority and completeness, to the ability to provide guidance, is undermined. In the face of the "chasm," of the graves of these dead, all that remains of the former instances of religion and art, of justice and legality, in whose name it was possible to speak, is a shattered heap of ruins. At present, it is possible to speak only in the name of this fragmentation itself. Thus, in its name, we are given the following words: "I pronounce you free." In this "acquittal" one also hears the unspoken formula "in the name of the law." As already indicated above, all the preceding lines of the "blessing" are thereby confronted with the norms, codes, and legislations of institutionalized religions, of traditional poetry, of conventional discourse. The estrangement of the divine word, the formal deviations from traditional poetry, the nullification of orderly logic in the chaos of references revoke legality as such, and free the voice speaking in the poem: "I pronounce you free / of the amen."

Amen: the final word in the traditional ritual of prayer means "So be it." It is the word of assent and the word of ending. The acquittal from the amen takes place here as a protest against consent to the world, against a resigned acceptance of events to which the death of the mother refers. It is also an expression of a refusal to speak the last word about the past, to get over it and bury it. In Celan's verse, the approval and affirmation of the state of the world is confronted with memory. In the refusal of the amen, the remembrance of the dead stands in opposition to the consent implied in the religious tradition—and in so much of the literary tradition. In a further sense, this acquittal from the amen is also the refusal to submit oneself to the laws of time, of forgetting. The addressees of the acquittal are multiple. First of all, with the "you," the mother who has been initially addressed in the poem is "pronounced free" of the ultimate death that occurs in oblivion: the counterword to the amen, to the yes-saying and the last-word-saying, lifts the final death sentence on the deceased because it liberates the memory that remains alive along with the cry of protest linked to it. In another sense, the pronouncement of freedom from the amen also sets itself against unthinking assent, against blind agreement with the commandments of those in power. In these lines Celan points to the fatal consequences of an amen pronounced by millions to a murder committed a million times over.

This pronouncement of freedom from the amen is to be understood as programmatic for the whole of Celan's poetry. It stands against the amen as the blessing of what exists and as a last word to finish the work of remembrance. The hermeticism of Celan's poems, the revocation of conventions—of traditional poetry, of the established symbolic order, indeed of traditional communication and communities based on consensus altogether—is in this sense to be understood as an assertion of autonomy and resistance. It is an act of liberation in the sense suggested in the "Meridian" speech: it is in one's "innermost straits," away from common signification, that the poetic word is "set free" (CGW, 3:200).

> I pronounce you free
> of the amen that drowns our voices,
> of the icy light on its edges
> where, high as a tower, it enters the sea,
> where the grey one, the dove
> pecks up the names
> on this and the other side of dying

In these verses the amen is qualified: in the affirming setting of a seal upon what is, in the sealing up of what has occurred, in the fading of memory, the chorus of amen-sayers "drowns" or deafens (*übertäubt*) the individual prayer of memory. The amen drowns "our voices" (*uns* [us], as the line has it in the original version). This "our," this "us" is a conjuration of a community constituted by the reunification of the dead and those who mourn them. This impossible community stands in opposition to the collective amen proclaimed in the name of a common cause—the murderous crimes of the past, the consensus of forgetting the dead in the present. This "we" unites poet and reader, but it also unites in sworn alliance the "I" of the speaker with the "you" of the dead mother: the amen is rejected because its affirmation of communal unison makes the living deaf, indifferent, and unfeeling; it suffocates the voices of the dead and threatens their commemoration in the present.

Unlike the "warm" light of the candle, of the eternal light of memory, the amen is "edged," ringed, surrounded by "icy light." "Edged" calls to mind trimming, a border (and the original German—*säumt*—suggests not only "seam" but also *Versäumnis*—omission, neglect), and the "icy light" an apocalyptic waste of cold brightness. The "icy light," that "high as a tower enters the sea," sketches the picture of a lighthouse, an authority that once provided orientation, but has now "entered the sea," the flood of the deeps, the ocean of tears and blood. Looking over the sea the tower stands in opposition to the "I" that bends down, that "loosens the hair of the trees in the chasm." The amen, the light "high as a tower," continues to point heavenward, continues to reinforce approval of what exists and of the authority of the gods.[8]

> where the grey one, the dove
> pecks up the names
> on this and the other side of dying

The dove is originally the sign of rescue and of peace. Here, however, it is not a white dove, the love symbol of the romantics, which can also be found in Celan's poems—e.g., "Der Tauben weißeste flog auf: ich darf dich lieben!" (CG, 47) (Of doves the whitest flew up: I may love you!). It is now a grey bird of peace, sign of a grey peace, perhaps a designation of the post-war period, of the present time, of the poem's Now. It—this dove, this time—"pecks up the names / on this and the other side of dying." "Dying" is used here in contrast to the earlier "being dead": the dove, which is where the amen is, assents to and carries out the laws of time, swallowing up the dead in an irreversible forgetting.

"Name" (*Namen*) constitutes a further contrast to "amen." The amen of collective convention is a negation of names, of individuals: in the general assent, in the indifference, they are "pecked up" and annihilated. With the disappearance of the names "on the other side of dying," with the forgetting of the dead, the name, the identity of the living is also lost. As the birds in the fairy tale peck up the crumbs the children have dropped in order to find their way back, so the dove that stands beside the amen "pecks up the names on this and the other side of dying," thereby destroying the trail, the link between the survivors and the dead. This connecting line consists of names, and their path is trodden in the naming of their names, as here in the invocation of the mother, in order to counter the grey dove, the dove that "drowns our voices" (in the German: *die Taube*—dove; *die übertäubt*—that "deafens").

"Names," however, is also a reminder of the list of "in the name of [. . .]" in the first part of the blessing, where the instances of Jewish, Christian, and literary tradition are seen as shattered. "The names / on this and the other side of dying" then also refer to the responsibility of these human and divine instances for the "dying," a responsibility the dove, in pecking up the names, ignores. The metaphors of the lighthouse and of the grey dove may also be understood in this way: the light, "high as a tower," of these former beacons of civilization, which "enters the sea," no longer provides any orientation. The divine and human "names" that professed to guarantee direction, rightness and right, no longer count. And in a much wider sense the "names" here refer to a "language of names" (*Namenssprache*), to a poetic language that "gives names" to object and creature in their specific identity. Where the amen, the word of routine and automatism, of convention and consensus rules, there is no poetry.

The following line is, as the colon after "dying" announces, the true "acquittal" from the amen, an incantatory cancellation of the legitimacy of time, of transience and forgetting:

> you remain, you remain, you remain
> a dead woman's child,

Oath, spell, stubborn exclamation of a child, mimetic actualization of persistence, a designation, a determination of identity, a "name-giving": you are, you remain "a dead (one's) child," eternally, indissolubly joined to the mother, who lives on in the child, in the "being dead's daughter," in the candle of memory,

> to the No of my longing consecrated,
> wedded to a fissure in time

The reinforcement of the oath takes the form of a poetic estrangement of biblical signs pointing to the covenant with God: of consecration and marriage. Here, however, no covenant is made with God. Instead, a bond is affirmed with the "No of my longing," with the impossible realization of bringing the dead back to life, and with the No of refusal, the counterword to the amen. The bond with this time also conflicts with words from the ritual Jewish prayer for the dead: "The mourners may You, God, give comfort and peace! [. . .] that they may find comfort and peace in Your divine words, which assure and promise us all a godly life; so that *each wound be healed,* each pain be stilled [. . .][9] The "fissure in time," recalling the wound of ritual circumcision, is a sign not of a divine covenant, but of an irrevocable, everlasting pact with the past, the only possibility of union with the dead.

Schrunde (fissure) can also mean "crack," "tear," or "rip." The threefold repetition of "you remain" is itself a "fissure in time," a crack in time that ought to be struck in order to entreat time to stand still:

> wedded to a fissure in time
> to which I was led by a mother's word

The fissure not only refers directly to the painful memory of the mother's death, but also points back to the opening lines, where the mother's command to shape the candlestick, the word of the mother, is given as the origin of the poem. Close to the end, by returning to its starting point, the poem denies to some extent its own course, its own temporality: it itself becomes a "fissure in time."

In the last three lines, the conjuration announced earlier is pushed to the threshold of its realization as an event. It shifts from oath to plea and ends with a spell:

> so that once only
> a tremor should pass through the hand
> that again and again reaches out for my heart!

With "so that" (*auf das*), with this liturgical formula of a prayer, there unfolds the desire and hope for an actual event, for a sign of life, for a revelation. All the preceding lines now appear as prerequisite, as condition of this longed-for experience. The hope that "once only / a tremor should pass through the hand" both appears utopian and was already anticipated in the trembling word written by the hand.

With the invocation of the moment at which the hand could tremble, the hand reaching out for the heart becomes a living gesture of pain, of sorrow,[10] but also of an oath of loyalty. The "tremor," the trembling, would be a sign of life of those to whom loyalty is being sworn here. The hand which "again and again reaches out for my heart" is also the hand of death. Its trembling would be a hesitation, a stumbling of the inevitable passage of time, of fatal transience. "You remain, you remain, you remain": conjuration of persistence; "so that [. . .] / a tremor should pass": conjuration of a utopian coming to life. By inscribing perpetuation into this utopia, the bond with the dead is eternalized in the poetic event.

The poetic utopia of "In Front of a Candle" lies in the hope that the poem itself will come alive. The writing hand that "reaches out for my heart" describes a transfer from the sign on the page to the poetic seat of feelings, to the core of life; the tremor signifies the coming alive of reality in the word. This climax of poetic aspiration is a mystical moment. A text on the Kaballah notes:

> In Lurianic (cabbalistic) prayer a special place was reserved for *yihudim* (acts of unification), which were meditations on one of the *letters of the Tetragrammaton or on configurations* of such names with different vocalizations [. . .]. As employed in such individual *yihudim,* these prayers were detached from the regular liturgy and became independent instruments for uplifting the soul. They also were sometimes used as a method of communing with other souls, *particularly with the souls of departed zaddikim* [the Just].[11]

In the German the last two lines of the poem read "erzittre die Hand, / die je und je mir ans Herz greift!" (a tremor that should pass through the hand / that again and again reaches out for my heart). The first letters of "Hand," "je," "je," and "Herz" (heart), HJJH, make up an incomplete, faulty combination of the tetragram JHWH, the name of God. Celan once more evokes and blasphemously transforms the convention: in Hebrew, HJJH (*Hajah*) means "it was." The past has taken the place of the name of God. The pledge to commemorate this past implies, for Celan, the refusal of any continuity reaching across this "fissure in time" and of common bonds based on religious, cultural, and literary traditions in the name of an imaginary, impossible communion with the dead.

Roots against Heaven: A Motif in Paul Celan

In his "Meridian" speech, Paul Celan describes the poem as "the place where tropes and metaphors are to be carried *ad absurdum*" (CGW, 3:199), where communal consensus and complacent continuity can be counteracted. This process occurs through a "durchkreuzen"—a "crossing through" that is also a "crossing out"—of literary images and figures of speech that have become commonplaces and thereby partake in the pre-reflexive affirmation of a tradition that has lost its validity. Among the traditional tropes and metaphors used to describe communal belonging, none is more loaded with weight, meaning, and history than the figurative use of the word "roots." This organic metaphor suggests natural continuity, a life-sustaining link with one's origins, and an implantation in the soil that implies a privileged relationship with a single place shared only with those stemming from the same location. From his first to his last poems, Celan invokes "roots." His oeuvre is indeed characterized by the difficult quest for a language that would root his poetry in his origins, experience, and remembrance while simultaneously expressing the historical uprooting to which these origins were subjected. The transformation of this metaphor in the course of his oeuvre perfectly illustrates the process implied in carrying a poetic figure "ad absurdum" and reveals the complex relationship Celan entertains with "the Jews," the literary tradition, and the German language.

The question of roots, in its varied meanings, has been addressed by a number of Jewish writers, among them Kafka, whose work was a profound influence on

Celan. One of Kafka's enigmatic little parables narrates both the human dream of feeling at one with the earth and the illusion of this dream:

> For we are like tree trunks in the snow. They seem to be resting smoothly as if one could push them away with a slight nudge. No, one cannot, for they are firmly attached to the ground. But see, even that is only appearance. (1995, 48)

"For we are," someone claims, "like tree trunks in the snow." It is winter and cold, we do not touch each other, we have no leaves, we are exposed and vulnerable. Fortunately, this is only the surface of things. Appearances are deceptive: beneath the desolateness of what is apparent lies the foundation of our existence. We have a place, we feel at home. We are upright, we sense that we belong and believe that we are safe and secure. This is something that cannot be seen at first, but it is real, or rather, it is what we want to call reality in order to feel firm ground beneath our feet. "But see, even that is only appearance": laconically, someone robs us of our deepest certainties, unmasks the dream of security, reality, and roots. Even beneath the snow, he says, even one layer deeper, our rootedness is an illusion: we are abandoned, insecure, mortal. "But see," someone says here, addressing someone else, addressing us. All we can see is the snow and the tree trunks; what we can hear, however, is the beginning of a conversation.

We have taken Kafka's parable at its word here, at a possible word. Let us now take it by its metaphor. It appears to rest flatly on the surface: there seems to be no binding connection between the parts of the metaphor, between tree trunks and us. Metaphors are products of the poetic imagination. Nothing is easier than proving them wrong. But no, one cannot do so. Once they have been united, the parts of the metaphor are linked to each other and cannot be separated again, and the metaphor is connected with us: once it has been planted in the fertile ground of our linguistic subconscious, one cannot just think it away. The way it grows and changes shape is linked to our history, which in turn is shaped by language, a language interspersed with metaphors. But see, even that is only appearance. We are tangled up in language but not imprisoned by it. We are not like tree trunks. "Whereas trees have roots, men have legs" (1967, 177), George Steiner says. And when we walk, burdened by history inscribed in metaphors, we carry them along with us, and further.

All metaphors have their history. Once they have originated from a poetic spark or from the vernacular, they become common property, change their meaning, their function, and their context, and involuntarily carry the traces of their earlier manifestations with them. History can be read from the paths and detours taken by the evolution of metaphors, especially from those that have made history themselves. Among them, one of the most loaded in the twentieth century is the metaphor of rootedness, the idea—transferred to humans—of being organically connected to a region, a landscape, a soil.

The originally mystical and romantic root metaphor became a political issue in 1897 at the latest, when Maurice Barrès published his novel *Les Déracinés* (The Uprooted). The novel, an at-the-time highly successful *roman à thèse* of little literary merit, describes with nationalistic enthusiasm and anti-Semitic undertones the destructive consequences of young people from the country being uprooted by urbanization, by the establishment of universities and democratic institutions. *Les Déracinés* triggered a public political debate, called *La Querelle du peuplier,* in which Charles Maurras, Léon Blum, and André Gide, among others, took part. The most important movements of thought at the time crystallized in this controversy as the metaphor spread and deepened. Political and ideological issues of the day—decentralization, reformation of the educational system, xenophobia—were translated into a botanic vocabulary. What was debated, for instance, was the question of whether uprooting a tree in order to transplant it would prompt it to thrive, or whether transplanting benefited only those trees that were already strong, while being detrimental to weak ones. The talk of the necessity of being rooted in the soil became the shibboleth of conservative nationalism, while the big city, distance, and aimless traveling represented the world of the dandy, the flâneur, and the Bohemian. Barrès himself, a charismatic figure, an *homme de lettres* and eloquent politician who also wrote an election pamphlet entitled *Contre les étrangers,* was especially popular with younger people and contributed to the making of a generation that saw in Pétainism not only a last resort or a compromise, but an inner rescue of the stability and health of the nation.

The talk of the uprootedness of modern man, which Barrès targets, was initially understood in a concrete way as leaving one's local, usually rural surroundings and became the epitome of all evils of modernity for conservative thinkers: it was associated with the loitering big-city mob, with the isolation of the individual and the loss of individuality in society, with the loss of a sense of community, of morals and vital energy. The manifestations of this critique of modernity range from a transfigured nostalgia for the way earlier forms of existence were rooted in the soil, to philosophical abstractions of a loss of existential security, up to the state-sanctioned destruction of foreign elements on one's "own" soil. Under the regime of the national socialists, Barrès's merely theoretical xenophobia turned into the most murderous reality.

The relationship between the German blood-and-soil ideology and the national socialist murder of the Jews is partially based on the idea of the Jew as personification of the eternal wanderer. The mythical rootlessness of the Jews, which was always an element of Jewish self-understanding, was reinforced by the fact that Jews, far into the modern age, were not allowed to purchase land and also that they have had a centuries-old history of persecutions and expulsions. After the Second World War and the destruction of the Jewish-European world, but also in face of the foundation of a Jewish nation-state, the role of the "wandering Jew" had to be newly conceived from a Jewish point of view. This is particularly true for those Jewish intellectuals who did not want to identify with the young state of

Israel. Many chose to reinforce the Jewish myth of eternal wandering and exile, as well as to stress the superiority of being spiritually rooted in the word, the book, and the law over having national or geographical roots. Ultimately, these writers invert the negative evaluation attached to the old metaphor to the point where diaspora Judaism becomes the exemplary paradigm of resistance to all forms of nationalism. Those seeing themselves in this light often refer to the centuries-old tradition of Jewish exile-identity. This gesture, however, is not unproblematic, as it celebrates uprootedness and "nomadism" as a counter-metaphor to a despised identity politics while continuing to refer to the identification of the individual with a community whose self-understanding is based on a historically uninterrupted tradition, on a common myth. A perfect example of this attitude can be found in George Steiner. In an article dedicated to Elie Wiesel, Steiner writes:

> The rootlessness of the Jew, the cosmopolitanism denounced by Hitler, Stalin, by Mosley, by every right-wing hooligan, is historically an enforced condition [. . .]. But though uncomfortable in the extreme, this condition is, if we accept it, not without a larger meaning [. . .]. Nationalism is the venom of the age [. . .]. *Even if it be against his harried will, his weariness, the Jew—or some Jews at least—may have an exemplary role. To show that whereas trees have roots, men have legs and are each other's guests.* Even a Great Society is a bounded, transient thing compared to the free play of the mind and the anarchic discipline of its dreams. (1967, 177)

Steiner's rhetoric is enticing. As a person without a homeland, the Jew with his exceptional position here embodies a universalist—and seemingly universal—ethic. Yet in his desire to make a strong point, Steiner covers up a problem he is very well aware of when he inserts the relativizing clause "or some Jews at least." But the issue here is not thus resolved: if not the Jew as such, but only "some Jews" embody the function of rootlessness, the question remains whether this role must be chosen and defended "against his harried will" or whether Jews play this role *as Jews,* in the name of their belonging to the Jewish people or its inherited tradition.

Bernard-Henri Lévy, another advocate of Jewish exile-identity, refers not to the myth of the wandering Jew, as Steiner does, but directly to the biblical tradition:

> One doesn't understand anything about the grandeur of the Biblical message if one sees privilege, chauvinism, nationalism in an election for which, in reality, the first concern is to uproot the subject from its ageless place, these archaic geographies, these savage and unmediated roots which are always and inevitably the source of cruelty. (1979, 160)

Lévy's as well as Steiner's arguments evoke a chosenness linked to a refusal of roots. Although they embrace an ethical mission, Steiner and Lévy are ultimately trapped in the paradox of wanting to subvert the ideology of a potentially violent, exclusionary, and sacrificial nationhood in the name of a communal identity.

While they may not be concerned with geographical roots, their celebration of a "good rootlessness" of the Jewish people *as a people* adheres to a way of thinking that presumes to speak in the name of an unquestioned transhistorical identity.

As a poet deeply attuned to the experiences of expulsion and exiled existence, Paul Celan constitutes a significant example of the kind of figure for which Steiner's and Lévy's tropes of rootlessness seem highly germane. However, Celan goes a step further. An examination of the metaphor of roots in his poetry illustrates the scope of an uprootedness that is thought through—and lived—up to its end. In contradistinction to Steiner's and Levy's understanding of rootlessness, Celan's trope emerges as a poetic gesture of quiet and consistent self-questioning that finally denies itself firm ground beneath its feet.

The genealogy of the root metaphor in Celan tells a history itself. His oeuvre is characterized by the difficult quest for a language that would root his poetry in his origins, experience, and remembrance, while simultaneously expressing the historical uprooting to which these origins were subjected. The metaphor of the root, used here for Celan's idea of the relationship between poetry and being, is not arbitrary. One of Celan's very early poems makes this clear:

Wunsch	**Wish**
Es krümmen sich Wurzeln	Roots writhe
Darunter	Beneath
wohnt wohl ein Maulwurf.	a mole probably dwells.
oder ein Zwerg . . .	or a dwarf . . .
oder nur Erde	or only earth
und ein silberner Wasserstreifen . . .	and a silver strip of water . . .
Besser	Blood
wär Blut.	would be better.
(CG, 373)	

Celan places this poem, written in 1937, at the beginning of a small notebook that he gave to a female friend from his youth after the war and that contains the poems he wrote during the war, mostly in forced labor camps. "Wunsch" (Wish) dates from the time shortly before the war. Situated at the beginning, it announces the poetological program of the young writer and is influenced by a romantic notion of poetry as a subterranean, poetic treasure. It bears witness to the poet's hope of going "deeper" than harmless nature poetry or fantastic fairytale magic. "Blood would be better"—to write with blood: this reverberates with pathos and existential urgency. The poem is to nourish itself with the sap of life, like roots that draw strength from within the earth. It is to be organically linked with the human, with one's own existence, which is conceived as the firm place and fertile soil of the living word. "Would be better"—perhaps this poetics, expressed only as a wish, confesses a youthful lack of experience, a romantic yearning for passion and intensity. But this combination of poetry, blood, and soil, which is here still evoked without hesitation, is soon to become impossible for Celan not only in terms of the fateful history of this vocabulary, but in terms of his own existence. A few years later, in the midst of the war, Celan ends a poem called "Wandlung" (Transformation) with these verses:

Nicht mehr mit den blühenden Zweigen kann ich die Welt zu mir neigen.	With the blossoming twigs I can no longer bow down the world to me.
Sondern rings um mein Haus reiss ich die Wurzeln heraus.	Instead, all around my house I tear out the roots.

(CG, 401–402)

These explicit, almost childishly defiant lines follow a nostalgically transfig- ured self-reflection on the enchanting power of the poetic word. It arises not from the landscape of a *Heimat,* a homeland, but from poetic language itself, which has become questionable in the face of historical horrors. The dwelling—in the sense of Hölderlin's famous "poetically man dwells" (*dichterisch, wohnet der Mensch*), which Heidegger famously singled out as the guiding line of his later philosophy— may still remain untouched, the root metaphor still unreflected, but these youthful verses, all the same, signify the first step on a path Celan will later take in increas- ingly encrypted language. In his post-war poems, he rejects the possibility of being at home in the world and inscribes this fundamental sense of uprootedness into the language itself.

In 1955, Celan is living in Paris, and his book of poems *Von Schwelle zu Schwelle* (From Threshold to Threshold) is published. The first poem of the book takes up the root metaphor again in an altered sense.

Written in past tense, the poem suggests a narrative, the reminiscence of an event that occurred in an earlier time. It is written from a point in time after what is narrated has already taken place and thus designates the *pre*-conditions of its own speaking. It simultaneously, as in "Wish" and "Transformation," conceives a poetic self-understanding. Here, however, the poem's self-reflection is based not on unmediated experience but on something that is remembered. And remembrance is the subject matter of the poem.

"Ich hörte sagen," "I heard it said": "Ik gihôrta dat zeggen" (in Glaser et al.

Ich hörte sagen	I heard it said
Ich hörte sagen, es sei im Wasser ein Stein und ein Kreis und über dem Wasser ein Wort, das den Kreis um den Stein legt.	I heard it said, there is in the water a stone and a circle and above the water a word that lays the circle around the stone

Ich sah meine Pappel hinabgehen
    zum Wasser,
ich sah, wie ihr Arm hinuntergriff
    in die Tiefe,
ich sah ihre Wurzeln gen Himmel
um Nacht flehn.
	I saw my poplar descend to the
	    water,
	I saw how its arm grasped down
	    into the depth,
	I saw its roots pleading 'gainst
	    heaven for night.

Ich eilt ihr nicht nach,
ich las nur vom Boden auf jene Krume,
die deines Auges Gestalt hat und Adel,
	I didn't hurry after it,
	I only gathered up that crumb
	    from the floor that has the shape
	    and nobility of your eye,

ich nahm dir die Kette der Sprüche
    vom Hals und säumte mit ihr den
    Tisch, wo die Krume nun lag.
	I took the chain of sayings from
	    your neck and hemmed with it
	    the table on which the crumb
	    now lay.

Und sah meine Pappel nicht mehr.	And saw my poplar no more.
(CG, 63)	

1984, 23): the title of Celan's poem echoes one of the oldest writings of German literature, the *Hildebrandslied,* to evoke the oral transmission of tragic events that were, in the subsequent Christian tradition, interpreted as occurrences consecrated by a divine will and passed on from one generation to the next. What does Celan's poem narrate? Once upon a time, facts were conveyed to an I. In deceptively simple language he was informed by words handed down, by rumors of the way things are. They are, he heard, clear, unalterable, static, like a stone in the water, the philosopher's stone in the stream of events, a hard, cold, and lifeless substance. The stone in the water would be pure nature, coincidence, a meaningless thing, if it were not for the circle, the magical designation of something meaningful. The stone attains meaning and weight only through the circle, which the divine word, floating above the water in the myth of creation, lays around it. "I heard it said": the biblical tradition perceived only as a rumor also provides the function of the word and of language: it serves to designate and encircle the stone, the unalterable, unshakable. Thanks to its aura the stone lies at the center, now a sign, testimony of divine presence.

The "I heard it said" of tradition is now juxtaposed with a three-fold "I saw," by the mediation of what was experienced. The biblical "there is" is confronted with an "I saw"—that is, with a testimony of a "there was." The eternal myth is confronted with an experience, tradition with history. It is the story of suffering of an uprooted tree going to the water for the sake of the stone: only the gesture of grasping downward bears witness to the fact that the stone itself still exists.

Pappel (poplar); *peuplier* (people): the etymology suggested in Celan's designation for "people"[1] is also evoked in one of his early poems, *Notturno*, written in 1942:

Schlaf nicht, sei auf der Hut	Don't sleep, beware
Die Pappeln mit singendem Schritt	The poplars stride singing
ziehn mit dem Kriegsvolk mit.	marching along with the people of war.

(CG, 393)

The romantic connection between man and nature is uprooted, is no longer a place of rest and peace; the nocturnal song is not a lullaby; and the uncanny—already present in romanticism—is no longer an abstraction, but historical violence.

In "I heard it said" the uprooted poplar pleads "'gainst heaven for night": "*My poplar,*" here, is "my people." The poet's people, the uprooted—Jewish—people, keeps on praying to the heavens above. With its roots reaching upward it begs for night, for peace. This tree, also a cabbalistic symbol, shows a way, but "I did not hurry after it": the refusal to follow the gesture of the poplar is a rejection of the simple reversal that would turn the habitual image into its negative: the poplar with its roots in the air. For Celan, such a movement in the opposite direction does not suffice.

In one of his preliminary notes for the "Meridian" speech, Celan insists on the distinction between opposition and inversion: "Gegenverkehr und Umkehr, das ist zweierlei" (1999, 131). The mere movement of opposition implied in the first term (literally "countertraffic") ignores the event taking place at the turning point and fails to perform the "second of inversion,"[2] an *Umkehr* that implies a truly transforming reversal. In another comment in the same cluster of notes Celan establishes a link between such a transformation, poetry, and Jewishness. This note introduces the notion of *verjuden,* of becoming Jewish, which Celan turns from a negative term indicating an abject contamination into an affirmative metaphor for poetic transformation itself: "Verjuden: Es ist das Anderswerden" (1999, 130)

(Becoming Jewish: it is the becoming other). Although Celan indeed reverses the "value" of the term, he is far from mystifying Jewishness as ultimate, auratic otherness. Instead, he writes in a somewhat jocular tone, "One can become Jewish. Admittedly this is difficult and many a Jew has failed in it; that is precisely why I consider it recommendable" (1999, 130). In another note he calls the poem, insofar as it constitutes an irritation, "the Jew of literature" and adds: "*Verjudung*, that seems to me to be a path towards understanding poetry." Yet another note starts with "*Das Jüdische*—" and ends on the laconic sentence, "*Das Gedicht ist eine Umkehr*" (1999, 131). Taken together, these fragmentary jottings indicate Celan's understanding that it does not suffice to turn the denigrating vocabulary captured in the word *verjuden* into its "positive" opposite. The inversion enacted in the language of poetry requires that the poetic words—and with them *das Jüdische*—are estranged (*verfremdet*), that they become strangers to themselves.

Similarly, it is not enough to reverse the metaphor of being rooted to convey the uprootedness Celan is referring to in "I heard it said." In the gesture of the poplar, the roots are indeed no longer in the ground—they reach "heavenwards"—but the image of a vertical connection between God and man remains intact. Celan's poem marks his reluctance to follow the direction indicated by the poplar's gesture through the suppression of a syllable in the use of the antiquated German word *gen*, which suggests a suppressed antagonism, a *gegen* that means not only "toward," but "against." The words of the poplar's plea are still founded on an understanding of language that originates in the biblical myth of God's word suggested in the first lines of the poem. The words "depths" and "heaven," but also "root" and "night," indeed still belong to a German-romantic vocabulary, which also makes reference to the divine origin of the poetic word.

The poplar continues to enact the grand metaphysical gesture: it calls upon nothing less than the depths of the waters and the height of the heavens. "I didn't hurry after it": in contrast, the poem's I enacts a small gesture: it gathers up from the floor—"only," as it stresses—the crumb, the remainder of a former entity, a reminder of the history it suffered, the smallest remains of past nourishment, and places it on the table to preserve it. "I only gathered up that crumb from the floor": there is an allusion to the act of reading (*lesen/auflesen*) here, while "table" (*Tafel*) can refer to the slate on which one writes. In this manner, the poem, too, refuses to mediate between the depths and the heavens, but rather wants to preserve what is lying on the ground by placing it on the table, on something that man built for man.

Crumb and table, instead of stone and water. The crumb is not a stone; it is not rounded off, resting in itself, unalterable and without history, but crumbled away from something larger, determined only in relation to something that once existed. This remainder is now in danger of being heedlessly stepped on and crushed. It is not a stone but what remains of a loaf of bread: the poet here gives in to the temptation to make earthly food out of dead stone, to transform the lifelessly inherited truth to a crumb, which may no longer be nourishing, but, in remembrance, still refers to the original loaf of bread.

The crumb has "the shape of your eye": the poem repeats the biblical story of creation. At first there is only water, stone, and the divine word; then there is organic vegetation, and finally, in the third verse, man. After desolateness, after the night in the forest, a "you" appears. Perhaps, like the "you" often alluded to elsewhere, this "you" is Celan's murdered mother; at any rate, however, it is an "other," a *Gegenüber*, or a "vis-à-vis," as Celan once called the "you" (CGW, 3:198). It originates from the crumb, the remembered rest. The "you" that is addressed and the "you" that is remembered are intertwined in the recollection of remembrance: "The poem becomes—under what conditions! [. . .]—it becomes a dialogue—it is often a desperate dialogue" (CGW, 3:198). The word is no longer an absolute designation; it finds its destiny in the orientation toward an other, in hoping for a dialogue. The "you" of this remembrance and this dialogue comes into being as an eye, as something capable of seeing, as a witness. "Nobody / witnesses / for the witness" (CG, 198)—the one remembering does not presume to represent the suffering of others. Remembering their *eye*, their view, their experience, Celan circumvents the instrumentalization of memory and the exploitation of remembrance.[3]

Instead of the stone in the water, instead of primary, eternal elements around which the divine word circles, the poetic word preserves the crumb on the table that refers to the human realm, to the meager remains of a destructive history. In the face of this history, the originally meaningful circle of the inherited divine word appears as a mere "chain of sayings": the sayings, or proverbs of the fathers, the inherited truths, once the jewels of humanity, have lost their credibility and are now only a chain and a burden. "I took the chain of sayings from your neck": the act of Celan's poetic word both negates the validity of the formerly precious adornment and frees language from the burden and confinement of the inherited word, which has become ossified into sayings, into pre-fabricated and therefore invalid phrases in the face of the experience of suffering, of uprooting and destruction. This act is expressed in the gesture of simplification—floor and table instead of depths and heavens—in the proximity of these verses to prose, and in the laconism of the last sentence. But the "chain of sayings," the tradition of the word and of language in general, insofar as it has always been something handed down, is not rejected as such. It is, however, to serve a different purpose now. "I took the chain of sayings from your neck, and hemmed with it the table on which the crumb now lay": the sayings, the handed-down word, and language in general can now be conceived only in an altered constellation, only in the face of the crumb, from the viewpoint of the eye that originates from the remains of remembrance. The word as the world-creating "let there be" is now engaged to serve the remembering "there was." The design of the crumb surrounded by a chain echoes the image of the stone and its circular aura. But here the word is no longer regarded as a signifying, auratic circle giving meaning to a static reality. It has, instead, itself become lifeless, degraded to empty phrases. Now, in light of the crumb and for the sake of its remembrance, these sayings should surround and hem all that remains after the destruction. "And hemmed with it"—in the German original an allusion to neglect, to omission is made here (*säumen, Versäumnis*): all that the chain of sayings, the old words, can do now is surround remembrance, but they fail in their attempt to signify it. In themselves, they have become empty hearsay.

Here, a momentous comparison suggests itself. "I heard it said" is the title of Celan's poem. This title reminds one of Heidegger's *Gerede*. Like Celan, Heidegger also complains about the "hearsay," the "lost, or rather never gained" origin of the word (1976, 170). For Celan, the conception of a divine language "which lays the circle around the stone," introduced by "I heard it said," has lost its authority, has become rumor in the face of what he saw. Heidegger also speaks of "Gerede," of rumor that as such "grows in influence and takes on an authoritative character" (1976, 169). Celan revokes the inherited language, showing it as a chain of phrases, while Heidegger speaks with a deprecatory gesture of a "*Weiter- und Nachreden*" (1976, 168), of "continuous and malicious gossip": "Das bodenlose Gesagtsein und Weitergesagtwerden reicht hin, dass sich das Erschliessen verkehrt zu einem Verschliessenden" (1976, 169) (the groundless having-been-said and passing-on suffices to transform the act of disclosure into closure). But Celan speaks of his uprooted poplar, of history, while Heidegger speaks of the "uprooted understanding of *Dasein*," of ontology. Heidegger presents "gossip" as existentially unavoidable; he himself is, as he says at the beginning, "far away from a moralizing critique" (1976, 167). For Celan, it was not an abstract rupture that destroyed the validity of the inherited language but historical experience.

"And saw my poplar no more": despite the dryness of these words, which conclude the separation between the lyrical I and the community, there is a note of sorrow and loss. Earlier, the I saw the uprootedness of its own people, saw them plea "heavenwards," but did "not follow them." Now it loses sight of its people by renouncing its tradition. It can no longer share its religious framework and the way it is mediated by language. It revokes the validity of the biblical tradition, the sense of communal belonging and the trust in the inherited language. It goes beyond inversion: Celan does not advocate any kind of negative theology and similarly avoids the celebration of the rootless Jew which, in its own way, establishes community and identity.

Celan refuses to reconcile and forget. In his poetry, he continuously seeks the expression of this refusal. He abstains from establishing himself in uprootedness, from affirming it as a negative myth of origin, and thus from securing his sense of belonging to a people for whom exile reverses itself into a communal identity. A direct revocation is not possible in the poem's striving to retain the residue as remembrance: the hearsay cannot be denied directly; it can only be undermined from within. Performing this subversion, Celan's gesture leads to a radical uprooting of poetic language from its traditional constitution: as opposed to the still-vertical poplar, which leaves the origin and destination of language untouched despite its inversion, the poem revokes the handed-down language and relinquishes its traditional legitimization as mouthpiece of the divine word. By excavating its own ground, Celan's language uproots itself. In his art, this leads to an extreme condensation and concentration, to a renewal of the poetic language as exemplified in the deferral of the root-metaphor that is carried further and away from its traditional origin and destination. In his life, the price Celan paid for the radical rejection of belonging, of rootedness and community, was too high. In one of his last poems, Celan with bitter irony remembers the wish of his youth, seeing it as wound and last possession:

Kleines Wurzelgeträum, das mich hält,	Little root-dreamgrowth, which holds me
blutunterwaschen,	washed in blood,
keinem mehr sichtbar,	no longer visible to anyone,
Todesbesitz.	possession of death.

(CG, 358)

The Voice of Israel:
Nelly Sachs's "Choirs after Midnight"

> A star, put it,
> put the star into the night
>
> —PAUL CELAN 1983, 191

Apart from Celan, Nelly Sachs is undoubtedly the most important German-Jewish poet writing in the aftermath of the Holocaust. Raised in an educated and as-similated family, Sachs was almost fifty years old when she fled from Berlin to Sweden in 1940.[1] The poetry and stories she wrote as a young woman in Berlin are more inspired by Christianity than Judaism and make use of traditional romantic imagery and themes. While Celan and Sachs are often mentioned in one breath and Celan was occasionally called Sachs's spiritual brother, the two poets repre-sent very different approaches to the means and aims of poetry "after Auschwitz." Hints about this disagreement can be found in Celan's poem "Zurich, at the Stork" ("Zürich, zum Storchen"), which he wrote as a response to their famous encounter in the Swiss city in 1960.

> Our talk was of Too Much, of
> Too Little. Of Thou
> and Yet-Thou, of
> clouding through brightness, of
> Jewishness, of
> your God.
> [. . .]

Our talk was of your God, I spoke
against him, I let the heart
I had
hope:
for
his highest, death-rattled, his
wrangling word—
[. . .]

Celan's poem suggests that they spoke about the difference between the richness and explicitness of her imagery and the extreme condensation of his "clouded," encrypted language, between her affirmation of a divine presence and his blasphemous, "wrangling words," between her traditionalism and his call for a radical rupture in the language of poetry.

Another difference, not explicitly addressed in Celan's poem but linked to their different attitudes to the religious and literary traditions, lies in their respective understanding of the role and status of the poet. While Celan traces the inspiration for his poetic commemoration to personal experience—in "In Front of a Candle" literally his "mother's instructions"—and directs his search for the poetic word toward his "innermost straits," Sachs writes: "It is entirely unimportant that it was me who wrote all this, it is the voice of the Jewish people speaking and that is all" (1984, 54). Throughout the post-war years, Nelly Sachs in various ways repeated this romantically inspired notion of herself as a poet[2] and even reinforced it by emphasizing that she "really did write all her own things at night [. . .] and in the darkness. But He was with me and gave me the words."[3] Subscribing to the idea of the poet who, appointed by a superior authority, allows herself and her consciousness to recede in order to lend her voice to a people, Sachs possibly wanted to lend greater weight to her solidarity with the Jewish victims. This echo of romantic ideas of poetic creativity,[4] however, encouraged a questionable appropriation of her poetry by those who yearned to cleanse their conscience in the years after the war. Her repeated renunciation of revenge and hatred toward the perpetrators could be assumed to speak for Jews in general and was taken as an opportunity to obtain absolution as if it came not only from the survivors but also from the victims themselves.

In the anthology *Nelly Sachs zu Ehren* (In Honour of Nelly Sachs), published in 1961, her poetry is explicitly described as the "manifestation of the spirit of a people" and as an expression of the "spirit of the Jewish people" articulating itself in "appeal, exhortation, lament and invocation" (in Dinesen 1985b, 131). What is striking in this description is the emphasis on speech acts that affirm the connection between "voice" and "people" so often invoked by Sachs herself.

Similarly, reviewers of her cycles of poetry published in 1946 repeatedly spoke of the "voice of Israel, the voice of the murdered millions" (Fritsch-Vivié 1993, 90) resounding in her poems. This voice, speaking without "a single word of hate" (Enzensberger in Aichinger et al. 1961, 47) and with "almost superhuman forgiveness" (Krämer 1994, 37), not only in the name of the survivors but also of the dead, provided for many the longed-for comfort after the catastrophe. Jewish authors likewise mention the conciliatory, healing, and cathartic[5] effect of Sachs's poetry. The poet and survivor Ilse Blumenthal-Weiss expresses her gratitude to Sachs with the words: "Through your poetry, in your poetry each and every one of our dead has found his place of rest and his blessing."[6] In an open letter honoring Sachs, the poet Hilde Domin associates this thought with the metaphor of the voice: "You have," she writes to her fellow poet, "given these dead a voice. With your words they have taken the path—lamenting, but nevertheless—the path the dead take." Domin continues: "You are the voice of these unfortunate dead. And at the same time you release [us] from the disaster." In keeping with the tradition of epitaphs, it is, in Domin's words, the living voice given to the murdered that allows their spirits to come to rest: "When I was reading your poems in the winter of 59/60," Domin writes, "hence, almost 15 years afterwards, you buried my dead, all these strange, terrible dead who visited me in my room" (in Aichinger et al. 1961, 191). Domin ends her open letter with the words "so that the dead shall not be interred in vain by you: in the *German* word" (in Aichinger et al. 1961, 197; emphasis by Domin). Sachs's poetry apparently not only pacified the souls of the dead but also appeased the living. For Domin, Sachs's poetry served to bury not only the dead that came to haunt her but also the rupture between Germans and Jews embodied by these dead. After repeatedly calling Sachs the "voice of the dead," Domin goes on to address her as a voice "that is German in its entirety." Domin's words prepared the ground for the praise bestowed on Sachs when she was awarded the German Peace Prize: Sachs was praised for lending a "German voice to the Jewish dead" and thereby "without any disagreement reconciled the German and the Jewish." The Israeli scholar Margarita Pazi called this assertion in the *laudatio* on Sachs a "breathtaking insensitivity" (1994, 153).[7]

Even in more recent appraisals of her work, Sachs continues to be celebrated as a "genius of forgiveness" (Grundmann in Lermen and Braun 1998, 7). This praise is accompanied by a strikingly frequent use of the metaphor of the voice. Her poetry is not only "the voice of these unfortunate dead," but also the "voice of wisdom, of experience, of reason," the "voice of fear, of suffering and of comfort" (in Lermen and Braun 1998, 8). Several critics, however, have attempted to counter these views by emphasizing in their readings of Sachs's poems their literary character, their textual, rhetorical, and structural intricacies, rather than the soothing presence and immediacy of her voice. Already in the sixties, well before the reception of her work turned into often fierce criticism of the poet herself,[8] some critics described her poems as "calculated texts of linguistic and logical permutations" (Geissner 1968, 28) and insisted that her motifs constitute "parables" rather than poetic conjurations of the "voice of creation."[9] This approach was followed in the eighties by close analyses of her metaphors, her "alphabet mysticism," and the epigrammatic dimension of her poetry. While the more traditional interpretations of her work continued well into the nineties to emphasize the motif of the voice—for instance by using quotations such as "Stimmen vom Nesselweg her" (Voices from the Nettle Path)[10] in titles of monographs on Sachs—more recent accounts of her work stress the constructed versus the spontaneous aspect and the textual versus the vocal dimension of her poetry. These interpretations of Sachs's work have drawn on poststructuralist theories of the sign. A strong example is the portrait of Sachs in the anthology *Deutsche Dichter des 20. Jahrhunderts,* published in 1996: following a description of the misuse of the poet as an "auxiliary to repression," a "conscience decorator," an "exoneration expert," and a "conscience stronghold at festive events and congresses, behind evergreen shrubs," the overview stresses the fundamentally textual character of her work. Sachs's own use of "voice" and "people" is not mentioned. Her poetry is now seen as "text surface," "textual event in writing," "web of signs," "signature of vital movement," "epochal text" (Jeziorkowski 1996).

It is striking that those readers who focus on the text—as opposed to celebrating the voice—and who try to save Sachs from associations with a problematic tendency toward romanticism and the associated "complicity" in the aforementioned attempts of appropriation, almost exclusively refer to the later works written in the sixties and seventies.[11] It is undoubtedly true that clear references to romanticism as well as the gesture of lending a voice to a communal "we" increasingly disappear from Sachs's work. However, it would not do justice to her early post-war poetry to reduce it to problematic borrowings from a romantic *Volksgeist*-poetics and hence declare it obsolete. Perhaps Sachs's significance lies not so much, as has often been claimed, in the poetry of her later years, even though those poems indeed conform more easily to contemporary conceptions of modern poetry, but rather in the earlier cycles of poems precisely because they reflect the conflict between a more traditional and possibly anachronistic poetics and one that is only beginning to emerge. This conflict manifests itself as a tension between a poetic mode inspired by romanticism and the demands placed on poetry by a commemorative awareness after Auschwitz. The clash between voice and sign—contrary to the usual perception—is already present in her poetry of the early post-war years and expresses itself not only in her poems but also (albeit not necessarily consciously) in Sachs's statements about her own work.

The tension between voice and sign manifests itself in various, often hidden ways. Sachs's own statements about the voice sounding through her are not always consistent. In a letter to Gunnar Ekelöf sent with some of her poems, she writes: "I enclose these words from the night. I cannot *speak* them, that is why I've been *writing* mute things for years. This is a secret . . ." (1984, 287; emphasis added). Another striking feature in this context is the conflicting metaphor in one of the many passages in her letters referring to her role as a mouthpiece of the Jewish people. "It is also of no consequence at all whether I wrote [my poems] or whether someone's voice was heard. But some voice must be heard to gather the bloody footprints in the sand" (1984, 68). The voice with its implicit assumption of presence and immediacy is hardly suitable for collecting footprints. While the desire for sublimation, for the transformation of material signs of a bygone time into a living, breathing presence exists here as well, the overstrained metaphor reveals its problematic character. What shows in the lines of the letter in fact runs through much of Sachs's poetry of those years, displaying a clash between a romantic po-etics[12] and a poetic commemoration of the Holocaust that becomes particularly evident in her so-called Jewish poems,[13] written between 1943 and 1946.

In her account of the religious undercurrents in Sachs's work, Margarita Pazi has revealed its peculiar and in many ways inconsistent blend of Christian and Jewish elements (1994, 153). As Pazi points out, the echoes of resurrection in this poetry, the orientation to a Beyond, and the mysticism of death and rebirth are diametrically opposed to basic Jewish belief, while the call for commemoration and the modes of mourning in Sachs's work are very much in keeping with Jewish thought and ritual. Sachs's early post-war poetry bears witness to this contradic-tion and the conflict between the invocation of a resurrection of the people of Israel through a vocal "we" on the one hand, and inconsolable grief borne out in indicative traces and signs on the other.

In den Wohnungen des Todes (In the Dwellings of Death, 1965), a volume of poetry published in 1946, is marked by the tension between restoration and resignation, forgiving and futility, poetic consolation and traumatic grieving—however laced with messianic hope—over an irretrievable loss. In this tension, the interweaving of voice and trace, of unmediated presence and referring sign, testi-fies to Sachs's ambivalence between ideas of presence and fullness and a poetics of absence and loss. This ambivalence applies in particular to the fourth and last cycle of the volume, "Choirs after Midnight" (1965, 94–107). Consisting of fourteen se-quential poems, this group constitutes the dramatic climax of the volume. It leaves behind the genre and "medium" of the preceding cycle—"Epitaphs written in the air"—and presents a collective voice, already mentioned in the cycle's title, that is concretized in the title of the last poem, "Voice of the Holy Land." This cycle is the most exact manifestation of Sachs's assertion that in her poems "the voice of the Jewish people speaks and nothing else." However, the rupture is inscribed here as well: the fulfillment of a poetic restitution of the "body of Israel" that has "gone up in smoke" is revealed to be an illusion and any redemption is presented as deferred, a messianic anticipation at most. This deferment is accompanied by a repeated undermining of the unifying and "soul-giving" voice speaking in the name of a "we" throughout the poems. The impossibility of a restoration and consequently of all reconciliation and harmony is inscribed through a shift in emphasis from vocal presence to trace and sign, the decoding of which is yet to come. The voices of the poem's ubiquitous "we" still sound, but they now speak of the loss of wholeness, presence, unity, and fullness, and not least of the loss of voice itself.

In "Choirs after Midnight," as in the preceding cycles of the volume, Sachs resorts to an older genre of poetry: after the passion poems, the laments, and the epitaphs, this fourth cycle introduces a form of poetry reminiscent of the choral poems of antiquity in which the "lyrical I" in the modern sense—the original articulation of a singular subjectivity—has not yet taken shape (Adorno 1981, 53). The symbolism, however, as well as the motif of the attunement of man and nature and the implicit idea of poetry as a quasi-magical power approximating the divine act of creation, are reminiscent of a romantic poetics. This combination of a nonsubjective, collective poetry and a romantic "horizon of expectations" (Gadamer) corresponds to Sachs's idea of the withdrawal of her own person and contributes to the notion of the "missing I" which, as Ruth Dinesen points out in her reception analysis, "was a scandal" to many critics of Sachs's poetry of the immediate post-war years (1985b, 130).

With few exceptions, each chorus begins with "we": we, the rescued, we, the wanderers, we, the orphans; but also we, the dead, we, the shadows, we, the stones, we, the stars. Sachs calls up the rescued, the wanderers, and the orphans along with the dead but also summons the trees, the shadows, and the clouds to raise their voices in mourning and to announce a new beginning. Although the dominant tone is one of lament, the coexistence of the survivors and the dead and natural phenomena—all on the same level—radiates an almost comforting cosmic harmony that embeds man in a universal context. This harmony, however, is questioned again and again as each "we" constitutes a defined group confronting another group indicated by "you": the perpetrators and bystanders of the crime. The lament about the indifference of nature in the face of human suffering, repeatedly reflected in later poems by Sachs, is still alien to this poetry. However, while the cycle is undoubtedly conceived in the spirit of Sachs's idea of herself as mouthpiece of a communal "we" and a corresponding unified voice, it also contains a countermovement whose poetic gesture evokes a gathering of traces[14] and the decoding of signs. In bestowing attention to the broken, the lost, the deserted, this gesture captures the destruction and marks the failure to achieve restoration. The voices speak, but what they say is that there is no voice—no wholeness, fullness, presence—*yet*.

As a sequence of thirteen choirs and the concluding poem "Voice of the Holy Land," the cycle programmatically stages a development toward an attempted restoration and revival of the people of Israel decipherable as a coherent, continuous development. This poetic recovery, however, remains unfinished. It is interwoven with contradictory statements oscillating between lament, accusation, and reconciliation. The cycle begins "after midnight," after complete darkness has set in, with a "Chorus of Abandoned Things" situated in the barrenness of a deserted space where the forsaken objects—a jug, a candle half burnt, a single shoe—bear the signs of former lives that have now been extinguished. They call for a re-creation of the world to be brought about by a backward-looking gathering of signs and traces.

The "Chorus of Abandoned Things" consists of three monologues spoken by objects that have been left behind in the rubble after the destruction, and one concluding chorus in which the objects speak together in one voice. "Was I?" asks the jug, "I saw," says the light, "I am," the shoe. The "jug in the rubble" is a reminder of a lost world of wholeness; the candle with its "I saw" bears witness to the crime committed against the star of Israel; the single shoe, epitome of what is now lonely and incomplete, sends the lament of Israel's suffering heavenward. What has been lost by the destruction is indicated in the initial question, spoken by the jug: "Was I the jug from which the evening flowed like wine / and sometimes for the rose

Chor der verlassenen Dinge	Chorus of Abandoned Things
KRUG IM SCHUTT	JUG IN THE RUBBLE

War ich der Krug daraus der Abend
    floss wie Wein
Und manchmal ein gefangener Mond
    zum Rosenstock?
Die Sterbenacht der Greisin fing
    ich ein
Als schon ihr Atem keuchte wie die
    Geiss am Pflock
O Krüge, Krüge! In ein Abschiedmass
    gezwängt
Ist was wir halten; rinnende Natur,
Wir sind wie Herzen, draus es
    weiter drängt
Und stille steht wie Zeit in einer Uhr

Was I the jug from which the
    evening flowed like wine
And sometimes for the rose tree a
    captured moon?
The old woman's death night I
    caught in
When her breath already heaved
    like the tethered goat
Oh jugs, jugs! Forced into a
    measure of parting
Is what we hold; liquid nature,
We are like hearts from which it
    presses on
And stands so still as time inside a
    clock.

EIN HALBVERBRANNTES LICHT

A HALF-BURNED CANDLE

O Schattenspiegel mein! Ich sah in
    dir, ich sah—
Die Hand aus Grabesstaub, die sich
    an einem Stern verging.
Die Zeit in ihrer Sterbeswiege schrie
    —ich sah
Israels Mund in Qual, gebogen wie
    ein Ring.

Oh shadow mirror of mine!
    I saw in you, I saw—
The hand from dust of graves
    defiling a star.
Time in its dying cradle screamed
    —I saw
Israel's mouth in torment, twisted
    like a ring.

EIN SCHUH

A SHOE

Verlorenes Menschenmass; Ich bin
    die Einsamkeit
Die ihr Geschwister sucht auf dieser
    Welt—
O Israel, von deiner Füsse Leid
Bin ich ein Echo das zum Himmel
    gellt.

Lost measure of man; I am the
    loneliness
Seeking its sibling in this world—

Oh Israel, from your feet's suffering
I am an echo shrieking
    heavenwards.

(TRANSLATED BY ESTHER KINSKY FOR THIS BOOK)

tree a captured moon?" In keeping with a romantic idea of poetry, the jug here integrates—like poetry itself—what is manmade into the cycle of nature. Not unlike the poet's mouthpiece, the jug holds the ongoing rhythm of nature—the flowing transitions, the waxing and waning of the evening and the moon—and, through the touch of a human hand, passes it to the wine and the water for the rose tree. The jug, like poetry, thus draws man into the cycle of nature. This notion of poetry remembered by the jug, however, is now declared invalid. Following the traumatic experience of the "old woman's death night" the jug no longer recognizes itself; its function of mediating harmony between man and nature is now "forced into a measure of parting," belongs to the past. The "Choirs after Midnight" thus invoke the poetic vocabulary of romanticism and simultaneously state that this mode has been lost.

In the concluding collective chorus, the lament of the abandoned things begins with a "But we" and calls for the revival of Israel. This occurs in a contradictory combination of the evocative voice of the "we" as the chorus sets in and the act of reading, of gathering and collecting the traces of the past for which this "we" calls:

Wir aber sind, seitdem wir Erde waren
Getrieben schon durch so viel Tod—

Bist du ein Band gepflückt aus Totenhaaren
Hier ist ein Buch darin die Welten kreisen
Und das Geheimnis flüstert hinter einem Spalt—
Wirf es ins Feuer, Licht wird nicht verwaisen
Und Asche schläft sich neu zur Sterngestalt.
Und tragen wir der Menschenhände Siegel
Und ihre Augen-Blicke eingesenkt wie Raub—
So lest uns wie verkehrte Schrift im Spiegel
Erst totes Ding und dann der Menschenstaub.

But we have, after being earth, already floated through so much death—

Are you a ribbon picked from corpses' hair
here is a book in which the worlds go round
And the secret whispers from behind a crack—
Throw it to the fire, light will not be orphaned
and ashes will sleep themselves anew into the shape of stars.
And as we bear the seal of human hands
and their eyes' glances imprinted like prey—
so read us like a reversed writing in the mirror,
first the dead thing and then the dust of man.

(TRANSLATED BY ESTHER KINSKY FOR THIS BOOK)

The first movement of these lines consists in a comforting sublimation of terms associated with the people of Israel: the Book of Books and the bond with God. The "book in which the worlds go round" has been burnt. The bond is now a ribbon made of corpses' hair, left behind after the destruction. But the lines suggest that nothing is really lost: the material book is dispensable because its spirit is not tied to its concrete existence. The book may burn, but it will not be destroyed. However, this new creation arising from the burning of this book—an obvious allusion to the Nazi book-burning and to the burning of the Jews as the people of the book—will now have to be compiled from material signs: it does not emerge directly from the ashes. The objects left behind now want to be *read* as signs and translated into a new reality. The invitation "so read us like a reversed writing in the mirror / first the dead thing and then the dust of man" is no longer a matter of immediacy. The revival cannot take place through direct invocation and recalling of a voice, but only by way of the detour of reading the traces that lead in a slow, groping journey backward[15] to the past. With the metaphors of reading and writing, the material quality of the signs as traces of what has been destroyed inscribes itself in this revival. Unlike the original creation, the new one can no longer come into existence through the word of God, but only through following the trail of traces back toward the past. This path backward leads through the destruction toward the recovery of a previous, unscathed life.

This call of the introductory poem to return to an earlier time of wholeness is carried out by the subsequent poems. The following twelve choirs indeed set out on a path leading step-by-step backward to the time before the destruction, to a rebirth. This revival takes place as a passage in which the "Rescued" of the first chorus after the introductory poem are the ones most deprived of hope, while the dead in the middle of the cycle pronounce the first lines of hope, before the as yet "Unborn" appear in the penultimate poem as "fragrant with morning." These "Unborn" announce a future redemption that will not, however, come to pass within the cycle. This sequence is largely consistent with the Christian resurrection narrative, but the *restitutio in integrum* fails to materialize.

The first three of the twelve choirs are spoken by the living: by the Rescued, the Wanderers, the Orphans. As each successive speaker is introduced, bereavement and death inscribe themselves with greater urgency, and yet the poems also point in the opposite direction: each poem moves further away from the traumatic experience and embarks on a step-by-step journey toward a new beginning. The Rescued, despite the positive connotation of the term, are those who bear the deepest wounds and show the least signs of hope. The Wanderers of the next poem raise their voices from the midst of a painful present marked by homelessness and abandonment, but already a very first hint of a distant future appears: grains of dust "beneath our wanderers' feet" begin to "sprout forth (*treiben*) blood in our grandchildren." However, the hope is faint: the double meaning of the German word *treiben,* which also suggests *Vertreibung* (expulsion) foretells a future without real possibility for change. Accordingly, the final lines of the poem augur death:

"Our death will lie like a threshold / in front of your closed doors." The Wanderers will remain excluded until their death. This warning is ultimately addressed to those who keep their doors locked at the sight of the victims: the "death on their threshold" also locks them up in their own houses. In the following poem, "Chorus of the Orphans," which deals with the experience of the loss of parents, the dead for the first time receive a voice of their own and attest their comforting presence "through the black folds of night." The orphans, however, refuse the consolation offered by voices from beyond. They respond: "Stones have become our playthings, / Stones have faces, father and mother faces." Here, consolation is still explicitly figured as an illusory substitute and self-made projection, and the last line of the poem—"We are like no one in this world anymore"—refuses all comfort. The next poem, "Chorus of the Dead," refers to Israel for the first time in this sequence. The poem is set as a dialogue between the murdered and the living and it reiterates the unbridgeable separation between the two. "Oh you, who still greet the dust as a friend / you who, talking as sand to sand, say: / I love you, / We say to you . . . We, Israel's dead say to you: / We have reached a star ahead / Into our concealed God." The dead affirm their severance from the rest of the world. They turn away from human bonds but declare their greater closeness to God, thereby giving the cycle a transcendental and hopeful turn.

The following choirs, those of the "Shadows," the "Stones," and the "Invisible Things," which all give a voice to what is inanimate, are also the most conciliatory of the whole cycle. The "Chorus of the Stones," the one that lends a voice to what is most lifeless, forms the exact middle of the cycle. Its conclusion constitutes one of those instances in Sachs's early post-war poetry that fed the image of her conciliatory stance, her absence of hatred, anger, and revenge.

The poem constitutes an exemplary blend of Jewish and romantic elements. The stones are "memorial stones," pebbles which, in the Jewish ritual, are placed on graves instead of flowers. But in the poem they are also magical elements of nature that partake of the life of human beings and absorb their experiences. Evoking romantic imagery, they keep "the roots of dreams hidden" and "let the airy angels' ladders sprout." These angels and ladders are also those which appear in Jacob's dreams in the Bible: they prophesy for Jacob, whose other name is Israel, the destiny awaiting his people. In the last stanza, avenging anger is equated with blasphemy, and revenge is replaced by a kiss of forgiveness and reconciliation. These verses may well have provoked Paul Celan's poetic reaction to Sachs as cast in his poem "Whichever stone you lift":

"Chorus of the Stones" is, along with "Chorus of the Orphans," one of the first poems by Sachs that Celan read (Dinesen 1985a, 119).[16] Celan's first stanza is a literal reference to Sachs's "Chorus of the Stones"; the second stanza refers to the metaphors of tree, branch, firewood, and kindling in her "Chorus of the Orphans." In the last stanza Celan seems to address Sachs directly. It is not a coincidence that it is the most conciliatory poem in this cycle that provoked the powerful indictment expressed in Celan's last verses. Klaus Jeziorkowski identi-

Wir Steine	We stones
Wenn einer uns hebt	When someone lifts us
Hebt er Urzeiten empor—	He lifts the foretime—
Wenn einer uns hebt	When someone lifts us
Hebt er den Garten Eden empor—	He lifts the Garden of Eden—
[. . .]	[. . .]
Wenn einer uns anrührt	When someone touches us
Rührt er eine Klagemauer an.	He touches a wailing wall.
[. . .]	[. . .]
Rührt er die Wegscheiden der Mitternacht an	He touches the forked ways of midnight
Klingend von Geburt und Tod	Sounding with birth and death
Wenn einer uns wirft im Zorne	When someone throws us in anger
So wirft er Äonen gebrochener Herzen	He throws eons of broken hearts
Und seidener Schmetterlinge.	and silken butterflies
Hütet euch, hütet euch	Beware, beware
zu werfen im Zorne mit einem Stein—	of throwing a stone in anger—
Unser Gemisch ist ein von Odem durchblasenes.	Our medley is saturated by God's breath.
Es erstarrte im Geheimnis	It petrified into a secret
Aber kann erwachen an einem Kuss.	But can awaken at a kiss.

(TRANSLATED BY ESTHER KINSKY FOR THIS BOOK)

fies in Sachs's lifting of the stones a "classical Gnostic idealism of cleansing: Up from the dark depths of the material, to the shining heights of the dematerialized ideal" (1996, 357).[17] This movement turns stones into a living organism containing breath. Such a romantic, rather un-Jewish endowment of nature with soul accompanies the renunciation of anger in Sachs's last stanza. Celan's poem counters this Christian-inflected reconciliation and calls up the Jewish tradition: the stones on the grave are, in his poem as in Sachs's, memorial stones, but for Celan they are not associated with flowers or wreaths, the symbols of hope and resurrection invoked by Sachs. Instead, his stones mark and fix the separation between life and death. To Celan, "lifting" the stones in an act of sublimation from the material to the spiritual sphere would be a betrayal of the dead. The dead are, for Celan, in need of a protecting separation, a "grief made of stone." Only then shall the living too

Welchen der Steine du hebst	Whichever stone you lift
du entblößt,	you lay bare
die des Schutzes der Steine bedürfen:	who needs the shelter of the stones:
nackt,	naked,
erneuern sie nun die Verflechtung.	they now renew the entanglement.
Welchen der Bäume du fällst	Whichever tree you fell
[...]	[...]
Welches der Worte du sprichst—	Whichever word you speak—
du dankst	you give thanks
dem Verderben.	to the destruction.

(TRANSLATED BY ESTHER KINSKY FOR THIS BOOK)

be saved from a (Christian and romantic) "entanglement" of life and death. This entanglement, which is explicit in Sachs's representation of the stones as "sounding of birth and death," is in a sense already inherent in the fact that the dead are being endowed with a voice. What Celan ultimately rejects is the presumptuousness of speaking in the name of the dead and of forgiving in their stead. Celan responds with a meta-reflection about poetic remembrance, addressed to a "you" that might well be read as a criticism directed at Sachs herself: "Whichever word you speak— / you give thanks / to the destruction." Every act of speaking that does not aporeti-cally take itself back, that does not mark its own impossibility and presumptuously claims to actually revive the dead by speaking in their name, implies for Celan a denial of the destruction.

Celan's response to the conciliatory ending of Sachs's "Chorus of the Stones" goes to the heart of the relationship between these two poets, a relationship Jean Bollack described as the "history of a struggle." Bollack writes: "Celan saw very clearly that Nelly Sachs betrayed his position" (1994, 122). Bollack sees Celan's crit-icism confirmed in a letter from Sachs where she approvingly quotes Hans Mag-nus Enzensberger's view of her poetry: "Your work contains not a single word of hatred. There is forgiveness and no threat for the murderers [. . .] There is no curse for them, no revenge." For Bollack, each one of Enzensberger's words "was directed against Celan." In his eyes, Sachs here served "as an alibi or allowed herself to be used as one. Whoever claimed, like Enzensberger, to be a champion of some form of reconciliation was in Celan's eyes party to an obfuscation of history" (1994, 123). Sachs's "Chorus of the Stones" on its own is no doubt one of her contestable poems. Within the cycle, however, it merely marks one moment in a movement which, in the end, revokes or at least queries this conciliatory stance.

"Chorus of the Stones" is followed by three poems—"Chorus of the Stars,"

"Chorus of the Invisible Things," and "Chorus of the Clouds"—that represent a change of tone and focus. After the lament and resignation of the first poems and the conciliatory tone of the middle of the cycle, the recurring key word now is "longing": the earth as "richest in longing," "the longing for new splendors," "how much longing has shaped us." This yearning note drives toward a messianic hope and emphasizes that the renunciation of anger does not imply recovery and restoration. Step-by-step, the speakers of the poems return to earth: from the stars to the clouds, and then to the trees, that romantic vertical link between the celestial and the terrestrial, between God and man. The speakers of the last two choirs are human again, "Those Who Comfort" (*die Tröster*) and the Unborn (*die Ungeborenen*), who both receive and communicate the tidings of the future revival. What the speakers of the choirs have brought back from "up high," from the stars and the clouds, is a hope of redemption. The poems after "Chorus of the Stones" express the presentiment of an organic new beginning—"angelic floating seed," "splendors which are sprouting"—and are directed toward a future: "Then [. . .] you shall see again," "new seed shall [. . .] be drawn." And yet, the more insistently the message of hope articulates itself, the more explicit is the deferral of an actual recovery: the "wound / which shall not close / Which must not heal." This is explicit in "Chorus of Those Who Comfort": "The flowers of comfort have sprouted too young." The voice of "Those Who Comfort," however, merely *announces* the coming of a still absent "nightly singer," a future poet who *will* give comfort. For no salvation has yet come to pass. Only once, in "Chorus of the Invisible Things," we read: "Now the angel with the baskets / for the invisible things *has arrived*" (emphasis added). This is the angel who gathers and collects the traces and the tears. It is explicitly stated that these residues of the destruction are "already being gathered in." The only verses that do not announce, conjure up, or hope for something in the future, but name what is already present, relate the unfinished act of "gathering" the broken remains of the past. From these remnants the messianic hope for a revival arises, but it remains an anticipation for a redemption that is yet to come.

While the earlier temporal indications—"still" and "not yet"—now gradually make way for the "already" of the angel collecting the traces of desolation, the last chorus before the concluding poem, "Chorus of the Unborn," takes one step further toward redemption.

The final destination of the Unborn, their birth, completes the return of hope. In the sequence of "already," "still," "already," "until," the temporal structure of this final chorus points to the "Holy Land," the ultimate goal of the last poem. The cycle's evolution from resignation toward messianic promise is marked by the transformation of the relationship between "we" and "you." The Rescued of the second poem have lost all bonds—as individuals, as a community of survivors, and in their relation to those unaffected by destruction. Throughout the cycle these separations are never truly overcome. Only the Unborn of the penultimate poem, who, "fragrant with morning," bear the promise of a new beginning, announce a change and the possibility of contact and exchange: "We are those who begin

Wir Ungeborenen	We the Unborn
Schon beginnt die Sehnsucht an uns zu schaffen	*Already* the yearning has begun to plague us
[. . .]	[. . .]
Noch liegen die Schatten der Zeit wie Fragen	But *still* the shadows of time lie like questions
Über unserem Geheimnis.	Over our secret.
[. . .]	[. . .]
Schon zieht uns euer Atem ein,	*Already* your breath is inhaling us,
Nimmt uns hinab in euren Schlaf	Drawing us down into your sleep
In die Träume, die unser Erdreich sind	Into the dreams which are our earth
Wo unsere schwarze Amme, die Nacht	Where night, our black nurse,
Uns wachsen lässt,	Lets us grow
Bis wir uns spiegeln in euren Augen	*Until* we mirror ourselves in your eyes
Bis wir sprechen in euer Ohr.	*Until* we speak into your ear.

(TRANSLATED BY ESTHER KINSKY FOR THIS BOOK; EMPHASIS ADDED)

to live in your glances, / In your hands which are searching the blue air— / [. . .] / Until we mirror ourselves in your eyes / Until we speak into your ear." Unlike the Rescued at the beginning of the cycle, who "might dissolve before [the others'] eyes," the Unborn here begin to live in the glances of the others. Yet it is suggested that only the voice entering the ear of the addressed would complete the recovery. This event, however, is still waiting to occur.

"Voice of the Holy Land," the title of the final poem, makes the whole cycle appear as if it has been moving directly toward this reviving, unifying voice of a people that would accomplish the resurrection of Israel. This poem contributed significantly to Sachs's reputation as the spokeswoman of the Jewish *Volksgeist*. In fact, the poem resumes the movement of the entire cycle and thwarts its own evocation of a voice. It ends on a poetic sign that points to grief about the past and hope for redemption yet to occur.

Like the entire cycle, the poem begins with a reminiscence of the bloody destruction of Israel. The central part, framed by the repeated question of the speaker, the Holy Land, contains a renunciation of revenge and anger which is, however, cast into doubt immediately afterward. The "Voice of the Holy Land" reveals that the cycle does not lead into restoration and resurrection but, emphasizing stars and dreams, ends on a faint suggestion of hope.

Despite the singular voice mentioned in the title, there are, in fact, several voices speaking in this poem. The "Holy Land" is involved in a dialogue with the

Stimme des heiligen Landes	Voice of the Holy Land
O meine Kinder,	Oh my children,
Der Tod ist durch eure Herzen gefahren	Death has run through your hearts
Wie durch einen Weinberg—	As through a vineyard—
Malte *Israel* rot an alle Wände der Erde.	Painted *Israel* red on all the walls of the world.
Wo soll die kleine Heiligkeit hin	What shall be the end of the little holiness
Die noch in meinem Sande wohnt?	Which still dwells in my sand?
Durch die Röhren der Abgeschiedenheit	The voices of the dead
Sprechen die Stimmen der Toten:	Speak through reed pipes of seclusion:
Leget auf den Acker die Waffen der Rache	Lay the weapons of revenge in the field
damit sie leise werden—	That they grow gentle—
Denn auch Eisen und Korn sind Geschwister	For even iron and grain are akin
Im Schosse der Erde—	In the womb of earth—
Wo soll denn die kleine Heiligkeit hin	But what shall be the end of the little holiness
Die noch in meinem Sande wohnt?	Which still dwells in my sand?
Das Kind im Schlafe gemordet	The child murdered in sleep
Steht auf; biegt den Baum der Jahrtausende hinab	Arises; bends down the tree of ages
Und heftet den weissen, atmenden Stern	And pins the white breathing star
Der einmal Israel hiess	That was once called Israel
An seine Krone.	To its topmost bough.
Schnelle zurück, spricht es	Spring upright again, says the child
Dorthin, wo Tränen Ewigkeit bedeuten.	To where tears mean eternity.

(TRANSLATED BY ESTHER KINSKY FOR THIS BOOK)

dead, who reply to its questions. The last verses of the poem—and hence of the entire cycle—are voiced by a child. In the first line of the poem, the voice of the Holy Land unites the survivors, the murdered, and the unborn of the preceding poems in a recollection of the crimes committed against the "children of Israel." It is no coincidence that the name of *Israel* appears as a written sign set in italics. This sign marks the dispersal of the people. It is a bloody portent, an inextinguishable trace, and a warning that now appears on all the walls of the earth. In contrast to the uniting, uniform *voice* of the "Holy Land," writing here becomes the medium of exile and dispersal.

In the following line, the "Holy Land" questions itself; in the face of destruction it is searching for the destination of its "little holiness," which is all that remains in the aftermath of destruction. The voices of the dead answer, literally speaking through a mouthpiece, through the "reed pipes of seclusion." Their response to the vengeful writing on the wall uttered by the Holy Land is an appeal to lay down the "arms of revenge." Their message of reconciliation combines the biblical command to turn swords into ploughshares with the romantic idea of a harmonious embrace of all things in nature. This appeal of the dead to forgive rather than take revenge forms the center of the poem and corresponds to the conciliatory voice of the stones in the middle of the cycle. There and here, where the voices of the dead resound through the "reed pipes of seclusion," life and death become "entangled" in different forms of living death or deadly life. In both the cycle and in this final, recapitulating poem, vocal revival and the renunciation of revenge and wrath are combined to create this entanglement, but in neither case has the last word been spoken. The renunciation of anger in "Chorus of the Stones" is followed by the second, "yearning" half of the cycle. Similarly, the message of reconciliation in the middle of the final poem is followed by the question "What shall be the end [. . .]?"[18]

The Holy Land obviously rejects the pacifying message of the dead and ultimately even their vocal presence. The last stanza suggests an alternative to the conciliatory *voice* of the dead. The beginning of the poem, describing death running through Israel "As through a vineyard" and leaving Israel behind as a bloody *trace*, a *writing* on the walls of the earth, brings to mind the Eucharist of wine turning into blood (implying an analogy between the murder of the Jews and the martyrdom of Christ). The end of the poem, however, rejects any incarnation in the present as well as the enactment of a *restitutio in integrum*. Accordingly, the poem ends by thwarting the prophesying voice alluded to in its title and in the words of the dead that speak in it. The voice of the dead appealing for reconciliation and the refusal of the Holy Land to accept such reconciliation are followed by a surprising and complex reversal. After the vocalized invocations and laments, the entire cycle ends on a coded and opaque act that conveys the intended effect of this cycle of poems. In the last stanza a narrator describes an allegoric scene in which the "child murdered in sleep," the personification of murdered innocence, addresses the "tree of ages," the history of mankind. The child bends the tip of the tree toward himself to pin his star—the star of David, the star of Israel?—to it and places it back in the sky by saying, "Spring upright again." The star "that was once called Israel" has survived, and the child now places it back in the sky. The star would thus be the brightness that survived the extinction of Israel just as the light in the first poem of the cycle has survived the burning of the book. In this interpretation, the resurrected child becomes the allegory of hope born out of the cycle of poems itself. The allegory arises from the poetic transformation of the tears of despair into a guiding star, bearing both grief and a promise for the future, which the child *places* in the sky, no longer a natural phenomenon but an artificial, a "constructed" light.

This star "breathes" and with its breath brings living voice and indicating sign together. Although the child *speaks* his final words, this is no longer a voice speaking directly as it did in the poems starting with "we." The allegoric and narrative form of the last stanza and the insertion of "says the child" annul the evocative structure characterizing the medium of the mouthpiece. The "white, breathing star / That was once called Israel" resumes the association of Israel and the star set forth in the first poem in the cycle. The name of the star "that was once called Israel" remains, at the end of the cycle, torn and scattered all over the earth: a trace of blood and a warning written on the wall. The child who was murdered in its sleep rises again, but this is no reawakening, no resurrection. The call to read a reversed writing from traces in the mirror, uttered by the "Abandoned Things" at the beginning of the cycle, remains unheeded. The wholeness of the name vouchsafing presence is not restored. In the final image, a star shines far away, above, outside of space and time, but the name of Israel is not reinstated. The traces of destruction and the signs of mourning are transformed with this star into an eternally shining hope, but the scenery carries the trace of tears and the star remains a sign pointing toward a redemption that is still to come. It is not the conciliatory, romantic-Christian *voice* of the dead that grants presence to the remaining holiness of the land, but the meaningful *sign* that keeps this messianic hope alive. This place, to which the child refers with his words "Spring upright again, [. . .] To where [. . .]," points heavenward, but also to the preceding lines, to the poem and the cycle, and ultimately to poetry itself as the place where this hope resides (West 1996, 101). In the poem, Sachs indicates this place in the act of the child who, after the destruction of the "natural" star, places the sign of poetry itself in the darkened sky.[19] Here Sachs is not so far from Celan, who writes: "A star, put it, put the star into the night" (CG, 111).

Coda

In a strange letter, written in verse, to his wife Gisèle in January 1965, Paul Celan describes with bitterness Nelly Sachs's appropriation by the German cultural establishment and regrets her involvement in this manipulation. "Former Hitler youths," writes Celan with bitterness,[20]

Halfen ihm [Celan bezeichnet sich hier selbst] aus seinen Erlebnissen heraus	Helped him [here Celan names himself] out of his experiences
und hängte sie derjenigen über, die sie nicht gehabt hatte und sich willig ins Konzept fügte.	and clothed [Sachs] in them who hadn't had them and willingly complied with the concept.
Von der Ehemaligen Gnaden wurde sie zur schlechthinnigen Jüdin. Man nannte sie königlich— wovon war ihr Purpur rot? "Mag sein," verkündete sie, "dass das Schicksal meines Volkes an mir leuchtet." Mag sein. Doch wie? Aber das aus ihr selber Leuchtende töteten sie.	By the grace of the former lies she became the Jewess per se. She was called queenly— what made her crimson red? "May Be" she announced, "my people's fate shines on me." May be. Yet how? But what shone out of herself they killed.[21]

She was, writes Celan, needed as the "Jew per se," as the representative of the Jewish people, and she obliged, seeing herself as mouthpiece of the Jewish victims whose fate and voice "shone" on her. In Celan's view, those who celebrated her as the voice of the Jewish people did not recognize her true light: that which "shone out of herself," out of her eternally maimed and mourning "innermost straits" (CGW, 3:200).

PART FOUR

CONTENTIOUS COMMEMORATIONS

A Broken Ring: The *Gruppe 47* and Ilse Aichinger's Poetics of Resistance

The intellectual and literary history of Germany in the immediate aftermath of World War II was, for a long time, fraught with blind spots covered up by a celebration of half-hearted attempts to face the immediate past.[1] Locating that heart's other half—the darker side of the cultural *Wiederaufbau* (reconstruction)—from the vantage point of the present requires caution, contextualization, and a suspicion of self-righteous hindsight. This is particularly true where methods derived from historical analysis are applied to literary texts in order to reconstruct—and ideologically indict—a bygone period. An alternative consists of reversing this procedure by looking at a specific moment through the prism of a contemporary literary text. The third option, chosen here, combines the two perspectives and superimposes the outlines of an important component of post-war Germany's literary culture with the analysis of a short text by one who both was and was not part of its core.

The moment is the height of the post-war restoration period, the particular component is the group of writers referred to as *Gruppe 47*, the text is "Der Engel" (1991a, 113–21),[2] a short prose piece written in 1962 by Ilse Aichinger. Aichinger was a member of the *Gruppe 47* but came to be considered, along with Paul Celan, Wolfgang Hildesheimer, Ingeborg Bachmann, and a few others,[3] as one of the group's "internal outsiders." These authors had, as Klaus Briegleb euphemistically explains, a different past than the majority of the group and wrote from within a different memorial space (*Gedächtnisraum*) (1997, 29). Considering the traces of this memory, some of Aichinger's work can be read as a consistent condemnation of the literary "disremembering" of the national socialist crimes and represents a so far insufficiently acknowledged, early contribution to a post-Holocaust poetics.

In the first years following the war up to the student movement of the late 1960s, the talk of a radical new beginning, of a *Stunde Null* (zero hour) and its literary equivalents, *Kahlschlag* (clear-cutting) and *Trümmerliteratur* (rubble literature), arose from the intention of marking a break with the Third Reich. These terms have by now been largely discredited because it has been shown that such slogans were not really put into practice and that continuities of different kinds persisted in Germany's political, institutional, and aesthetic practices of the period. The emphasis on the needs of the day and the orientation toward a better future involved an amnesia about certain aspects of the immediate past, even when that past was recognized as the measure against which the future was to be conceived. Furthermore, the hopeful orientation toward a new and different Germany, a new and different literature cleansed of the uncomfortable past, also came down to encouraging oblivion.

The *Gruppe 47* was an instance in which lucidity was mixed with blindness. From 1947 until 1967 this loosely knit association of writers dominated—some said monopolized—the German literary landscape. The group, a *Freundeskreis* (circle of friends), as it was called by its main founder and organizer Hans Werner Richter, met once or twice a year in different places and was conceived as a *literarische Werkstatt*, a literary atelier where mainly younger authors presented their unfinished work and subjected it to the criticism of the other members. The list of its participants, oscillating between 17 and 125, included the most prominent German writers of the post-war era: Böll, Grass, Eich, Bachmann, Enzensberger, Andersch, Jens, Rühmkorf, and many others.

The *Gruppe 47* originated with a group of German war prisoners selected by the Americans to participate in a reeducation program through the publication of a literary journal called the *Ruf* that was concerned with reestablishing the broken traditions of German literature. The group itself came into being after the dismantling of the *Ruf*, which was suppressed by the Americans, who disapproved of its increasingly leftist radicalism and its association of capitalism with fascism. Hans Werner Richter, one of the main editors of the *Ruf*, became the head of the group and remained in this position until its dissolution in 1967. From the start, the group's declared enemy was "fascism." Yet, in Saul Friedländer's words, this "overall tag, along with the new awareness it created, shielded many [. . .] from the *specificity* of the Nazi past" (1994, 257). The group explained the success of fascism solely in terms of an irrationality of the masses. This perception of the Third Reich hindered a more differentiated analysis of the past and in many ways furthered the period's suppression and mystification of the actual Nazi crimes.

In its beginning, most members of the group either had a socialist background or belonged to a generation too young to have participated in Nazi crimes. Members typically posited the assumption of a *Stunde Null* at the end of the war and formulated their self-understanding in terms of a radical new beginning, "unburdened by the past." It is in these very words, quoted here from different sources and different accounts of the attitude of the *Ruf* and the *Gruppe 47* in its early period, that the group's complex relation to the past becomes manifest. Dismissing not only the past, but its *burden* (Arnold 1980, 79; Kröll 1979, 29), the group's members did not fully measure this past's influence on the present and on themselves. Though theoretically the group called for a radical *Traditionsbruch* (rupture with tradition) and a new start, it did not, at least in its beginnings and as Urs Widmer convincingly demonstrates, ever entirely escape remnants of the national socialists' language (1967, 328–35).[4]

In terms of an aesthetic program, which was never made statutory, the authors of the *Ruf* and of the early *Gruppe 47* were searching for "a closed form," for a healing narration that would provide new meanings.[5] They proclaimed the necessity of a new kind of "honest" literary realism, and they rejected all versions of formalism, but also, at first, of any explicit social or political criticism. For this reason, the emerging "novel of persecution" (*zeitnaher Verfolgtenroman*)—along with the literature of exile—was dismissed by the group. The editors of the *Ruf*, and Richter himself, defended this stance by arguing that any kind of explicitly political literature would repeat the old link between aesthetics and politics practiced under Hitler's regime. Meanwhile, they and other members of the group explained the rejection of works written by those who were driven into exile in 1933 by saying that literature could only be relevant if it remained in touch with the society out of which it sprang (Richter in Arnold 1980, 53).

The group's realist ideal of an unmediated and directly communicative language, which mimetically and truthfully reproduces the present, was accompanied by the imperative of an absolute focus on the present (*unbedingter Gegenwartsbezug*): "It was to orient itself not to the past, not to the future, but to the problems of the present" (Arnold 1980, 77). The insistence on renewal and the belief in an actual "point zero" blinded many members of the group to the restorative tendencies and repressive continuities in the social, ideological, and institutional structures of the Adenauer period and led, for the majority of the group's members, to a more or less unwilling tabooization of texts about Nazi crimes. It was both more pragmatic and more convenient to defend a general anti-fascism and pacifism than to face the Jewish emigrants and survivors. These, it was feared, could disrupt the group's idea of a generation's shared experience (*ein gleiches Generationserlebnis*) (Arnold 1980, 142). The name they gave to this past was *Faschismus* and *Weltkrieg* (fascism and world war) and not Auschwitz. This attitude partly explains the utter incomprehension and even "aggressive contempt" with which the group reacted to Paul Celan's reading of the "Todesfuge" and other poems during a 1952 meeting (Briegleb 1997, 53). Celan's poetry was chided for its bathos[6] and (in the words of

Peter Rühmkorf published in the group's 1962 almanac, edited by Richter) its "luft-und leuteleerem Raum" (airless and unpopulated space) (in Briegleb 1997, 65).

A letter by Richter concerning a controversy about the publication of Celan's poems in the group's almanac reads: "Mit kranken Narren kann man nicht seine Zeit verbringen" (one cannot waste one's time on sick fools) (Briegleb 1997, 63). Nevertheless Richter wanted to include Celan's poems in the almanac: "His absence would, in a few months [. . .] be interpreted as a measure against Celan" (1997, 336). Concerning another Jewish author, Hermann Kesten, Richter writes in a letter from January 1961: "Kesten is Jewish, and where would we be if we now dealt together with the past, which means that I don't consider Kesten to be part of us, although he thinks he is" ("Kesten ist Jude, und wo kommen wir hin, wenn wir jetzt die Vergangenheit untereinander austragen, d. h. ich rechne Kesten nicht uns zugehörig, aber er empfindet es so" (in Briegleb 1997, 78).

The group's exclusion of such emigrants was defended in a 1997 interview by Joachim Kaiser, a critic and former member of the group:

> For example, one did not invite the emigrants who later complained very much about this and even claimed that the *Gruppe 47* was anti-Semitic. But then, one did not invite the older German authors either. Richter would never have had the idea of inviting, let's say, Ernst Jünger [. . .] who, God knows, also belonged to German literature.[7]

The choice of Ernst Jünger, considered by many a proto-fascist writer, may, in this context, not have been the best way to ward off accusations of the group's exclusion of emigrants. Kaiser continues:

> Emphatically said: The people who met in the group were beaten by history, they had [. . .] been in the workforce, or in the army and had met—if they were lucky—in the U.S. camps for war prisoners.[8]

The criteria for acceptance, "zeitgeschichtlich geschlagen" (beaten by history), which is here applied to German soldiers and their experience as war prisoners, seems hard to defend in the face of the exclusion of those Jewish writers who had come back to Germany with *their* experiences.

A radical indictment of the *Gruppe 47,* and of H. W. Richter in particular, has been made by Klaus Briegleb. He speaks not only of a "tiefe Befangenheit," a "deep malaise" vis-à-vis Jews writing in German (1997, 43), but of "antijüdische Affekte" and of the group's participation in the collective denial of the past: "The group as a whole succeeded in covering up the 'Third Reich' in their own biographies."[9] Describing its suppression of national socialist crimes, Briegleb explains how the group's cohesion prevented possible disruptions of this silencing (1997, 29). Asked about Günter Eich's involvement with national socialism, Richter answered: "I didn't know anything about him, not about his life before and after the war, nothing about his youth, his childhood. In this period, a few years after the war, this was unimportant" (in Leer and Guntermann 1995, 37). "The group,"

Briegleb concludes, "took itself to be *the* antifascist association of the time but in reality was united in the fear of learning more about each other than anyone wanted" (1997, 51).

For a while, Briegleb's critique of individual members of the group such as Günter Grass seemed exceedingly harsh, but as the recent disclosure of Grass's participation in the Waffen-SS in his autobiography *Beim Häuten der Zwiebel* (2006) indicates, Briegleb had good reasons to be suspicious.[10] Among the number of analyses, histories, and comments about the *Gruppe 47* published since the mid-nineties (Parkes and White 1999), mostly on the occasion of the group's fiftieth anniversary, only Maxim Biller, a German-Jewish *provocateur* and author of *Land der Väter und Verräter* (1997), is more radical than Briegleb. Biller calls the group "entnazifizierte Reichsschrifttumskammer" (denazified Chamber of Literature), a "Vereinigung ehemaliger Nazi-Soldaten und HJler" (an association of former Nazi soldiers and members of the Hitler Youth), and even included some of the group's "internal outsiders" in his critique of its retreat to a position of "nonaccountability" ("Rückzug auf eine Position der Nichtzurechenbarkeit") (in Leer and Guntermann 1995, 37–38). Few went this far in their disparagement of the group. Earlier and more frequent criticism addressed the structure of the group as such, its existence as a powerful community that imposed its opinions on the literary market. Some spoke of dictatorship: "literarische Polizeiaufsicht," (literary police surveillance) "demagogischer Clan" (demagogic clan), and "Meinungsterror" (opinion terror).

How did Ilse Aichinger fit into all this? Although she was part of the group from 1951, was married to Günter Eich, another important member of the group, and won one of its annual prizes in 1952, she both did and did not belong. The "space of memory" Briegleb refers to consists, for Aichinger, of separation and loss experienced as a result of the Nazis' invasion of Austria while she was a young girl. After 1938 her non-Jewish father had his marriage dissolved, causing his wife to lose her privileged status. Aichinger's twin sister emigrated to England while Ilse stayed in Vienna to protect her mother, who was Jewish and spared from deportation only because she was the caretaker of a half-Aryan daughter under the age of twenty-one. Aichinger painfully experienced the persecution of friends and family members and above all the deportation of her beloved grandmother, who later died in a camp (Lorenz 1997, 152). It seems that Aichinger rarely evoked her past in the group, but the importance for her work of the Jewish fate during the Nazi years is obvious in her first novel, *Die grössere Hoffnung* (translated as *Herod's Children*), which was published in 1948 and is considered to be one of the important literary documents of early German post-Holocaust literature.

Like the other members of the *Gruppe 47*, Aichinger refused the ornamental "Schönschreiberei" (calligraphy) practiced by many older German writers after the war. But Aichinger went further, increasingly refusing the group's own early literary program of realistic representation and narrative closure. Above all, her work set itself off from the group's practice of "disremembering" and lent a quiet but disturbing voice to the silence that, in her view, ought to mark a rupture in the continuity of German literature and culture. She also became increasingly suspicious of the way the group functioned, especially when it lost its role as primarily a *literarische Werkstatt,* became more and more institutionalized, and, in spite of its growing political activities, such as organized protests against the wars in Algeria and Vietnam, the German rearmament, and the manufacturing of atomic weapons, slowly integrated into the official marketplace of the German *Literaturbetrieb* (literary industry). In the early sixties Aichinger started distancing herself from the group (Arnold 1980, 166). It was during this time that "Der Engel" (The Angel) was written.

Like Celan's poetry, Aichinger's prose became increasingly hermetic, following a similar development from a lyrical, narrative mode to a more laconic and obscure language, and from thematic references to the murder of the Jews to an incorporation of this memory into the very form and texture of her writing.

The stories she first presented when she joined the *Gruppe 47* in 1951 translate this dimension—if at all—in a barely recognizable form. The extreme obscurity of Aichinger's texts dating from the late fifties and early sixties was seen as primarily motivated by formal experimentation and was hailed in the group as the manifestation of a literary renewal that would help German literature rejoin the developments in European modernism.[11] "Der Engel," a paradigmatic example of her prose work of this period, contains hidden poetological reflections revealing the motivations behind this obscurity and points to a hermeticism of resistance and commemoration reminiscent of Paul Celan's textual practice and its "strong tendency towards silence" (CGW, 3:197).

"Der Engel" is a radically obscure short prose text—less than ten pages—published in Aichinger's volume *Eliza, Eliza* in 1965. It has rarely been discussed in critical studies of her work, and when critics do mention it, they usually offer descriptions of its incomprehensibility rather than attempt to make sense of it. At a first reading, the enigma is indeed complete: in the absence of an obvious plot, it seems practically impossible to paraphrase the text's content. Most of the references to people and places seem incomprehensible, and at first no coherent pattern of themes and motifs can be established. One critic mentions that, in a private conversation, Aichinger explained the situation of the text as the monologue of an angel in a cemetery, but did not specify any further (Lorenz 1981). The monologue is interrupted by scene instructions in italics describing the actions of the angel, who addresses different absent figures: "My sisters, my brothers, my child [. . .]" (AE, 115). This angel often bows down, sometimes to read a name. The angel appears to address himself to the dead. Repeatedly he says, "I'm going now," "I'm leaving" (AE, 113). At the end he once more announces his departure and asks for one more breath before his voice will disappear and be taken over by "them," by some mysterious "Pförtnersöhne" (AE, 121) (gatekeepers' sons), heirs to former guardians.

Between the first word, "stumbling," and this ending there is a juxtaposition of sentences, an incoherent stream of words, exclamations, memories, warnings, unrecognizable quotes. The only progression of a possible plot consists in the announcement of the angel's disappearance. The text thereby functions as a sort of testament of the angel. The first word after "stumbling" is "ring." Does the angel stumble over a ring, an old German designation for an association of like-minded people?

The monologue starts with the following sentences: "Ring- und Kupferschmiede! Diese Langweiler, die man immer wieder trifft. Die Luft sollte einem im Kreis ausgehen, Nägelrost, jedes Mal frisch, keine Zeit für Seufzer" (AE, 113) (Ring- and coppersmiths! Those dawdlers one encounters time and again. Someone in the circle should lose his breath, rust of nails, each time fresh, no time for sighs). Later, a "Kreis der Freunde" that are "beisammen" is mentioned, a circle of friends that are gathering; there are "prizes," "jubilees," "patrons" ("Schirmherren" hiding in "Schirmhändler" [AE, 114]), a "Gesellschaft für Glasfluss" (AE, 118), "und am Ausgang einer mit einem scharfen Hund" (AE, 117) (and at the exit one with a dog). Obviously these passages refer to a sort of semi-official association, though one about which the speaker says, "I see little possibility for the union there" ("Ich sehe wenig Möglichkeiten für die Vereinigung" [AE, 117]). Hidden in the text is the actual key: "Children of the raven, alight on my shoulders, seven on the left, four on the right, I can bear quite a bit." In German: "links sieben, rechts vier, ich vertrage da einiges" (AE, 117). *Vertragen* indeed means "bearing," but literally also signifies transporting, carrying over from one place to another. What has been changing places here is the sequence of digits in the number 47. This hint establishes the connection with the repeated gathering of "smiths" at the beginning of the text and appears to refer to the *literarische Werkstatt,* the literary atelier, in which literature was discussed as *Handwerk,* as craftsmanship.

With a similar associative method, another passage, in which the angel seems to be enacting a confused self-interrogation concerning past events, reveals its references:

> I saw all of you, the shoes you were wearing, and your hands, stretched out toward the ceiling, yes, I saw you. A flask dashed from the roof and wasted you against the slates, *cunningly, triumphantly* that's how it happened, isn't it? And I? Booed you, scattered you over the threshing floors. Interfered in the toy coffins, divided you in lodges, tore heaven from your breast. Can any of you claim I have not been with you? Didn't I wind up clouds and secret help, and yet didn't do anything, looked at the numbers and how they didn't get mixed up under the lee? Didn't appeal to anything, although it was left to my discretion, *desperate* but self-praise sounds weak, and I don't praise myself. I don't, do I? Who wants to extol the short end with me, the old lot of rails, whom do I pull from the row. (AE, 119–120)

Confusing as these sentences are, the references are unmistakable, evoking worn shoes, marks on the ceiling (those shown in Alain Resnais's film *Nuit et*

Brouillard?), the flask, the rails, the rows, the numbers, mixed with alternations of self-accusation and self-praise, evoking both guilt and pain, a hiding and a facing of facts. The passage ends in the present tense: "Whom do I pull from the row" (AE, 120), merging connotations of saving someone from death rows and an invitation to desert the ranks.

Another recognizable reference points in the direction of an actual concretization of such a resistance. It is contained in a name:

> Hey, you there at the front, was it you who bent down and scrawled on the stone with black chalk? Your Sofie is dead, I found her between the rubble cans. [. . .] Now she'll soon hide and keep stooping forward, vanishing along the walls. Sofie-i! Little Sofie! (AE, 113)

"Sofie" can refer to "wisdom," and could be interpreted meaningfully as saying that wisdom is now to be found in the rubble. But there is another, real Sofie closer to Aichinger's framework. In several lesser-known texts, Aichinger previously paid tribute to the group of young Catholic resistance fighters Die Weisse Rose, organized by the students Sophie and Hans Scholl, who, in 1942, paid with their lives for opposing the Nazi regime. One of their actions, called *Schmieraktion,* consisted of writing "Down with Hitler" seventy times on the walls leading to the university, and "freedom" over its entrance. All this was scrawled on stone walls with black chalk. On Thursday, 18 February 1943, they filled a valise with pamphlets calling for an uprising against the regime and threw it into the university hall. The gatekeeper of the university, named Schmidt, denounced them to the Gestapo. They were beheaded shortly after. In her earlier non-fiction texts about the Scholls, Aichinger honors their attitude as the highest ideal to be followed: resistance to power, to the specific murderous power opposed by the Scholls.

Placed under the sign of this resistance, Aichinger's text indicts the literary practice of false harmonization and denial of a rupture after the war. In "Das Erzählen in dieser Zeit" (1991b, 9–11), an earlier text in which she reflects on the possibilities of narrative representation "in this time," Aichinger describes earlier narrative practices with the metaphor of a flowing river, of a tranquil "Erzählfluss," a literary form she declares to have become invalid. Among the references to the *Gruppe 47* in "Der Engel" there is the phrase "Gesellschaft für Glasfluss" (AE, 118) (society for glassflow), which, with glass implying transparency, expresses her critique of the group's poetics of a harmonizing, flowing realism. For herself she fears, in "Das Erzählen in dieser Zeit," that "unter dem Eindruck des Endes man den Mund nicht mehr aufbringt" (1991b, 9), that under the impact of the end, speaking is becoming impossible.

Perhaps this moment of hesitation, this sense of the impossibility of going on speaking and telling stories, is what the first lines of "Der Engel" are calling for. After evoking a ring, a closed circle, the "immer wieder" (over and over again) of continuation, of an eternal return, the lines state that "one in the circle should lose his breath": "Die Luft sollte einem im Kreis ausgehen [. . .] keine Zeit für Seufzer"

(AE, 113)—"no time for sighs." A reference to rusting nails negates the possibility of putting the scattered rubble back together and making things whole (AE, 113). There ought to be a break, a rupture, a caesura stopping the rhythmical breathing, the smooth continuation of the flow. Anything that creates connection and coherence and hides the tear, for Aichinger, participates in a false healing, a treacherous covering-up of a wound. A space must be left open, interrupting the ongoing circle. Later in the text an alternative to the "ringsmiths'" craft is suggested: "We want to agree on farriers" (AE, 115) (*Hufschmiede*), smiths who make horseshoes, "and the moon crescent above, but only one," "um das Geschwätz abzuhalten, das Sonntagsgerede" (AE, 115) (to ward off the prattle, the Sunday-twaddle), "the dissolved luster" (AE, 115). What horseshoes and the single crescent of the moon have in common is their open shape, and in contradistinction to the coherence, continuity, and fullness of ring and circle, these signs bearing an interruption, a gap, become emblematic for Aichinger's own poetics. They oppose the Sunday-twaddle, the official, self-satisfied, and lofty tone, and conjure up "the soundless, silent day" ("den lautlosen Tag" [AE, 114]). A suggestion that the gaps should be closed, should be filled with meaning, is rejected by the speaker: "Füllen heisst es? [. . .] Heisst es nicht Kugelwind, Gehorsamspflicht?" (AE, 118). In a play on the double meaning of *Füllen*—"young horse" derived from the horseshoe, and the verb "filling in"—traditional, realistic "full" narration becomes associated with submission, this old excuse, the duty of obedience. But the speaker refuses to comply with the orders and expectations: "Hinweg, hier bleibt es still" (AE, 115) (Get away, it remains silent here).

In hidden allusions, in puns and paronomasias, the text also foresees that it could be misunderstood as a mere aesthetic experiment. It fears that its "torn-up lantern stumps" (*zerrissene Laternenstümpfe*), the violently fragmented remnants of a destroyed poetic luminosity, will be mistaken for comforting "slumber pillows" (*Schlummerrollen*), and its "frozen leaves" (*Eislaub*), those pages coming from the cold, for pretty "chambermaid's cushions" (*Zofenkissen*) made of lace. But the angel warns: "Die Kunstblumen werden ab heute ins heilige Recht geführt, braun mit goldenen Staubfäden" (AE, 115). The artificial flowers, the fake artistry adorned with golden threads of romantic poetry, now have the brown tint of the past.

At one point the angel speaks to the graves, calling on the dead to follow him. He turns around, saying, "Come! Let's see what can be saved of this lamentation, the healed bones" (AE, 118). Like Walter Benjamin's "angel of history" from his *Theses on the Philosophy of History,* written in 1939, Aichinger's angel looks back and sees a heap of rubble. The difference is that Aichinger's angel asks how something of the lament, the expression of despair, can be saved in the face of the *healed* bones that no longer show their trauma. Benjamin's "angel of history" wants to awaken the dead, but the wind of progress carries him off. Aichinger's angel is also carried away by those who strive forward in the name of the future, leaving no time for sighs. Before disappearing, he leaves behind this text, and at its end a warning: "Lasst euch nichts gesagt sein" (AE, 120), "don't believe what they tell you," "beware of false bird's swarms," of "falsche Vogelschwärme, gezielt und zugespitzt" (AE, 121), of false prophets purposefully manipulating with their promises, of "Vorstadtpfeifer" and "Perückenmacher," of seducers and false players who claim authority, dry the tears, and promise with a voice reminiscent of Nelly Sachs at her most Christian that "the sky will beget you anew" ("Der Himmel zeugt euch neu" [AE, 121]). They will, the text says at the end, "tell you with my voice," in an angelic tone: "There is nothing here apart from us." There is an addition in italics: *the latter sentence as if it had already been shouted by many voices, those of the gatekeepers' sons*" (AE, 121).

The gatekeeper's descendants, perhaps the sons of the one who denounced the young resistance students to the Gestapo and, more generally, of those *Ordnungshüter* (guardians of order) who imprisoned, excluded, and executed, who murderously marked the line between same and other, now speak with the fake voice of an innocent, heavenly messenger. But, Aichinger's angel warns, they are not to be trusted. Their promises of a radical renewal are misleading and their exclusionary practices carry echoes of the past. In the end, usurped by the gatekeeper's sons, the angel's own voice disappears, leaving behind a memory of true resistance, a call for vigilance, and a void that ought not to be filled.

II

After the Silence: Holocaust Remembrance in Contemporary Austrian-Jewish Literature

For decades, literary approximations of silence determined the poetics of Holocaust remembrance. This poetics assumes that only silence can truly render what occurred and convey the horrors of this past in a language uncontaminated by inadequate discourse. Since the ultimate witnesses, the dead, are silent and speak only through the living, it is silence itself that is summoned. Silence is the language that corresponds most closely to the absolute speech of the dead. Only silence itself, the interruption of communicative speech, the empty space between words, the self-erasing trace of the non-representable, the open wound of the abyss, the caesura, the rupture, the stuttered, stammered word approaching silence is true.

Variations of this conception can be found in Holocaust literature and theory from Nelly Sachs to Paul Celan, and from Theodor W. Adorno to Giorgio Agamben. The claim about the necessity of silence, of emptiness, of interrupting the word-stream as an act of opposition against soothing representations and biased discourse, was initially put forward by the first post-war generation of survivors. It mirrors the sensibilities and demands of a "damaged life" (Adorno), whose deep traumatization made any harmonious lyrical speech seem barbaric and every narration dishonest. Silence, on the other hand, interrupts connections, sunders relations, and forestalls closure. It designates the past as an all-consuming abyss, the present as emptiness, and the future as an always postponed redemption from an irremediably wounded life. Restraining from rendering as present what has to be experienced as absent in its essence became, for many years, the highest imperative of Holocaust literature. In this insistence on the limits of representation, however, silence risks sacralizing the past in a negative aesthetics of the unsayable and positing an absolute as a norm that disregards specifics.

Not surprisingly, silence as a literary mode could not endure. In eternal repetition, emptiness empties itself out, nothingness negates itself, silence goes dumb. The last witness, the last trace, the final word, and then there is only silence. But before long, some begin to stir again, to reproduce and represent, to reenact and mimic this last word, so that the silence splits open, is robbed of its absoluteness and indivisibility, is disseminated in space and time.

Initially, silence is still the issue: the silence of repression and of shame, the silence of guilt, bewilderment, awe, indifference, and ignorance, both genuine and feigned; the silence of approval and shock, of respect and contempt, of forgetting. But gradually an awareness arises that talking about absence and the impossibility of words itself turns into speech. And, unnoticed at first, one finds oneself in the midst of dialogue and conversation.

Multifarious silence is one of the main topics in contemporary Austrian-Jewish literature written by the so-called second generation of survivors. In this literature, the abysmal past is still omnipresent, but it is embedded in layers of reflections, controversies, and discussions and is accompanied by ongoing comments about the very fixation on this past. Silence is often referred to in deliberately direct and over-explicit language that attenuates the demand for authenticity that had, for decades, motivated the post-Auschwitz aesthetics of the abysmal, the unsayable, and the sublime. Authors such as Robert Schindel, Robert Menasse, and Doron Rabinovici turn to literary forms that draw the various silences of the past—the hushing of the initial post-war period as well as the various imperatives to refrain from representation in the decades that followed—into a turbulent excess of words.

The protagonists of three important novels written by these authors after 1989, Schindel's *Gebürtig* (Born-Where), Menasse's *Vertreibung aus der Hölle* (Expulsion from Hell), and Rabinovici's *Suche nach M.* (Search for M.), are children of the dead or of survivors. They too are damaged, and their speech revolves constantly around the traces of their injury; yet they are also injured by the widespread silence itself and ceaselessly talk about this wound. Their talk is usually neurotic, a drunken, exaggerated, provocative form of speech. Their words do not reconcile or heal anything; nothing decisive is said. Only the talking itself stretches like a tenuous web over the abysmal past. However, this surface of words eventually turns into the very scene on which new possibilities of reconstructing a life—albeit one permeated with remnants of the past and lacking reassuring foundations—are being explored.

"Malgré tout" is an expression used in the title of an essay by Georges Didi-Huberman (2004) on the problem of representation under the sign of Auschwitz.

Schindel's drunken Danny Demant and his coffeehouse companions, Menasse's paranoid Viktor, and Rabinovici's schizophrenic Mullemann are stricken offspring who, "malgré tout," in spite of everything, initiate debates and arguments, make up stories, waste and squander words, and try somehow to come to terms with life half a century after the destruction. All these figures search for what Robert Schindel, in his novel *Born-Where,* calls "a committed but not devouring relationship [to the past]."[1] These works seem to say that neither an identification with the suffering of the parents nor an obsessive hatred of the perpetrators should determine the present to the point of delegitimizing the weight and importance of the now. They suggest that it is only by bringing their own present into the picture, or rather, into the writing of the past, that a true commemoration of the Holocaust by the generation of the survivors' children can take place.

The present time of Schindel's, Menasse's, and Rabinovici's novels is haunted by ghosts rising from the abyss of Austrian history and its aftermath. While Germany, especially after the student revolts in the late 1960s, practiced an overt if often problematic *Vergangenheitsbewältigung* (mastering of the past), both Jews and non-Jews in Austria hushed up the past for a longer time. It was not until 1986, when it was revealed that Kurt Waldheim, the former United Nations Secretary-General, had covered up his activities during the Second World War and Austrians reacted to the international outcry by electing him president, that Austria's role in Nazi crimes was openly discussed. The long silence allowed the unacknowledged guilt of the perpetrators and the repressed trauma of the survivors to linger under the surface and to proliferate in the form of unconscious resentments and pathological neuroses. Consequently, in the Austrian-Jewish literature of the second generation of survivors, the past repeatedly appears as a ghost, a phantom, or a specter.[2] These ghosts haunt all the novels under discussion here. Just as the dead of the past turn up as *Wiedergänger,* as *revenants* in the truest sense, the words that evoke them seem themselves like shadows from the past that have already been spoken. They are only quotes of silence, and deliberately give up any claim to authenticity.

Schindel, Menasse, and Rabinovici, each in a tone of colloquial irreverence and light-footed artfulness, quote, plow through, and dissect previous expressions taken from Holocaust literature, such as Celan's poetry, where the past is endowed with the aura of a negative sublime and the poetic self is wholly defined in terms of this past. This denial of the present and of the literary forms that accompany it is questioned by the authors of the second generation. At the same time they call for a relentless commemoration of what happened and refuse calls for a "normalization" (Schindel 2004, 22).[3] They also call into question the hope of staying connected with the dead through poetic conjurations of the magic word that, in Celan's formulation in his "Meridian" speech, stands in the "light of utopia" (CGW, 3:199). The work of Schindel, Menasse, and Rabinovici purposefully undoes such utopian expectations. As Dorothee Kimmich puts it apropos Schindel's novel: "No one here waits for a new, unscathed language, no one awaits redemption, but they all toughly, ironically, bitterly, funnily, sometimes romantically, then again cynically, often failingly, but persistently seem to fumble for an everyday language that would at least be bearable [. . .] At no point does language become endowed with a redemptive function" (1996, 105). While Celan's poetic project participates in an art that, in the words of Jean François Lyotard, "doesn't say the unsayable, but rather says that it cannot say it" (in Kimmich 1996, 45), contemporary Austrian-Jewish authors convey the point that the unsayable is unsayable, but that it is possible, maybe even imperative, to keep on talking.

One of the strongest lines in Schindel's *Born-Where* makes this demystifying gesture explicit. Irreverently distorting the weighty oxymoron "zwei Mundvoll Schweigen" (two full mouths of silence) from Celan's poem "Sprachgitter" (CG, 99), Schindel has Danny Demant say: "Ich hätte noch gern ein Maul voll Schweigen, aber der Vorrat ist aufgebraucht" (SG, 183) ("I would like another snout full of silence, but the supply is used up" (SBW, 146; translation slightly modified). As a result, talking sets in, and with it, conversations about remembrance, identity, and the relationship between them.

In the place of an auratic silence meant to reach beyond words in order to overcome the inevitable failure of language to grasp the abysmal catastrophe, contemporary Austrian-Jewish literature is talkative to the extreme and merely wavers about the key in which this talking should occur. Authenticity is no longer the issue: "Nothing about me is genuine? I should hope so," says one of Schindel's narrators in *Born-Where;* "what's genuine, the cat can have it" (SBW, 11). In a dialogue between Danny Demant and his girlfriend Christiane in the same novel, it is the non-Jewish woman who says, "When we talk everything is lost, or more accurately: everything is named and becomes known." "I don't understand," replies her Jewish lover as he rejects this mystifying refusal of words: "Are you one of those who always claim that all feelings are talked to death? [. . .] But I like talking. I want things that are known and things that are named" (SBW, 35). Later, Christiane accuses him, or rather "them," the Jews, of "talking and talking," of "always talking about Auschwitz" (SBW, 159). It is unlikely that Schindel approves of his protagonist's excessive talking or his desire for things known and named.[4] The exaggerated drive to talk—and always talk about Auschwitz—is rather to be read as a violent and neurotic reaction to the various forms of silence predominant in the previous generation. In Schindel's novel very little is actually *said* about Auschwitz. Instead, the novel tells stories about those who incessantly talk about the past.

As in Schindel's *Born-Where,* the protagonists in Rabinovici's *Suche nach M.* (Search for M., 2000)[5] talk all the time about "back then." Mullemann, the central figure, is literally a phantom who haunts the city of Vienna. Wrapped in bandages that both protect and hide a mysterious skin disease symbolizing the wounds of the past, the phantom compulsively adopts and thereby exposes the guilt that is woven into the very fabric of his environment. This phantom turns out to be a mask worn by Dani Morgenthau, the son of survivors who kept silent about the past. Dani, a paradigmatic representative of the "second generation," is called "a

clump of pain made of numerous deaths and nothing more than a bundle of commemoration" (RS, 76), whose self risks disappearing under the stifling effect of
his parents' wounds, which have inscribed themselves into his skin. Rabinovici
insists that it is the task of the second generation to uncover the hidden past, yet he
simultaneously warns that an exclusive and obsessive concern with this past may
turn into a neurosis of guilt and revenge: "The search for the culprit turned into an
addiction" (RS, 31). However, Dani is quite successful. With satirical verve, Rabinovici caricatures Mullemann's fame: He becomes a hero, a "Zoro in white." He
receives fan mail, and his image inspires fashion designers and the entertainment
industry: "Mullemania everywhere" (RS, 251). While his own existence behind the
Mullemann disguise dissolves, his bandages increasingly take on a linguistic life of
their own. The texture of his masking, which initially still refers to the treatment of
a real skin ailment, becomes a textual material that weaves his entire environment
into a comprehensive semantic net. Mullemann relentlessly exposes the participation of the "Gesamtverband der Gesellschaft" (RS, 182) (all-encompassing bonding
of society) in repressing the past until he also perceives his own obsession as an
enmeshment. He arrives at an alternative form of experiencing the past: "Not to
be tied down by the shackles of time like a mummy, to reject all the techniques of
preservation, to shed the layers, undo the knots, to go after the knotting, to feel
for the lumps, to unlace and remove the straps: this is the work of memory" (RS,
180–81).

The passive form of "being tied down" is gradually replaced by actions. Commemoration, Rabinovici suggests, consists not in passively indulging in a com-
pulsive identification with the victims but in an active unraveling of the past that
involves the living self of the one who commemorates. This imperative can be
formulated in Walter Benjamin's words as an attempt to shake off the burden of
the past that has accumulated on the back of humanity in order to get it into one's
hands (2002c, 268).

Similarly, Robert Schindel verbalizes the precarious attempt to avoid both an
excessive identification with the victims as well as any falsely understood gesture
of reconciliation. In a section of *Gebürtig* a survivor named Hermann Gebirtig
is honored by Austrian officials for purely self-serving purposes. The Viennese
municipality decides to bestow the highest honors on Gebirtig, a writer and former Viennese emigrant who had to flee from Vienna to New York at the time of
Hitler's annexation of Austria. Actually, Gebirtig comes back to his native city only
because a young, politically committed woman convinces him to testify against
a former Nazi criminal. Gebirtig is decorated and celebrated by the Viennese officials, but in the meantime the Nazi torturer is acquitted. While this plot obviously satirizes the corrupt Austrian juridical system and its treatment of former
Nazi criminals, the last pages of the novel suggest the futility of thinking of the
past primarily in terms of revenge. In the final scene of the novel, the Jewish lector
Danny Demant figures as an extra in a concentration camp movie. Freezing on
the film set during the shooting, he dismisses the desire for retribution: "It hits me

that the anti-Semites should be the extras. Let them stand there not an hour and a half; but, say, sit and stand for three hours in the snow like that at minus twenty-two centigrade. On the other hand, if they freeze, our kind still won't warm up, not then, and today a tea will do."[6] In provocations, contradictions, and linguistic excesses, contemporary Austrian-Jewish authors evade both the undertow of an all-consuming past and leveling conciliatory stances. This refusal is not exercised by way of silences and gaps, but is instead extensively and explicitly carried out, back and forth across boundaries.

The dialogues between Jews and non-Jews in these novels are woven out of everyday expressions of attraction and animosity that are largely determined by the past, out of coarse misunderstandings and attempts at mutual exposure, out of experiments to get closer that fail more often than they succeed. However, in their relentless talking, these children of the perpetrators and the victims stand together in opposition to the negative consensus of a collective, homogenous silence. As soon as talking sets in, differences that are presumed to be forever seated in the depth of historically determined collective and individual identities come to the surface and become enmeshed and entangled in situations of the present.

A passage from a dialogue in *Born-Where* reveals how Schindel's use of language and dialogue undoes and reconfigures unified concepts of identity. After they spend the night together, and at the very moment when their different backgrounds prove to be an obstacle to their relationship, the Jewish lector Danny Demant playfully asks his girlfriend Christiane what she would like to be. Christiane answers that she would like to be a man, or a woman, "or I want to be somehow I" (SBW, 36) ("ein Mann, oder auch eine Frau [...] oder ich will sein irgendwie ich"). Danny enigmatically replies: "You are I when you are in the not-I"[7] ("Ich bist du, wenn du im Nicht-Ich bist"). Danny is quoting, or rather misquoting, a verse from Paul Celan's poem "Lob der Ferne" (Ode to Distance). However, Celan's words "I am you, when I am I" (CG, 37) ("Ich bin du, wenn ich ich bin") suggest that the boundaries of the self should not dissolve in an encounter with the other since the "I" can be addressed as a real "you" only as long as it does *not* lose itself in this other. Schindel transforms the quote into its opposite and has Danny suggest to Christiane that she is truly herself only when she *does* "lose" herself in him. Meanwhile, in a barely noticeable move, Schindel possibly undermines Christiane's wish to be "herself" in the very words she uses to express this desire. The odd structure of her sentence, "ich will sein irgendwie ich," in which the object is placed behind the verb—in German it would have to be "ich will irgendwie ich sein" (I want somehow to be I)—has a slight Yiddish ring. Unwillingly, Christiane is caught in the "Nicht-Ich" of her Jewish interlocutor.

What this passage performs at the individual level occurs in many of the novel's scenes where collective identities are discussed. In a dialogue between Danny Demant and Masha Singer, the young Jewish woman insists on the difference between the fragmented and torn identity of Jews and that of the non-Jewish Austrians whom she considers to be rooted, whole, and united: "They [the Austrians] remain locals. The victors. And me they cut off. And I exist in fragments. And what I am is foreign to me" (SBW, 8). Demant objects to this distinction and suggests that the Austrians too are fragmented and no longer exist as a unified whole. Almost hysterically, Masha replies, "But the Danube connects them" (SBW, 8). Some three hundred pages later, Gebirtig, who returns to Vienna for the first time since his enforced exile before the war, enters a tobacco shop and asks for a brand of cigarettes called "Donau" that he used to buy for his father as a child. The same shopkeeper who sold these cigarettes before the war replies, "Donau we don't have any more [. . .] Oh, they don't make them any more." Lost in thoughts, Gebirtig repeats, "So the Donau doesn't exist any more" (SBW, 245). In this exchange and its link with Masha's remark about the unifying powers of the Danube, Schindel implies that today, at least in Vienna, even the legendary river has lost its unifying force. Since the war, the Jewish and non-Jewish citizens of Vienna can no longer rely on this precarious geographic and symbolic bond to hold them together. Although Schindel continues to emphasize the difficulty of overcoming the "glass wall" between Viennese Jews and non-Jews, he puts his hopes for the future in the awareness that the war has revealed the illusory nature of all beliefs in homogeneous and self-enclosed social, ethnic, and national communities and groups.

In many accounts of a post-Holocaust poetics, auratic absence of language and irreconcilable gaps and differences are accompanied by the silence of messianic postponement, the mark of the unredeemed, of a wholeness lacking. As a last trace of transcendence, the dead of history are witnesses of a future under the sign of an awaited messiah. In countering this posture, contemporary Austrian-Jewish literature reveals itself to be radically worldly. Robert Menasse's *Expulsion from Hell* (2001)[8] shows Rabbi Manasseh's belief in a coming redemption to be as pitiful an illusion as Viktor's faith in the Hegelian notion of a gradual deployment of the "world spirit." The ancestors of the novel's main character, Viktor Abravanel, are described as "famous politicians, poets, scholars. And one asked in each generation: the messiah? No! Highly talented people, but no human God" (ME, 412). The novel has parallel plots where the lives of the historical Rabbi Manasseh and the contemporary historian Viktor Abravanel echo each other continuously, but at the end of the book the two life stories diverge on a crucial point. Before he dies, Rabbi Manasseh loses himself in phantasms about his role as Redeemer, or at least as a messenger of the messiah. In the book's last lines, his death is described as an apocalyptic explosion of the rising sun that suddenly breaks through his window: the explosion signifies a last revelation before his death. Like Rabbi Manasseh's life, Viktor's story also ends on an explosive light, but the difference in content and tone between the two experiences captures the spirit by which the novel dismisses eschatological expectations. Toward its end, Viktor sits in a bar with Hildegund: "Suddenly it became very bright, the light glared up with a blinding shine in the midst of cold flames, no, it was only a spot that had wandered through the bar, as an invitation to dance" (ME, 483). This bar, where the apocalyptic light of redemption turns out to be nothing more than an invitation to dance, is called Eden, which, as Viktor laconically remarks, both ridiculously and significantly rhymes with *reden* (ME, 480) (talking).

Similarly, in *Suche nach M.*, Rabinovici dismisses the idea of religious redemption along with an aesthetic sacralization of suffering. The art expert Sina Mohn, Mullemann's girlfriend, associates Mullemann's obsession with pain and wounds with a baroque tradition based on the Catholic idea of redemption through suffering. The iconography of "those bandaged-up forms wrapped in gauze and racked with pain" (RS, 136), which she recognizes in the works by Viennese avant-garde artists—a group that can be easily identified as the "Wiener Aktionisten" Hermann Nitsch and Arnulf Rainer—in turn makes her think of an earlier art form widely practiced in Austria. Sina Mohn associates the work of these artists who paint over portraits and depict pain, injuries, scars, and blood orgies with Catholic depictions of Christian saints "pierced with arrows, impaled on stakes, nailed to crosses, roasted in fires, and battered by stones," with "bodies in extreme pain that found their way to redemption through martyrdom" (RS, 136). Rabinovici suggests that an aesthetic wallowing in wounds would emulate this baroque tradition. The end of the novel shows that Mullemann, the Jewish son of survivors, indeed is not redeemed through suffering but is healed by a more active mode of remembering—and the loving care of his girlfriend Sina Mohn herself.

In the last section of *Born-Where* mentioned above, one of the most grotesque but also most memorable scenes in the entire corpus of contemporary Austrian-Jewish literature, Schindel's Danny Demant travels to Teresienstadt with a group of other Viennese Jews, who, because of their authentic Jewish noses, were selected as mute actors for a concentration camp film. There, in this staged past, today and yesterday fold into each other and the present, which was "pressed into the past's mask" (SG, 342), frees itself. It appears at intersections of reality and virtuality and manifests itself where empathic reenactments derail and where memories flash up in the midst of banal perceptions of the present day.

In the last lines of the novel, Danny Demant is standing in the freezing cold on the set during the shooting of the concentration camp film and senses that it is his bodily discomfort in the present that creates a link "von damals nach heute" (SG, 353), "from then until today" (SBW, 285). Shivering next to him, doctor Klang, a man in his seventies, recites in a barely audible voice an irreverent imitation of the most basic Jewish credo as articulated in the prayer "Shema Israel," transforming its original words, "Hear, O Israel, the Almighty is our God, the one and only," into "Sch'ma Jisruel, kalt is ma in die Fiss, Sch'ma, die Fiss so kalt, oj is ma kalt in die Fiss Israel. Sch'ma Jisruel, in die Fiss is ma soi koit in die Fiss adonai" (SG, 353) or "Sch'ma Jisruel, cold is me footsie; Sch'ma, footsies so cold, oy me ma footsies Israel. Sch'ma Jisruel, in the footsies is me so coldy, adonai" (SBW, 285). Overhearing this disrespectful complaint introduced into the holiest of Jewish prayers, Demant reflects: "There, I think to myself, when the feet finally warm up and the head stays wonderfully cool, it can happen that there comes not the Messiah, but a beautiful feeling" (SBW, 285). The evocation of Israel and the addressing of God are mixed with fragments from liturgy, everyday speech, and tavern jargon. The prayer resembles jabbering mumblings, and the messiah turns into a dispensable promise.

To be sure, Schindel, Rabinovici, Menasse, and their living figures continue to commemorate the horrors of the past, but they know that if the dead were actually to come back and speak out, or, less metaphorically, if an absolute language of witnessing were to be found, if a poetics of silence had the last word, this would mean the end of stories, and the end of remembering the past in the medium of literature. Traces of nostalgia for an absolute literary testimony remain, but in the work of these contemporary authors a hope grows within the language of the living that one might stand accountable for the dead and their lost lives not by approximating a pure and awesome silence in which the ranks of the commemorating community would be closed in perfect communication, but within the tarnished and limited speech of the living and in the midst of everyday concerns about a cool head, warm feet, and the heat of a passionate discussion.

Jewish Voices, Human Tone:
Robert Menasse's *The Expulsion from Hell*

Given the variety and pervasiveness of Jewish topics in Robert Menasse's novel *The Expulsion from Hell* (*Die Vertreibung aus der Hölle*), it is tempting to see in it the expression of a "Jewish voice" in contemporary German-language literature (Stumpp 2004; Reichmann 2001). In a short, untitled polemic Menasse resists such categorizations. To him the "philo-Semitic inquiry as to Jewish voices," which is always on the lookout "for peculiarities, for unmistakable characteristics" that are "clearly distinguished from [those of] other people" is analogous to being consigned to the ghetto, and he counters it with the demand that his particular voice be "heard as that of someone in whom the human condition finds its very own tone."[1] In the same text, however, this rejection of a determination of the specifically Jewish aspects in his writings is restricted to the *effect* of the question and does not refer to the question itself: "I don't really believe," Menasse writes, "that the question as to 'Jewish voices' [die Frage nach 'jüdischen Stimmen'] is only intended to ascertain who is to be assigned or consigned to a virtual ghetto—but that is the effect." Obviously, without going into further detail, Menasse does concede that there may well be a point to the inquiry into Jewish aspects of a text. The search for Jewish "peculiarities" and "unmistakable characteristics" is itself part of the Jewish thematic of *The Expulsion from Hell* and also constitutes the point at which this question becomes one of universal human interest. It addresses the general tension between an affirmation of collective identity, a community based on specific historical and cultural experiences, on the one hand, and a desire to free oneself from collective determinations altogether on the other. The warning expressed by Menasse against a consignment to a "virtual ghetto" in the determination of Jewish aspects in his writings leads straight to the heart of the novel's treatment of Jewish history and Jewish identity, as well as to the medium through which this tension manifests itself there—language, writing, literature itself.

"How do you know that he's a Jew?" In the middle of the novel, this is the question with which Esther, the sister of the protagonist Mané/Manuel Manasseh, challenges the latter's assertion that Miguel de Cervantes Saavedra, the author of Don Quixote, is a baptized Jew (ME, 246). In Mané's answer, "We know it, because we can read," the response to the question of whether an author is a Jew appears very much a matter of knowing an ascertainable fact, and moreover, the cognizant, perceiving subject appears as a "we" referring to a Jewish collectivity: "Because *we* can read." The speaker continues: "We had to learn to look behind the letters and behind people's masks" (ME, 246). The knowledge about what is Jewish can, he believes, be ascertained from texts, although only to the extent that one does not abide by the words on the page but is capable of reading what is hidden beneath the surface. The ability to look behind the letters, behind the masks as it were, is presented as a special Jewish characteristic. This "talent," however, is nothing natural, but something acquired through history, something that has emerged out of the experience of danger and threat. In this sense, Mané's reply to the question "How do you know that he's a Jew?" points to the crucial aspects of Jewishness in Menasse's novel: it involves a history of suffering, an exceptional position emerging from that historical experience and from a special relationship to texts.

The people with a history of suffering, the people with exceptional talents, the people of the book: making use of such traditional ideas of Jewishness, Menasse stages a skillful game, one that at once revives these popular conceptions and also questions their acceptance as a uniform and unchanging definition of a collective identity. In a variety of ways the novel intertwines two Jewish lives, that of the Portuguese Marrano, Manoel Dias Soeiro, born in 1604, and that of Viktor Abravanel, born in Vienna in 1955. Thus, it draws on a large range of what must be considered to be stereotypical Jewish motifs and figures, but deploys them in unexpected contexts, provocative demystifications, and subversive parodies.

Jewish history—historical events, conceptions of history, and forms of remembrance of the Jewish past—is revisited on several levels. The motifs of exceptionality, of the outsider, of otherness provide the impetus for the Jewish figures' search for identity. By tying into the themes of writing and reading, as well as scholarship and intellectual dispute, the poetological dimension of the novel reflects the role that the historical and individual search for traces of the past, and the transmission of tradition and of story-telling itself, play in the discussion of Jewishness in Menasse's work. In the alternating accounts of the intertwined biographies of Rabbi Manasseh in the seventeenth century and of Viktor Abravanel, a child of Holocaust survivors, the realms of history, identity, and writing are associated with traditional definitions of Jewishness. Simultaneously, they are altered by literary means to the point at which the stereotypes borne by the various concepts are unsettled and the effect of a "consignment to the ghetto" is undone.

Menasse's novel reflects a variety of approaches to history and suggests the literary implications of these approaches. The disclosure of a repressed past, the archival collection of historical facts, the transmission of experiences through the generations, as well as mimetic, often detailed accounts of life stories and, above all, a great diversity of forms of remembering—and indeed forgetting—traumatic events run through the novel. History is looked at from the perspective of the present and a space is opened up for projections of new stories, which inscribe themselves against the background of the old tales and in the gaps between them. "The study of history," Viktor declares at a reunion of his high school class and its teachers, "is nothing other than a preoccupation with the conditions of the course of one's own life" (ME, 20). The consideration of history from a perspective of the present is offered as an alternative to a positivist neutralization of history and to historicist determinations. The viewpoint of the present, together with its open possibilities, becomes urgent when those born after the historical catastrophe are trying to free themselves from the burden of a past, making it difficult for them to gain access to their own present and future.

In *The Expulsion from Hell,* Jewish history appears not only as the background to realistically narrated scenes from the seventeenth and twentieth centuries, which mix fact and fiction, but also as a recurring motif in reflexive insertions and conversations. The historical settings range from the pyres of the Inquisition to the crematoria of Auschwitz, from the "swine hunt" after the Marranos to the national socialist hounding of the "Judensau" ("Jewish swine"), from the lives of those who were able to escape the Spanish and Portuguese persecution of the Jews by fleeing to Amsterdam to those living in post–World War II Vienna. These events are accompanied by reflections on the significance of historiography and the meaning of history itself, as expressed by the protagonists. In the novel, narrated and reflected history refer to one another and are overlaid by a conception of history that is implicitly developed from the analogies and differences between the two historical periods and the narrative time of the novel itself. Menasse uses the motif of the archive to signal the distance from a positivist understanding of history. Hence, Mané is repeatedly associated with an archive of one kind or another: he is the scholar, the "man as archive of facts" (ME, 475). "But in the archive of his head," it is remarked of Mané, an unsuspecting child involved in the tracking down of "secret Jews," "everything was of equal value and unalterable" (ME, 74). The limitation of this positivist attitude to the past becomes even clearer when Mané loses out to Aboab, his rival for the position of Chief Rabbi in Amsterdam, because in his speech the latter does not resort to facts but emphasizes their relevance for the present. Aboab discusses how "biblical passages can be made topical" and considers "the relevance of Genesis, chapter 11, for the situation in the New Jerusalem," that is, in the Amsterdam of his time (ME, 405).

The point of view of the present in the novel is also contrasted with the repeatedly rejected or even mocked idea of a meaning in history. Admittedly, in the accounts of both historical periods, ideas of a historical teleology are mentioned, yet on every occasion they are revealed to be absurd by the ensuing course of events. *The Expulsion from Hell* uncovers Rabbi Manasseh's faith in the future as being just as pitiful an illusion as Viktor's trust in the Hegelian idea of a progressive unfolding of the "world spirit." The correspondences between the two lives appear to invite interpretations of history as eternal recurrence. However, precisely because of this comparability, the differences between the two historical periods prove to be greater than all possible analogies. Thus the interweaving of the two time frames incites a literary refutation of both the positivist approach and the beliefs inherent in a Hegelian philosophy of history. For Menasse, history is guided neither by a goal, an inner logic, nor by an organic dynamic. There is no historical linearity linking the Spanish Inquisition to the Holocaust, but rather, as Menasse states in his acceptance speech for the Hölderlin Prize, they are linked by the "modified long-term effect" of an ongoing sympathy for certain destructive "historical patterns" on the part of the actors of history, of the "political elites (with the assent of a majority, even if it is silent)" (2002, 57).

"History," as Menasse points out in the same speech, "when it really is history, is always something alien" (2002, 57). In view of the history of Jewish suffering addressed in his novel, the premise of a historical meaning—whether teleological or cyclical—is untenable. There is, as is also noted in the novel, no "historical logic"; the individual is no "tool of history" (ME, 479). The responsibility for history and its interpretation, which can never be conclusively fixed, rests with the individual. The examination of what has occurred in the past must be renewed in every present moment, becoming both an indispensable duty and the only possible means of being liberated from the burden of history in order to shape a different future.

The explicit and implicit reflections on the "course of history" correlate with individual remembering and forgetting. Here, too, the primacy of the present is posited as a counterweight to an obsessive fixation on the past. Like the novels of other Austrian-Jewish authors, *The Expulsion from Hell* structures the pervasive power of a repressed past as a double silence by the generation of perpetrators and of victims. The novel begins with a twenty-fifth reunion of a high school class attended by both former pupils and teachers, at which Viktor, the son of a Jewish survivor, suddenly begins to read out the Nazi Party membership numbers of his old teachers. The teachers react to this revelation with outrage and leave the dinner. Although the membership numbers Viktor reads out ultimately prove to be pure invention, he is not so far off the mark: two of the teachers were indeed Nazi collaborators. The scene implies that Viktor's fictitious accusations have hit upon an unacknowledged truth, yet at the same time Menasse maintains a self-ironic perspective regarding his generation's obsession with the national socialist past.

Menasse's self-irony should not, however, be seen as a conciliatory gesture: the gulf between the offspring of the Jewish survivors and of the Austrian perpetrators can perhaps never be closed, not even in the case of Viktor and the woman he loves. Their responses to the pasts of their respective parents, which remain unmentioned in both families, are just as different as those pasts themselves. As a child, Viktor was asked by one of his teachers: "Is the Nazi period talked about in your home? In your family they no doubt talk about what happened." He replied by lying and saying "Yes" (ME, 137). Later, when Viktor asks the woman whom he is courting, and whom he familiarly calls "Gundl," where her parents were during the war, she replies, "What did my parents do before? They lived. In their time. Now they're dead. And my name is Hildegund" (ME, 25). So nothing is entirely certain: Viktor, the son of survivors, insists on the power of the past, yet affectionately calls his girlfriend, whom Menasse characterizes as a "typical Austrian Nazi family child," by her pet name. She, on the other hand, buries history and her deceased, and responds to Viktor's demonstration of love with a proud insistence on her clearly Germanic name.

Despite his implicit claim that the next generation has to some extent the right to live in the present (ME, 345), Menasse mistrusts any gesture of pacification. As the historical alter ego of Viktor, he introduces the character Rabbi Manasseh, whose parents had survived the Spanish Inquisition and who subsequently makes a passionate commitment to the cause of reconciliation in his theological work *Il Conciliador,* thereby gaining the respect of his non-Jewish contemporaries. The historical Rabbi Manasseh had, it is reported, "taken a millstone from the neck of the Christian world" (ME, 418). Viktor, on the other hand, continues his "struggle" against the old Nazis. Menasse's work hardly follows the harmonizing approach of the Rabbi. Nevertheless, on an individual level, Viktor and Hildegund, the "Nazichild," will continue trying to become closer to one another.

The often unexpected irruption of the repressed memory of past events into the present is illustrated by sudden emotional clashes, misunderstandings, and hostilities between Jews of the second generation and their non-Jewish contemporaries. The present demands its rights in the form of tentative manifestations of love and understanding between individuals from both groups. These hesitant steps toward a new closeness on an individual level can be taken only outside of the public eye and in full awareness of the shadows of the past, in accordance with Gershom Scholem's prediction that "fruitful relations between Jews and Germans"—in this case Austrians—"must be prepared in secret" (1970, 46). Menasse's novel depicts this obligation as a complex undertaking that brings numerous existential and political traps in its wake. Its starting point is the recognition that the gulf between the present and the past cannot be bridged, but that it is just this impossibility that represents a new literary space in which the concerns of the present and the confrontation with the past can be reflected upon in new ways.

Menasse subverts notions of a fixed and essential Jewish identity in a variety of ways and repeatedly blurs its contours. Particularly provocative is the way he deals with the demarcation of Jewish and German identity and origin. He quotes at length from Walther Wilhelm Friedrich Maier's seventeenth-century book *Die*

Begründung teutschen Lebens durch den jüdischen Stamm Shem (The Foundation of German Life by the Jewish Tribe of Shem), according to which a descendant of Noah had settled beyond the northern frontier of the Roman Empire. It was from him that the Friesians and the Saxons were ostensibly descended, and Maier concludes with an apparent overstatement: "Germans are therefore Jews, the Dutch are Jews [. . .] By descent they are a rediscovered lost tribe of the Jews" (ME, 471). How serious this statement is intended to be is irrelevant; more important is the clear desire to unsettle demarcations and affiliations and to demonstrate the absurdity of the hostility between these groups.

It is true that situations, figures, and conversations that summon up Jewish characteristics or stereotypes are repeatedly described or mentioned in the novel, yet these are immediately retracted, contrapuntally refuted, or parodistically subverted. In a scene where Viktor's uncle Erich, a professional mime, is threatened by thugs who take him to be a Jew, he gestures "appeasingly" in self-defense; however, these very movements "only confirmed anti-Semitic prejudices: Jews talked with their hands" (ME, 274). Erich's farcical burial should be understood in the same way. His sister wants to give him a Jewish funeral, although he not only had been baptized but was himself a "fervent anti-Semite." So enthusiastically and convincingly had he imitated Jews to mock them that "yiddling" "had become second nature with him," and he himself had not registered that he was slowly "becoming what he so much despised: the yiddling idiot" (ME, 212). Authenticity itself becomes performance. Appropriately, the yiddling attributed to the Jewish businessman Grün only becomes "authentic" in Erich's imitative exaggeration: "See, that's exactly how a Jew was supposed to yiddle!" (ME, 210). Finally, as a result of the difficulty in distinguishing genuine from acted Jewishness, he himself falls victim to an anti-Semitic attack. In the face of so many transgressions on both sides of the demarcation between Jewishness and non-Jewishness, every conceptual ghetto wall turns porous.

Every peculiarity, every characteristic to which the adjective "Jewish" could be attached in this novel has been accorded an opposite trait that is also "Jewish." The Jews are presented as heroes and cowards, scholars and brothel owners, successful businessmen and failures, geniuses and epigones. True of them all is what is said of Viktor's ancestor Isaak Abravanel: he was "a man torn by inner conflict, divided against himself. He was of Jewish birth" (ME, 132). The "existential ambiguity" of the Marranos, who were forced to conceal their Jewishness, is a symptom of the never-ending experience of "having to run with and run away" (ME, 53) and affects almost all the Jewish characters in both periods. This symptom arises not only from the historical predicament of the concealment of the Jews' origin, but also from their compulsion to conform to their surroundings. These experiences are, for Menasse, a major aspect of Jewish history, but he is somewhat skeptical of subsequent generations who invoke them as an unchanging basis of Jewish identity. He vividly describes the panic felt by the young Mané, whose existence during the Inquisition is repeatedly threatened by the fearful experience of "running with and running away." This fear gives him nightmares of having to run but being unable to run. A few pages later Viktor, whose father suffered under the Nazis, tells Hildegund of similar nightmares: "Hildegund! When you were a child did you have recurring dreams, nightmares, which kept. . . ." Interrupting him in mid-sentence, Hildegund rejoins, "Do you mean, where you want to run and you can't . . . things like that? Sure. Everyone has had dreams like that at some time." Indignantly Viktor asks, "What does everyone mean? [. . .] How do you know, that everyone has nightmares like that." Hildegund's response: "It's first-term child psychology. I studied psychology, you know that!" The dialogue ends with Viktor's laconic but significant reaction: "Oh yes. I forgot that" (ME, 56). With subtle irony Menasse rejects the presumption of the "second generation" of survivors to ascribe to themselves unconscious, traumatic symptoms stemming from the real experiences of their parents.

The question of Jewish identity is thrown up most forcefully in a lengthy scene in which, on a school trip to Rome, Viktor is enlightened about his Jewish birth by his Catholic teacher Hochbichler. When Hochbichler calls Viktor over to his seat on the bus and the latter asks himself why he could not sit with the others, the motif of exceptionality—of the Jew as the chosen one and an outsider—is evoked. Referring to examples of Viktor's extraordinary ancestors, who held on to their Jewishness, the teacher addresses the question as to what it actually is that Jews have in common and how Jewry was able to maintain itself over the generations. He mentions "love, respect, and blood." "Blood? Why blood?" Viktor asks himself. Hochbichler tells Viktor about three ancestors, all of them Abravanels, respected scholars, treasurers, and statesmen, who appeared to conform and assimilate, had themselves baptized, and were "worldly, urbane" men. Was it, asks Hochbichler, a "question of blood," was it "blood loyalty?" (ME, 137). His final example recounts the biography of Isaak Abravanel, who with his exceptional talents and Christian upbringing was chosen by the Archbishop of Coimbra to receive a special stipend, but stole away to Venice instead, had himself circumcised, and became a famous Jewish doctor. Hochbichler concludes his account by asking: "How do you explain it? Blood? No, please don't say yes! *Blood doesn't have a voice.* Because, if that were so, then the Inquisition would have been right, then the Nazis would have been right, and it would have been the victims themselves who would have proved it first" (ME, 140; emphasis added). The antithesis to the bonds of blood is evidently the "voice" here. This distinction is, however, far from obvious: like "blood," the "voice"—as in "the voice of the people"—is frequently used to designate a natural, homogenizing bond. It is precisely because a voice is always radically singular and specific to an individual that it has a unifying effect and denies the existing differences when it is said to emanate from a community. However, as in the short text mentioned at the beginning of this essay, Menasse either uses plural voices or speaks of "a voice" and never mentions "*the* voice," as for example Nelly Sachs does when she entitles her poem "The Voice of Israel." In Hochbichler's account, "a voice," unlike "blood," involves the individuality of a speaker, in this case that of Isaak Abravanel, who *decides* to return to Judaism.

When Viktor tells Hildegund how Hochbichler informed and enlightened him about his Jewish genealogy, he initially refuses to accept that the incident revealed his Jewish identity to him or had any effect on him at all. Nevertheless, he ends his story with a reflection that sums up his relation to Jewishness: "Somehow [Hochbichler] won the battle after all. Because he gave my story a direction [. . .] after that I learned Spanish, I studied history, and simply the question of whether I had been told at home about the Nazi period led me to asking questions, again and again" (ME, 145). Not blood, but rather an active engagement with the history of his origins, bestows upon Viktor a "Jewish voice": it no longer engenders a ghetto "effect," but lends him meaning and direction in the present.

The question of the "Jewish voice" of the novel also proves to be an issue of intonation and narrative form. *The Expulsion from Hell* is for the most part presented in a realist mode. This realism, however, is interspersed with narrative breaks and repetitions, with jokes, word games, self-reflexive loops, and intertextual references that rupture the surface of the novel and cause fissures in its double-tracked plot. The uneven tone of the work multiplies positions that have become bogged down, primarily in relation to Jewish concerns, to such a degree that they absolutely discredit one another. The humorous tone, the element of caricature, and the seeming lightness of the language ridicule any form of self-righteousness and hypocritical rhetoric that relies on authorities or certainties. This effect correlates with the tension between a secular modernity and echoes of traditional doctrines, such as the ban on images or the anticipation of the messiah. The relaxed colloquial language of the contemporary perspective, therefore, also takes on ethical and political dimensions.

At the literary level Menasse's novel draws its strength from the stylistic breaks between the dignified, often dramatic account of events in the seventeenth century associated with Rabbi Manasseh, and the colloquial, mocking tone of Viktor's memories of his participation in the student unrest of the 1970s.[2] The function of these divergent linguistic registers is reflected on in the novel itself. The elevated tone is deemed to be a disguise for hard-heartedness and inhuman behavior. In particular, pathos and the aura of the sublime are subverted wherever they are linked to terms such as "origin," "identity," or "authenticity." Against the claim that these and other "big words" connote truth, Menasse places an emphasis on the fluidity of meanings.

Profaning and provocative word games run through the novel, from the pious Jesuits of the Inquisition to the Jesuit Meadow (*Jesuitenwiese*) on which young boys play football, from the "sufferer on the cross" to Viktor's "having his arm pulled" (in German *aufs Kreuz legen* denotes being put on the cross but connotes being the victim of a practical joke), from the golden teeth wrested from the mouths of the murdered to the "treasure" (in German *Goldstück* means piece of gold), a term of endearment used by the grandmother for her grandson. These word games arise from the possible shifts and ambiguities inherent in language. Menasse explicitly derives this flexibility from an acute awareness of the Jewish tradition of the manifold interpretations of the Bible, in which signs do not correspond to a single and unambiguous reality. In both historical periods the protagonists reflect on the materiality of signs and the relation of word and reality. For weeks "the question why the world didn't function literally went through [Viktor's] head" (ME, 222). At one point, Viktor experiences a linguistic crisis stemming from the "gulf between the literal and the real," because "there were codes he didn't understand, meanings which didn't correspond to the meanings of words" (ME, 222). He experiences this difference when he slips a ring onto his girlfriend's finger that he does not know is a tab from a drinking can. What he regards as a token of love is contemptuously rejected by her: "He had thought: a ring! This means something. And she had thought: Trash! That means something" (ME, 228). Doubling the distance between "high" and "low" linguistic registers in the work, Viktor calls this incident his "ring parable." Similarly, Mané undergoes a crisis when he gets his instruction in matters of text and style from his sister Esther. After leaving the Jesuit boarding school, Mané is encouraged by his sister to return to his Jewish origins. "His sister," says a key passage, "had given him a lesson that wiped out the three years of seminary" (ME, 243). Indeed, Esther dismisses the "big words" which Mané brings with him from the seminary as empty rhetoric:

> Why are you talking so pompously [. . .] We are not Christians. The Christians interpret everything by the letter, that's the problem with them. When they read that men who don't believe in Christ are like dead branches, which should be burned, then they burn men like dry branches. If one takes everything literally, even if it has such consequences, then one must be quite without feeling. So they need other feelings. A substitute. That's the pathos. That is Christian feeling. The beautiful feeling above the world of feeling of the letter. (ME, 244)

This lesson reverses the Christian definition of Jewish loyalty to the law as adherence to the "letter" which "killeth," in contrast to the "spirit" which "giveth life" (2 Corinthians 3:6). Alluding to Cervantes's Don Quixote, Esther sums up her lesson with the judgment "Big words—absurd deeds! Very big words—murderous deeds!" (ME, 245) and concludes with the exhortation "So only use big words when you mean something else by them" (ME, 246). These words characterize Menasse's own literary program and his language, permeated as it is by ironic turns of phrase. His relinquishing of the big words is tantamount to an affirmation of the primacy of the present, not only over and against the auratic enthronement of the catastrophic past, but also over the expectation of a messianic future.

While the past nevertheless permeates the present and has to be faced relentlessly to prevent forgetting and repetition, utopian dreams are banned, or rather, they are relegated to worldly visions. A messianic redemption is indeed not in sight. Mané's dream of paradise is a new world modeled on a port where "strangers don't attract attention and don't raise suspicion, because there are so many strangers there from all countries on earth. Nothing was so familiar to the inhabitants of the big ports than this: the strangers. Manoel could not imagine paradise in any other form but this one: a port in another world. Strangers that don't attract attention, people without fear. And letters with all possible meanings with one exception: the literal" (ME, 247). A diversity of meanings without origin and authenticity is here linked to the end of the exclusion of the stranger. Quite inconspicuously, this idea of salvation flows into the title of the novel. The song of young people in a distant harbor town, "No one will ever see us / as we roast in hell," is commented on by the narrator with the words "There is no hell. That's why one will never be able to see them there . . . So many meanings. So little reality" (ME, 247). The "expulsion from hell" reveals itself to be a liberating departure from a defining, circumscribing, and excluding language into another one which, like literature itself, subscribes not to clarity and clearly circumscribed definition, but to an imaginative power moving in and between the words themselves, the playful deployment of which explodes the barriers of unyielding concepts—and with them the ghetto walls. The last sentence of the novel is "In the dark everything is conceivable" (ME, 493). Conceivable is a manner of dealing with Jewish history and Jewish identity that accepts contradiction and blurred contours, that simultaneously draws on and dissolves traditional ascriptions, and that bestows a Jewish voice upon language and literature which is capable of replacing the walls of the community's ghetto with the brackets of quotation marks and which, in its shifting inflections, encounters its own human tone.

PART FIVE

KAFKA'S COMPANIONS

Of Language and Destiny:
Paul Celan and Kafka

When the Romanian poet Alfred Margul-Sperber, an early mentor of Paul Celan, called the latter's first published volume of poetry *Der Sand aus den Urnen* (The Sand from the Urns) "the sole lyrical counterpart to the work of Kafka" (in Dor 1973, 282), he could not foresee just how influential Kafka would turn out to be in the poet's work. It is clear now that Kafka was a powerful presence for Celan throughout his life, from his early translations of several Kafka texts into Romanian (Chalfen 1983, 175) to comments about reading Kafka in letters written shortly before Celan's death.[1] In the 1950s Celan briefly considered writing a dissertation on Kafka (2001a, 576), and in his later correspondence he reports on preparing to teach a Kafka seminar at the École Normale Supérieure in Paris, where he taught (Felstiner 1995, 283). And while scholars noticed a number of references to Kafka in Celan's work early on, it was only after the poet's library became available to researchers in the Marbach Archive for German Literature that preliminary attempts could be made to register and explore the traces of Celan's reading suggested by the marks made in his Kafka books.[2] These efforts are still largely limited to uncovering and collecting references demonstrating the general importance of Kafka to Celan, and to reflections on ill-defined parallels in the two authors' works. As recently as 1988 it was still possible to write that "exogenous traces of Celan's reception of Kafka" are limited "to one poem and to individual motifs" (Sparr 1988, 140). Celan's literary estate, at least partially accessible at present, and the publication of previously unknown poems now disclose a far more extensive network of references, revealing the outlines of the figure of Kafka in Celan's work.

Paul Celan has entered modern literary history as the poet who found words for the inability "to say the unsayable" (Lyotard) and who gave the most masterful expression to the correlation between dark language and somber fate. In Kafka, he found a source of inspiration and an imaginary companion in difficult times. The draft of a letter by Celan to Klaus Wagenbach states his sense of fellow feeling for the older author: "In Franz Kafka's diary—on which side? The north side presumably—one can read, that K[afka]'s Jewish first name was Amschel. Amschel—and here we are soon back in the south again—is the original form of my surname Antschel and basically the Middle High German form of Amsel [blackbird]. (You see, this bird, too, is black, but not a raven!)" (CG, 746). By way of a shared Jewish name of German origin Celan traces here a "meridian" between himself and Kafka. For Celan, this imaginary connecting line, made famous by his Büchner Prize speech, the "Meridian" speech, designates a bond that is at once topographical and utopian and summons up an encounter between separate yet kindred spirits based on affinities of language and destiny (CGW, 3:187–202). In his letter to Wagenbach, Celan charges the analogy of their names with fateful significance. The fact that he imagines Kafka's Jewish first name to be found on the north, that is, the shadow side, while assigning Antschel, his own surname (which in the Romanian spelling provided the anagram Celan) to the south side, could derive from the geographical position of Celan's birthplace of Czernowitz in relation to Kafka's more northerly hometown of Prague. In a metaphoric reading of this constellation, Celan describes how the atmosphere becomes brighter and warmer at the very point where Kafka's and his own name meet. In the light emanating from this onomastic encounter, Celan distinguishes between the raven, a northern bird and omen of death, and the bird referred to in their common name, *Amsel,* the singing blackbird that signifies hope and life. Time and again, Celan will turn this imaginary meeting with Kafka into a topos of his poems. Out of the obscurity of a poetry that situates itself at the "edge of silence," Celan seeks out Kafka and conjures him up as a companion in his search for illuminating words for this darkness.

Vom Anblick der Amseln, abends,	From the sight of blackbirds, in the evening,
durchs Unvergitterte, das mich umringt, versprach ich mir Waffen.	through the unbarred that surrounds me, I hoped to gain weapons.
(CG, 209)	

These opening lines of a poem written in 1965, at the end of his stay in a sanatorium in Le Vésinet where he was treated for depression, correspond to a passage in a letter of that same day in which Celan tells his wife of an idyllic moment with sunshine, peace, and a blackbird hopping across the lawn (CG, 746). But the poem, invoking weapons, follows less peaceful paths. The I of the poem sees the blackbirds (*Amseln*), so significant for Celan's relationship to Kafka, through an unobstructed opening, presumably a window that, unlike the windows in the sanatorium, has no bars. As at the end of Kafka's "An Imperial Message," in which the "you" of the story sits at the window "when evening falls," expecting and finally dreaming up the redemptive message of the Emperor,[3] so Celan's lyric subject is on the lookout for a sign of possible rescue. The absence of a grating (*Gitter*), which here as elsewhere in Celan's work also signifies a grid of language (*Sprachgitter*), defines this hope for salvation: without the grid of pre-existing, petrified meanings, a more promising vision becomes possible. The gaze of the I falls on blackbirds, which evoke the common ground with Kafka. This sight is not obstructed but surrounded, encircled (*um-ringt*) "by the unbarred," evoking the sign of a liberating alliance (*Ring*). This bond offers the promise of "weapons," of strength, support, and protection: it echoes the hope Kafka invokes in the last sentence of his diary, a passage Celan had vigorously marked in his own copy: "More than comfort is: You too have weapons."[4] As for Kafka so for Celan these weapons are words, writing itself. In his poem, Celan makes of Kafka his brother in arms in the struggle for language.

The fate of language is at the heart of Celan's relationship to Kafka. "Key to Kafka himself?"[5] Written in faded grey pencil, yet clearly legible, these words are inscribed in the margin of a page in one of the seventeen books by Kafka found in Celan's library. Most of these books contain numerous markings and occasional notes that Celan scribbled in the margins. Celan's comment "Key to Kafka himself?" refers to a passage in Kafka's "Researches of a Dog" in which the speaker reflects on his relation to his forebears.

> I see only decline, although I do not mean that previous generations were essentially better, they were just younger; that was their great advantage, their memory was not yet as overburdened as ours is today, it was easier to get them to speak out, and even if no one ever succeeded, the possibility of it was greater; this greater possibility is indeed what so affects us when we listen to these old, really simple stories. Here and there we hear a suggestive word and we would jump to our feet, if we did not feel the weight of the centuries upon us. (KSS, 148)

The idea that an excess of history overburdens memory and has made authentic speaking impossible has, since Nietzsche at the very latest, become a commonplace of modernity. Likewise, the view that earlier generations did not speak "truly" either, but that the possibilities of language have dwindled through the ages, belongs to modern thought from the early romantics to Heidegger and beyond. As the following lines in Kafka's text indicate, the deterioration of language deplored by Kafka's speaking dog does not essentially concern its communicative function but its transformative power. Once, the speaker continues, dogs were

> not so currish as today; the structure of dogdom still had some play in it; at that time the true word could still have intervened, determined the construction, changing its tune, changed it at will, turned it into its opposite, and that word was there, or at least was very near, hanging on the tip of everyone's tongue, everyone could receive it; where has it gone today? Today you could dig into your bowels, and still not find it. (KSS, 148)

The "true word" has gone astray, and with it the possibilities of language to act upon reality. The burden of the centuries has had the effect of petrifying the present dismal condition. The open spaces in the "edifice of dogdom," which used to allow for change, are now closed. The power of language to exert an unmediated impact on the world—a power associated with ancient beliefs in the magic effect of words—has vanished. For Celan, the complaint of Kafka's dog must inevitably have summoned up the experience of a much more specific historical decline of language. In his "Meridian" speech Celan evokes the circumstances in which language only "recently" went through "thousand darknesses of death-bringing speech" and, after this catastrophe, could only "come to light again, 'augmented'"— that is, corrupted, weighed down, and burdened—"by all this" (CGW, 3:186). In the "key" passage he marked in Kafka's text, Celan must have recognized the core of his own poetics, the loss of the possibility of "truly" speaking as a result of a historical burden. However, for him, that burden was inflicted on language during the time that lies between him and his predecessor Kafka. For Celan, Kafka's words foreshadow this fate of language and consequently the starting point of his own poetry.

Between Franz Kafka and Paul Celan lies the weight of the first half of the twentieth century and, certainly from Celan's point of view, that rupture in its middle that put into question the possibilities of poetic speaking. If Celan is the paradigmatic witness to this occurrence, then Kafka has repeatedly been described as its prophet. Celan's designation of the "key to Kafka" goes beyond this philosophically and philologically contested reading of Kafka's work (on this controversy, see Rosenbaum 1998, 239–51, and Langer 1986, 113–45) and ends in an almost uncanny aporia. To Celan the words of Kafka's dog evidently not only represent a central point of Kafka's thinking, but, in providing him the "key to Kafka himself," they also offer him a description of his own relationship with his predecessor. In this relationship, Kafka becomes, from the perspective of Celan's identification with the words of the investigative dog, the representative of an earlier generation that was already aware of the decay of language but nevertheless still possessed a "greater possibility" of speaking now lost to Celan. The significance of this passage for Celan is rooted in the paradox that Kafka does recognize the historically determined loss of language, but that it is nevertheless still possible for him to address it in the flow of a narrative representation. While Kafka, in a (not exactly "childishly simple") story told by a dog soliloquizing for pages at a time, could still tell of the difficulty, indeed, the increasing impossibility of speaking, Celan is left with the search for a language that can only broach its own impossibility in halting, stuttering, cryptic, and elliptical half-words. It is in just such a language that Celan's poetry continually appeals to Kafka as an ally in the struggle against his own speechlessness and against a world that fails to recognize and admit both the present impossibility of speaking "poetically" and the historical tragedy that caused it.

Celan recognizes in Kafka's writing a premonition not only of his own experience with language but also of his own fate. The traces of Celan's reading in his Kafka books lead to another central point of engagement with Kafka: the motif of "Hunter Gracchus" (Günzel 1995, 119). Celan marked numerous passages of this story, which he read in his editions of *Beim Bau der chinesischen Mauer* (Building the Great Wall of China) and *Beschreibung eines Kampfes* (Description of a Struggle), as well as sentences from the "Hunter Gracchus Fragment" in the appendix to the latter edition and numerous passages in Kafka's diaries, letters, and other texts in which Celan recognized a reference to this motif. It is the story of a hunter from the Black Forest who for centuries has been wandering the earth in an old boat after he fell from a rock and died while hunting a chamois. He continues restlessly roaming the earth without any prospect of reaching the shores of the nether world. What evidently affected Celan was the idea of a living death, a state of "death in life" in the wake of a catastrophe, an agonizing, incurable half-death, or rather, half-life. In Kafka's "Hunter Gracchus" texts Celan primarily marked those passages that describe the similarity to death of life in this condition. Underlined for example is the Hunter's reply when, having claimed he is dead, he is questioned by the mayor of Riva: "'But you are alive too,' said the Burgomaster. 'In a certain sense,' said the Hunter, 'in a certain sense I am alive too.'"[6] In Kafka's letter to Felix Welsch of September 1913 from the sanatorium in Riva, Celan notes "Hunter Gracchus" in the margin beside the sentence "Sometimes I believe I am no longer in this world."[7] In Kafka's fragment "Vom Scheintod" (Whoever was once seemingly dead)[8] Celan underlines passages concerning the distinction between a death-like experience after which one returns to life and that incomparably more dreadful intermediate state, in which life itself is like death. In these lines Kafka is less interested in someone seemingly dead than in someone "seemingly alive," someone truly outliving his own death, who lingers on earth like a living shadow. Also striking is Celan's accentuation of the first lines of "Hunter Gracchus," in which everyday scenes at the harbor of Riva indicate the indifference of the world in the face of the arrival of the uncanny living-dead Hunter Gracchus. Celan, who repeatedly incorporated elements of this story in his own work, undoubtedly recognized here a description of his own condition. Referring to the "Hunter Gracchus" motif, Celan's poetry addresses a fellow-sufferer who, like himself, is driven out of the world, and, neither alive nor dead, writes against a world that is indifferent to the despair that gives rise to his poetry.

At two points a clear link can be made between the "Hunter Gracchus" motif and the key passage marked by Celan in "Researches of a Dog." In the "Hunter Gracchus Fragment" the hunter first says that he has, "over the centuries" of his wandering, "learned languages enough to act as an interpreter between this generation and their ancestors" (KCS, 231). Like the talking dog in the "key passage" marked by Celan, who surveys the degeneration of language, Gracchus is also described as a mediator between earlier generations and the present. However, when he is called on by the mayor to tell his story "coherently," Gracchus responds in a passage energetically marked by Celan: "Ask the historians! Go to them, and then come back. It's so long ago. How can I be expected to keep it in this overcrowded brain" (KCS, 234). Like the overburdened memory in "Researches of a Dog," so in the "Hunter Gracchus Fragment" does an overburdened brain prevent the past from being truly "spoken." Only the historians, who merely communicate information about what has occurred but do not attempt to render the past as an event that can be "experienced" in the very medium of their narrative, have "open mouths"; only they are able to speak "coherently." Hunter Gracchus, on the other hand, who after all should be an "interpreter," a spontaneous "translator," replies to the request that he tell his story "coherently": "Ah, coherent. That old, old story" (KCS, 233). He can convey his origin and the cause of his death—his fall in the Black Forest—in fragments only. The connections are broken; a smooth, harmonious form of storytelling is no longer possible for him. "Don't ask any more," says Gracchus; "Here I am, dead, dead, dead . . ." (KCS, 234). Adjacent to this line Celan notes, "So dead *in what way*?" Kafka's description of this death-like life, the fate of someone who outlives his own dying, and the impossibility of speaking coherently in the manner of "the old stories," of traditional historical narration, come together to form the central emphasis of Celan's reading of Kafka. Wherever in Kafka the fate of one who has outlived his death intersects with a language outlasting its own loss, Kafka becomes both Celan's alter ego and, paradoxically, his still-articulate predecessor. In numerous poems, in a language that takes into account his own "greater impossibility" of speaking, Celan summons up this "key to Kafka" and incorporates it in his own struggle for the "true word" that has been lost. At the same time he takes Kafka's "tropes and metaphors," evoking this condition *ad absurdum* (CGW, 3:199) by both enacting its sense of the impossibility of speaking and thinking it through to the end. For Celan the "true word" that is forever slipping out of reach now aims at the constantly thwarted message of the impossibility of speaking itself. The "meridian" drawn by Celan follows the path back to Kafka and to a language in which its impossibilities can still be uttered. This route goes against the flow of time, including the time leading back to Kafka, and remains a poetic utopia constituting the core of Celan's invocation of his encounter with Kafka.

Exactly when Celan found the "key to Kafka himself" or read "Hunter Gracchus" cannot be determined. On the inside cover of his copy of *Building the Great Wall of China*, which contains "Researches of a Dog" and a version of "Hunter

Gracchus," Celan wrote: "À Paris sur les quais le 23 Novembre 1951." However, the largest number of poems with clearly recognizable allusions to Kafka were written in the 1960s, at a time when Celan was increasingly suffering from the belief that the world was hostile to him and saw anti-Semitic attitudes at work everywhere. Apart from the trauma of the war years that defines Celan's whole existence as well as his poetry, the "Goll affair," in which he was accused of plagiarism, undoubtedly played a crucial part in his dejected state during those years. He felt let down even by his closest friends, from whom he expected unconditional defense and support, considered himself betrayed, and subsequently lapsed into persecution mania and an obsession with conspiracies that appeared pathological at times. He sensed that both he and his poetry were not understood by his readers and, through allusions and quotes in his poems, searched for real and imaginary companions in misfortune. In these difficult years, Celan entered into a poetic dialogue with fellow poets which is based on a shared experience of madness, pain, and loss. Kafka, like Hölderlin, Ossip Mandelstam, and Nelly Sachs, became such a companion.

In much of his work during this period, Celan sets out with Kafka to do battle with time in a threefold sense: against the impossibility of speaking because of the events he had witnessed during the war, against a forgetting of those who died in the course of these events, and against the indifference and hypocrisy of his contemporaries, who pretended to be unaware of what had happened. Accordingly, with Kafka at his side, Celan fights both against the debilitating effects of his trauma and against the danger of forgetting its origin. The enemies he battles most fiercely come from the ranks of his fellow-poets, who feign unawareness of the cause of his suffering: to him they are a horde of betrayers, whom he calls the "fehme-poets" (CG, 156–57),[9] the rhapsodists and "harmonizers" who continue to speak, sing, and write as if nothing has happened. In "Ars Poetica 62," a poem written at the end of 1962 that remained unpublished during Celan's lifetime, Kafka becomes both the counterweight to these traitors and, explicitly, Celan's alter ego.

As indicated in its title—a reference to Horace's *Ars Poetica* and the year the poem was written—the poem deals with the condition of poetry in the early sixties. It simultaneously situates Celan's own poetry in opposition to this mode and to the lyric tradition it transports, as well as to his own earlier poems, in which, as he repeatedly admitted himself, he still wrote "musical" poetry.[10] "Ars Poetica 62" is concerned with the relationship between historical date and lyrical euphony as intimated in rhythm, rhyme, and meter. The I at the beginning of the poem is presumably not limited to Celan himself: the popular elision *stands* (instead of *stand es* for "it stood") and the dialectical form *Wiesen* (instead of *Wiese* for "meadow") in the first two lines suggest a speaker who has taught poetry in the hymnic and rhyming style of Pindar, and also gives voice to the Swabian poet Hölderlin, author of the lyrical novel *Hyperion*.[11] Under national socialism Hölderlin received the "brown laurel" and was celebrated as the embodiment of the German poet. Allusions to Heidegger, who wore a moustache and was a well-recognized interpreter

Ars Poetica 62

Das grosse Geheimnis—beim Bärlapp,
  da stands,
auf der Wiesen.
Ich hätte es pflücken können, leicht,
  mit zwei Zehen.

Aber ich hatte zu tun, ich brachte

Hyperion die Sprache bei,

auf die es uns Hymniker ankam.
Er lernte gerne und brav.
  Beim Wort Hure
Wuchs ihm der brauen
Lorbeer schnell um Taktstock und
  Klaue: er hatte
Was man zum Reimen braucht, nach
  Pindar und einigen
Ungarn, Finnen und Pruzzen.

In seinem Vers
Stand die Zeit, im Licht ihrer
  schwäbischen Stunden,
schnurrbärtig, jung und gesamtstumm.

Sinnig,
hört ich mich sagen,
sinnig—: meinem andern, gestern

im Schwarzwald halbierten Nachbarn,
  dem Mann
mit der Dohle (und der vernähten
  Zäsur!) fehlte noch dieses Schatzwort.

(Sonst wär auch die zweite Hälfte
  gestorben
und aus
    leg
      bar.)

(CG, 473–74)

Ars Poetica 62

The great secret, by the stag moss
  it stood,
on the mead.
I could have picked it, easily, with
  two toes.

But I had things to do, I was
  teaching
Hyperion the language that
  mattered
to us, the rhapsodists.
He studied eagerly and well.
  Upon the
word whore the brown laurel grew
swiftly around his baton and
  claw: He had
what it takes to rhyme, according
  to Pindar and a few
Hungarians, Finns and Prussians.

In his verse
stood the times, in the light
  of their Swabian
hours, mustached, young and
  all-mute.

Makes sense,
I heard myself say,
makes sense—: my other neighbor,
  cut
in half yesterday in the black
  forest, the man
with the jackdaw (and the sewn up
  caesura!) had been lacking this
  treasure word.
(Or else the other half would have
  died too
and been inter-
    pret-
      able.)

of Hölderlin, as well as to the Hungarian Peter Szondi and to the author of the "Pruzzian Elegy," Johannes Bobrowski, may also be identified. The latter two disappointed Celan during the Goll affair (see CG, 934). Celan uses the word "whore" for these admirers of the poetic form of the panegyric and of elevating odes to the harmony of the world celebrated in rhyme and meter, and portrays them as venal betrayers. In Celan's wounded eyes they are the belated adherents of a hymnic tradition that was given the lie by history. In essence, they are the representatives of a euphemistic *Ars Poetica,* which in 1962 still cultivates a melodious poetry that is blind to the past and attempts the restoration of an anachronistic tradition of lyrical poetry that Celan himself still emulated in his own earlier "musical" poems. Against the hollow wholeness of this "whorish" conception of poetry still cultivated by the betrayers, whose lack of historical awareness and claim to everlasting poetic value literally cause time to "stand" still, the final verse of the poem turns to Kafka in mysteriously encoded language.

As the first verse tells us, its meaning can be disclosed only through a secret hidden "by the stag moss" (*Bärlapp*). According to an eastern European legend, the stag moss is "the last tree" that survived a massive destruction. The legend tells of a great storm that devastated the most magnificent of all forests, situated in the region near the Moravian-Austrian border. After this catastrophe "on the territory of present-day Central Europe," so the legend ends, only the "stag moss stood upright and lonely in the stone desert that had been created" until it too fell over and turned to stone. Even today, it is said, "the observant viewer can study the remains of this tree."[12] Evidently, the stag moss, in the vicinity of which the "great secret" can be found, is the lonely, surviving witness of yet another central European catastrophe. In the opening lines of a poem accusing those who continue to pay homage to German rhapsodies and their "brown" fame, Celan alludes to this historical destruction.

The last stanza counters this collective poetic betrayal with another community and another poetics. In contrast to the "all-silent" rhapsodists of harmony and wholeness, the I of these lines is itself split. The I speaks the word "sinnig" (makes sense) to his "other," literally his alter ego who, after the Hölderlin of the first verses, is his *other* neighbor." He speaks this word as commentary on and in opposition to the current state of poetry, which he has previously dismissed as "senseless." The "other" addressed here is unmistakably Kafka, Celan's geographical neighbor, whose name means "jackdaw" in Czech and whose "Hunter Gracchus" figure continues to live in a state of half-death after his accident in the Black Forest. Heidegger's Black Forest is here countered by the Black Forest of Kafka's Hunter Gracchus as the place of a violently acquired injury. Similarly, Hölderlin's metrical "caesura" is contrasted with the historical rupture alluded to in the wound of the half-dead Gracchus. In contrast to the presumed wholeness of the panegyrist Hölderlin and the poetics of his admirers, Celan points to a time and a history of pain and destruction after which life turned into half-death. In accordance with this fate, the I also speaks in half-words. Enigmatically, this I offers the precious words "makes sense" (*sinnig*) to the "man with the jackdaw" in order to preserve some remnant of meaning that is still alive. The "dead" part—the other half—is to be found in the omitted part of the word *sinnig*—"makes sense," in the word *Wahn* (delusion; *Wahnsinn*—madness; *wahn-sinnig*—mad). Celan's poetic corroboration of the meaningfulness of madness corresponds to Kafka's description of the half-dead Hunter. In its fragmented, encoded, dismembered language Celan preserves the maddening awareness of a post-war condition of living death in the place of a poetics of false totalities. Poetically enacting this awareness, Celan breaks up the word for the ascription of "making sense," the word "inter-pret-able" (*aus-leg-bar*), and implicitly gives away the motivation of the seemingly senseless, codified language of his poetry. The notion of poetic words "making sense" would deny that madness alone is appropriate to the destruction alluded to in the poem. Such words could not only be interpreted, but appropriated and eventually annihilated. The "secret of the stag moss," the last remaining witness of the destruction, would be lost and done with (*aus*, cf. *aus-leg-bar*); in the end it would lie there (*läge*) unresisting and flat on the ground, naked and defenseless (*bar*). It would be exposed to its enemies, against whom Celan goes into battle. In this fight, he is supported by Kafka and his words: tearing open the hidden "stitched-up caesura," the false closure of the wound, Celan invokes Kafka, the "man with the jackdaw" who helps him bring to light the only possibility of the "true word" that remains—the obscure half-word of half-death corresponding to destruction. In affirming madness as the only state of living and speaking that makes sense in the face of what happened, Celan also rescinds his indictment of his "other neighbor," Hölderlin, the poet of the uninterpretable sign ("ein Zeichen sind wir, deutungslos"), who spent decades in a state of mental derangement. With Hölderlin and Kafka, these two so very different "neighbors," at his side, Celan conjures up weapons against his enemies. In a time of utter isolation and despondency and in a language that shuns all "sensible" communication, Celan creates for himself an imagined community of incommensurable allies with Kafka as one of its most prominent and secret members.

Kafka's canine researcher had already been looking for an ally: "Where, then, are the fellows of my species?" (KSS, 147) he asks in a passage marked by Celan,[13] and dreams of a neighbor who would understand his obsessions. Straddling the time of the historical caesura, Celan replies to this call and reciprocates the hope found in such an encounter. The poem "From the Orchis," written one year later, rehearses such an anticipated meeting with Kafka.

The poem starts with an allusion to a children's game, the counting of steps, which in turn introduces a game of numbers: "Twelvenight" stands not only for midnight but also alludes to Shakespeare's comedy, *Twelfth Night,* in which the survivor of a shipwreck hopes to meet her brother again, which does then come to pass on the magical twelfth night. Celan's poem, too, grants itself such a meeting after a catastrophe. It speaks of a lost childhood, origin, and past, and sketches a place that has disappeared as magical and far away, a place from which, at mid-

Von der Orchis her—	From the Orchis—
geh, zähl	go, sum up
die Schatten der Schritte zusammen	the shadows of the steps up to it
bis zu ihr	
hinterm Fünfgeberg Kindheit—,	behind the fivemount of
	childhood—,
von ihr her, der	from it, from which
ich das Halbwort abgewinn für die	I gain the halfword for the
Zwölfnacht,	twelvenight,
kommt meine Hand dich zu greifen	my hand reaches out to grasp you
für immer.	forever.
Ein kleines Verhängnis, so groß	A little disaster, large
wie der Herzpunkt, den ich	like the heart dot I set
hinter dein meinen Namen	behind your eye
stammelndes Aug setz,	stammering my name,
ist mir behilflich.	comes to my help.
Du kommst auch,	You come too,
wie über Wiesen,	as if across meadows,
und bringst das Bild einer	bringing with you the image of a
Kaimauer mit,	quay wall,
da würfelten, als	where strangers—while
unsre Schlüssel, tief im Verwehrten.	our keys crossed like a coat of arms
sich kreuzten in Wappengestalt,	in the depth of the denied—
Fremde mit dem, was	cast dice with what
wir beide noch immer besitzen	we both still possess
an Sprache,	of language,
an Schicksal.	of destiny.

(CG, 195)

night's magic hour, the words of poetry may be won. As in children's tales, this faraway place lies behind the hills; it is as strange and remote as the place where the *Orchis* is found, which, to cite its more popular name, *Knabenkraut* (literally, boy's herb), refers to childhood, and is also a Zen symbol for poet (Pöggeler 1986, 265) and part of the sphere of the *gozan-bungaku*, the Zen "literature of the five mountains" (Ury 1992). Starting out from this exotic, unattainable location and simultaneously moving toward it, the poem stages a meeting with a familiar "you" who at the magic twelfth hour may be of assistance in finding the "halfword." The identity of this helpful "you" is indicated in the second verse: "behind your eye / stammering my name" lies the "heart dot" (*Herzpunkt*), the core of the encounter between the I and the "you" who share a common name and whose destinies are intertwined (*Ineinander-Verhangen-Sein; Verhängnis.*) Admittedly, Celan's "you" is always also an "I," and a meeting with "you" always a meeting with the self (CGW, 3:142). That this "you" also addresses Kafka, whose words were "given" to Celan long before their "meeting," is made clear in the last part of the poem. At the beginning of the third verse the one who "comes too" brings with him "the image of a quay wall" on which strangers "cast dice" with property shared by an "I" and a "you." This image, with which the eye of the "you" brings forth the name, the identity of the "I," derives from the first sentence of Kafka's "Hunter Gracchus" story: "Two boys were sitting on the wall of the wharf playing a game with dice" (KSS, 109). With this seemingly innocuous image used by Kafka to signal the indifference of the world to the arrival of the half-dead Gracchus, Celan delineates the hostility of a world against which his meeting with Kafka is set. The picture of the dice-playing boys is charged with additional meaning: Celan turns the allusion to the crucifixion of Christ, already present in Kafka, into the subtext of the poem's last verses. Just as the Roman soldiers cast lots for the garments of Christ, gambling for the last remaining possessions of the one crucified, so too do the strangers in Celan's poem rob, slander, and peddle the last remnant of the shared property of the poem's "we": language and destiny. This "we" facing the treacherous foes unites the "I" writing the poem with the author of "Hunter Gracchus," who offered to the lyric "I" the image of the quay wall. Another passage marked by Celan in Kafka's "Hunter Gracchus Fragment" reads: "the world runs its course and you pursue your journey, but until today I have never noticed that these paths have crossed." For Celan, "the world" is the enemy against whom his poem portrays the bond with Kafka in a shared emblem, their "keys crossed like a coat of arms." These keys are allegories of the secret that lies hidden "in the depth of the denied," the inaccessible place of the *Orchis* mentioned at the beginning: the site of childhood, of origin, fate, or destiny, and also of the poet's calling. At this confluence Celan receives the wounded half-words of his poetry from Kafka's "greater possibilities."

In the poem "In Prague," also written in 1963, the association with Kafka projected by Celan appears in the light of the common weapons of language. These lines evoke Kafka's life and writing with varying degrees of explicitness. Along with the name of Kafka's birthplace in the title, there is the allusion to the Alchemists' Lane (*Alchimisten Gasse*) in the Hradschin quarter where Kafka resided at various times in his life. Particles of Kafka's work appear in the reference to nocturnal writing, in the expression "born from wordblood," reminiscent of Kafka's famous diary entry describing the "birth" of "The Judgment" in a passage marked by Celan.[14] There is also the Tower of Babel from Kafka's story "The City Coat of Arms" and the Hradschin as a castle of language, but above all repeated images from "Hunter Gracchus": the half-death, which feeds on life, the "stairs of delu-

In Prag

Der halbe Tod,
grossgesäugt mit unserm Leben,
lag aschenbildwahr um uns her—

auch wir
tranken noch immer, seelenverkreuzt,
   zwei Degen,
an Himmelssteine genäht,
   wortblutgeboren
im Nachtbett,

größer und größer
wuchsen wir durcheinander, es gab

keinen Namen mehr für
das, was uns trieb (einer der Wieviel-
   unddreißig
war mein lebendiger Schatten,
der die Wahnstiege hochklomm
   zu dir?),

ein Turm,
baute der Halbe sich ins Wohin,
ein Hradschin
aus lauter Goldmacher-Nein,

Knochen-Hebräisch,
zu Sperma zermahlen,
rann durch die Sanduhr,
die wir durchschwammen,
   zwei Träume
jetzt, läutend
wider die Zeit, auf den Plätzen.

(CG, 194)

In Prague

Half of death,
nursed large on our lives
lay around us, the truth of an ashen
   image—

we too
were still drinking, soulcrossed,
   two rapiers
sewn to sky stones, born from
   wordblood
in the bed of night,

larger and larger
we grew through each other,
   there was
no longer a name for what drove us
(one of the how-many-
and-thirty was my living shadow,

climbing the stairs of delusion to
   you?),

a tower,
the half one built it for himself in the
   where-to
a Hradschin from sheer alchemists-
   No,

bone-Hebrew,
ground to sperm,
flowed through the hourglass,
through which we swam,
   two dreams
now ringing
against time, on the squares.

sion" and the "living shadow" climbing them, all evoke the figure of the half-dead Hunter of Kafka's story who is "always on the grand staircase [. . .] that leads up to it" (KSS, 111). In this poem, Celan again summons up the picture of shared weapons. As with the crossed keys the meeting with Kafka takes place under the sign of the crossed emblem of a coat of arms; "soulcrossed" here are "two rapiers sewn to sky stones." Pointing forward to the "bone-Hebrew" of the final verse, this image suggests in encoded form the identification of the common weapon as sign of resistance to Jewish suffering. The "soulcrossed [. . .] rapiers" are "sewn to sky stones." These sky stones are faded stars, onto which weapons can be sewn; doubtlessly they allude to the lusterless stars that were once sewn onto the coats of the defenseless Jews in Prague and elsewhere. In remembrance of these victims the poem performs an alchemistic transformation, in which the tower of scattered languages and the unreachable castle are sites of a rebirth. Hence, the poem executes an inversion of time: "the hourglass, / through which we swam, two dreams now, ringing / against time, on the squares." Contrary to the vertical down-flow of time in the hourglass, the "bone-Hebrew," the pulverized language of the Jewish dead, is to be revived to sperm and new life. This poetic dream of "ringing / against time," of resuscitating the dead in the awakening of memory, succeeds thanks to the "we," the joining of Celan's and Kafka's dream of defying the flow of time that separates them. The life-giving sperm swims against the flow of the hourglass to that place at the beginning of the poem where it was born from "wordblood." In the subsequent line it is nursed and fed, so that the experience of life as a "half-death," the point from which the poem resonates, may be spoken. The words for that utterance can be found in Kafka's "alchemists' No," in a negation that has turned to poetic gold and ensures an awareness of the state of living death. In order to find the words Kafka has "given" him, the engendering sperm of Celan's poem sets out as if in a dream, one that dreams with and of Kafka. With its ringing voice awakening from the mute course of time, this dreaming path of the poem flows back along the meridian to counter the direction of the hourglass, intersecting with Kafka in the Now of the poem. In its final words, the encounter "on the squares," defying the flow of time, literally takes *place*.

In another place, at another time, in the poem "Frankfurt, September," Celan encounters a Kafka counterfeit, a stuffed and "stitched up" jackdaw. Through the disclosure of the deception, Celan's words, borrowed from Kafka, bring to life again his true and wounded ally. Written in Frankfurt in 1965, the poem contains the most unambiguous references to Kafka in Celan's work and the first to be recognized by scholars. Their commentaries have stressed their limited knowledge of the circumstances referred to in the poem and the speculative character of their interpretations of these references.[15] Subsequent discoveries in Celan's papers not only make further decoding of the poem possible, but also provide insight into Kafka's importance for Celan during these troubling years in a world Celan increasingly experienced as hostile and treacherous.

Frankfurt, September	Frankfurt, September
Blinde, licht- bärtige Stellwand. Ein Maikäfertraum leuchtet sie aus.	Blind, light- bearded partition wall. A cockchafer dream illuminates it.
Dahinter, klagegerastert tut sich Freuds Stirn auf,	Behind it, in a grid of lament, Freud's brow opens up,
die draussen hartgeschwiegene Träne schiesst an mit dem Satz: "Zum letzen- mal Psycho- logie."	the tear, hardened by silence, outside, wells up with the sentence: "For the last time psycho- logy."
Die Simili- Dohle frühstückt.	The simile- jackdaw has breakfast.
Der Kehlkopfverschlusslaut singt.	The glottal stop sound sings.
(CG, 221)	

Various interpreters have recognized numerous references to Kafka in this poem, most unmistakably to the famous quotation "Never again psychology" from Kafka's aphorisms "Reflections on Sin, Suffering, Hope and the True Way," which Celan had indeed marked heavily in his edition of the volume *Wedding Preparations in the Country*.[16] The word "simile-jackdaw" (*Simili-Dohle*) clearly refers to the Czech meaning of Kafka's name and distinguishes the true author from his epigones.[17] Less obvious references have also been noted: the illuminating "cockchafer dream," which is to be found both in Freud's *Interpretation of Dreams* and in Kafka's *Wedding Preparations in the Country*,[18] and the contrast between the breakfasting bird and the singing glottal stop sound (*Kehlkopfverschlusslaut*), which simultaneously suggests Kafka's larynx tuberculosis (*Kehlkopftuberkulose*), the K sound in Kafka's and Josef K.'s names, and a key passage in "The Hunger Artist." In Kafka's story, the hunger artist, singing with the last vestiges of his strength, confronts his guards, "who have just been brought an enormous breakfast."[19] The images and words of this confrontation between the true, suffering artist and the prison warders suspecting and exploiting him are adopted by Celan from Kafka as weapons in his own struggle for a true, pained speaking in opposition to the sated language of his "well-fed" enemies.

The first lines of the poem can be understood in this sense. As Thomas Sparr and Rainer Nägele have pointed out, the Kafka quotation should not be taken literally as a rejection of psychology (Sparr 1988, 142; Nägele 1987, 237–65). In fact, the poem unfolds a topography altogether compatible with Freudian theory. The "blind partition wall" is first of all a screen, a wall without openings that usually serves to hide a disorder behind it. In accordance with the conceptions of psychoanalysis, this surface conceals a dark, "disordered" unconscious, which may, however, be illuminated by dreams. Lit up by a dream, Celan's wall becomes "light-bearded." This word, which appears in Celan's poem "Tübingen, January" as "light-beard of the patriarch" ("Lichtbart des Patriarchen,") (see commentary by Wiedemann in CG, 751), referring to a possible savior in the guise of the mad, stammering Hölderlin, also has an authoritative and "truth-saying" function in this poem. In Freud the light gives rise to "a cockchafer dream," a dream that deals with cruelty toward beetles kept imprisoned, one of which escapes while the other is squashed (1961, 295). In Kafka's *Wedding Preparations in the Country* it is the dream of the liberating independence of the beetle-like body, which, although consciousness is silent, "will manage everything efficiently while I rest."[20] In both cases the cockchafer dream is simultaneously traumatic and liberating. In this vein, the dream can also be set beside the cockchafer that Celan, in his poem "In the Air," quotes from the old children's rhyme "Cockchafer fly" (*Maikäfer, flieg*). In that poem there is a "Pomeranian, at home / in the cockchafer song which remained motherly, summerly, light- / blooded on the edge / of all jagged, winterhard-cold / syllables" (CG, 166) ("Ein Pommer, zuhause / im Maikäferlied, das mütterlich blieb, sommerlich, hell- / blütig am Rand / aller schroffen, winterhart-kalten / Silben"). In "Frankfurt, September" the bright cockchafer song becomes a dream that unites the trauma of a decimated home and the dream of a mother's song. This wounded cockchafer dream, longing for a liberating, bright song, illuminates the unconscious behind the partition and makes it known. What is then found there, however, is the unconscious, the repressed of the Freudian topography itself: "Never again psychology."

However, these quotations suggest that psychology may still apply this one, last time, as Celan applies it to Freud's theory itself. The cockchafer dream of a liberating, quickening song exposes Freud's own brow "in a grid of lament," barred by a language of mourning. It reveals that Freud's analysis addressing psychological backgrounds is in reality itself the result of a repression. According to these verses, what is repressed by Freud's search for unconscious motivations originating in the depth of the psyche is a tear, a mourning "hardened by silence." Kafka's call for an end of psychology frees what is left unspoken "outside" and allows the suppressed tear to well. Celan's poem implies that Freud's theory, which justifies and explains on psychological grounds, represses a different, more "direct" suffering and prevents the expression of outrage and the struggle against injustice. In a letter, which was never mailed, dated 8 January 1961 and addressed to Kurt Hirschfeld, Celan places the Kafka quote in the context of the Goll affair, exclaiming: "'Never again psychology!' It is not the description of the motives and considerations that matters but the exposure of the baseness (and its allies)" (CG, 752). In this letter Celan enters into battle against his opponents armed with Kafka's quotation and does not accept the validity of any extenuating circumstances of psychological origin—explanations such as envy, offense, or simply the disturbed psyche of his enemies—with which friends try to placate him. Celan rejects Freud's theory as a suppression not only of sorrow and pain but also of anger and resistance to hostility. The ability to express this objection to psychology granted to him by Kafka's phrase liberates Celan's own sorrow and he vents his anger in the last lines of the poem. With an allusion to Kafka's name, with his words, and finally with the sound of his diseased, mute speech organ, Celan's tear, suppressed until now, bursts out in these final lines; it frees itself violently like a weapon from the repressive grid of containment. Appropriately, it finds expression in the indictment of the "false" jackdaw, which—as the warders of the Hunger Artist do when confronted by his suffering—simply has "breakfast" as if it were the normal end of the night. "Nothing," we read in Kafka's story, "tormented the starvation artist more than such watchmen; they made him melancholy; they made his starving terribly difficult; sometimes during the hours of the watch, overcoming his weakness, he sang for as long as he could so as to show these people how unjust their suspicions were" (Kafka 2007, 87).[21] The song of the Hunger Artist, to which Celan's last lines allude, is proof of the truthfulness of his art of fasting and a weapon against the insinuations of his enemies. Yet, whereas Kafka's Hunger Artist can still wrest a true song from himself, albeit only with a great effort, the liberated expression in Celan's final lines is no more than a muted, stifled K-sound. Kafka himself, to whom Celan owes this last remnant of a "song," indeed still had "greater possibilities."

From Celan's point of view Kafka was fortunate to have greater possibilities not only of speaking, but also of living. In a short poem written in 1968, two years before his suicide, Celan writes of these possibilities.

Sprüchlein-deutsch:	Versespell-German:
entdinglichte Welt, er- fürchtet, erwirklicht,	de-reified world, be- feared, be-realized,
Konstanze, heute, wäre ein Tag,	Konstanze, today, would be a day.
Dora Dymant, heute, ein Leben.	Dora Dymant, today, a life.
(CG, 509)	

The name of Dora Dymant, Kafka's partner who stood by him until his death, makes the reference to Kafka unmistakable, but the rest of the poem appears initially puzzling. Indeed the very first composite word, "Versespell-German" (*Sprüchlein-deutsch*), already suggests a riddle or a charm. This impression is reinforced by the triad, the rhythm, and the alliterations, but also by the semantic fields of the subsequent words "de-reified," "be-feared," "be-realized." The remaining four lines, which seem to bear no relation to this beginning, set up a contrast between two women's names, each associated with a different notion of duration. Dora Dymant's name is the only immediately recognizable particle of reality. As for the other name, Konstanze, the commentaries in the appendix of the 2004 edition of Celan's *Collected Poems* note that "no allusion to a concrete person could be established" (CG, 953).

The first word, "Versespell-German" (*Sprüchlein-deutsch*), can be read as designation of a language of "little sayings" (*Sprüchlein* as a diminutive form of *Spruch*), thus a particular linguistic form of German. The colon after this word suggests that a definition or description of this language will follow. The first two lines describe in extreme condensation three moments of a process that takes place in and through this language: an undoing of alienation (*ent-dinglicht;* de-reified), a renewal generated by fear (*er-fürchtet;* be-feared), and a re-creation of reality (*er-wirklicht;* be-realized). "Versespell-German" evokes the oldest surviving form of German poetry, the Germanic spells, of which the earliest, the two Merseburg charms dating from before AD 750, are usually regarded as the beginning of German literature. These relics of pagan ritual practices are considered to be the embodiment of a magical language aiming at an intervention in reality. The poem "Versespell-German" refers to the enchanting power of this language, simultaneously reflecting on its impact and conjuring it up.

Einst sassen Frauen (Disen),	Once women were sitting,
setzten sich hierher [und] dorthin.	they sat down here and there.
Einige banden Fesseln,	Some tied fetters,
einige hielten das Heer auf,	some held up the host,
einige lösten ringsumher	some untied all around
die (Todes)Fesseln:	the fetters of death:
Entspringe [dem] Fesselband,	Leap out of the fetters,
entflieh den Feinden!	flee the foe!
(ROTHMANN 1978, 12)	

The first of the Merseburg Spells is concerned with the freeing of prisoners. The charm describes how female goddesses free captured warriors from their bonds. It concludes with the actual "magic" spell, contained in the last two lines, that is supposed to release the prisoners: "Leap out of the fetters, / flee the foe!" The form and content of this spell are the starting point of Celan's "Versespell-German." The conspicuous repetition of the prefix *ent-* (in the German "Entspringe [dem] Fesselband, / entflieh den Feinden"—"Leap out of the fetters, / flee the foe") is intended to have a loosening and liberating effect. These syllables have their correspondence in Celan's poem in the varied prefixes of the words "*de*-reified world, *be*-feared, *be*-realized" ("entdinglichte Welt, erfürchtet, erwirklicht"). Whereas the original spell invokes the transformation of reality in imperative verb-forms, Celan's words, in addition to the formal echoes of magical charms, contain a reflection on the impact they wish to conjure up. The process described in the three words of Celan's "spell" reflects his understanding of poetry altogether. "Reality is not," Celan writes in his "Meridian" speech; "reality must be sought out and won" (CGW, 3:168). The rejection of an alienating reality corresponds to the "de-reified world," which is, in Celan's self-definition of his poetics, the condition of the possibility of a poetic re-creation of reality, of a world "be-realized," brought into being by poetry. If the alienating material world in the Merseburg Spell is an actual imprisonment, then the "de-reification" in Celan's poem is directed at a liberation from an oppressive reality altogether. The means for this deliverance are generated in fear, in a refusal to be lulled by soothing appearances. The goal is "winning" a different, no longer alienating reality. In his search for a poetic language that has the power to undo reality and refashion it anew through the magic of words, Celan reverts to the earliest periods of the German language. Celan goes back to the most ancient poetic form in order to win back the "greater possibilities" of speaking that he feels have been lost. In Kafka, these possibilities of language were still available to earlier generations "unburdened by the centuries," at a time when the "true word" and its power could still "intervene," when it could still determine and change the whole structure of reality.

If this language still existed "today," as the poem emphasizes, then the spell would work and successfully entreat the goddesses to free the captured warriors. In Celan's present, the spell has become the diminutive *Sprüchlein* and gets no further than the conditional form in conjuring up an alternative reality and an imaginary rescue by female saviors.

Konstanze, heute,	Konstanze, today,
wäre ein Tag	would be a day.
Dora Dymant, heute,	Dora Dymant, today,
ein Leben.	a life.

Like the Merseburg Spell, Celan's poem invokes female figures who have the power to free men from imprisonment. The goddesses of the ancient spell, called "Disen," are also described as guides who succor the dying warriors and deliver them into eternal life.[22] The women's names in Celan's poem conjure up a similar hope. One can only speculate whether the name "Konstanze" really does not correspond to a real person or whether it refers instead to Mozart's notoriously unfaithful wife, who on the day of his death was not by his side but taking a cure in Baden. More significant is the contradiction between what Celan associates with the name Konstanze and its meaning derived from the Latin *constans:* constant, steadfast. Instead of bearing witness to a redeeming constancy, Celan's Konstanze rescues only a single day. In accordance with her inadequacy, the magic of her name, requiring a correspondence between word and essence, also fails. However, Konstanze's etymological meaning and the brief duration of her loyalty point to another, a literary source: the lack of steadfastness of female loyalty deplored in the poem "Women's Constancy" by the English metaphysical poet John Donne, whose work Celan translated into German. The first lines of this poem read: "Now thou hast loved me one whole day, / Tomorrow when thou leavest, what wilt thou say?" (Donne 1896, 12).

In contrast to the fickle Konstanze, Dora Dymant would be a companion for life. Her name, too, is laden with metaphoric meaning—diamonds are the most durable substance—yet her real identity, her role in Kafka's life, and her presence at his side as he was dying are undeniable. In the verse mentioning her name, the implied verb "would be" is still conditional, but this is no longer explicit: "Dora Dymant [. . .] a life." In this juxtaposition, the magic of language brings forth a "true word" in which name and meaning coincide. The bridge created here between this Eastern Jewish girl from a Hassidic home and the Germanic goddesses is one of the unexpected possibilities of Celan's own cryptic word magic. The life, however, that Dora Dymant gave Kafka before his death, the succor she granted this representative of an earlier, less traumatized generation, remains for Celan a dream of desire, about which he, wounded and "half dead," could only write poetry. Admittedly, Kafka, like Celan, was engaged in the struggle against a hostile world; admittedly for him, as for Celan, words were his only weapon; but Kafka, unlike Celan, was still able to write: "In the struggle between you and the world, act as second to the world."[23] Weighed down by the burden of his experiences, Celan could no longer bestow this support to the world, even as he nominated Kafka as his companion in the struggle to name these experiences. With his own end in the waters of the Seine, Celan followed Hunter Gracchus in the very hope of reaching the other shore, while we, his readers, continue to draw lots for what is left of his possessions, his language and his destiny.

A Permanent Shadow:
Ilse Aichinger and Kafka

Following her reading of one of her most acclaimed stories, "Mirror Story" ("Spiegelgeschichte"), at a meeting of the literary association *Gruppe 47* in 1952, Ilse Aichinger was given the nickname "Miss Kafka" (Endres 1995, 114; Torton Beck 1983, 565; Steinwendtner 1993, 147). Affinities between her work and that of the Prague writer have been noted ever since. Kafka was described as one of her "patron saints" (Piontek 1995, 224), and her perception of things was described as a vision "through Kafka's eyes" (Neumann 1995, 260). Her stories were read as a response to his stories (Nicolai 1997, 44; Hoffer 1993, 90; Arnold 1995, 255; Holthusen 1995, 195), and it was said that parts of her work are "unimaginable without Kafka's influence" (Arnold 1995, 255). In 1983, when Aichinger received the Kafka Prize, she gave a speech with the title "The Impertinence of Breathing" (1991d), in which she protested that she had never read any of Kafka's writings, with the exception of a single brief passage from one of his letters. In her speech she relates that reading these lines had frightened her so much that she snapped the book shut and resolved never to read another line of Kafka. "No, for as long as I can bear it," said Aichinger at the end of her address, "I am not reading on, as long as even the shadow of a memory [of this passage] touches me when I pass the bookcases with his books, I am not taking out one [of Kafka's] volume[s] again. And this shadow will touch me as long as I breathe and as long as I see the books there. No, I am not reading on. As long as I breathe, I am not reading on. It is one or the other" (1991d,

107). The name Kafka is repeatedly mentioned in commentaries on Aichinger's work, but it would be difficult to explain his influence on her simply as a shadow of the memory of reading a few of his sentences. Since it is evidently impossible to talk of Kafka's influence on Aichinger in a narrow sense, we may assume that this often-noted bond has a less direct origin.

In "Kafka and his Precursors" (1979) Jorge Luis Borges describes how Kafka could not only exert an influence on his successors but even "create" his forerunners retrospectively, that is, could also have an effect on writers who had never read him. After listing some very diverse texts—from Zeno's *Paradoxes* to Browning's poems and the stories of Lord Dunsany—in which he recognizes an affinity to Kafka, Borges states that while these texts do not share common features with one another, they nevertheless all display traits of Kafka's writing. "In each of these texts we find Kafka's idiosyncrasy to a greater or lesser degree, but if Kafka had never written a line, we would not perceive this quality; in other words, it would not exist" (1979, 236). According to Borges, without having a direct effect on the work of another, a writer can still have an influence in the past and in the future by revealing a specific mode of perception shaped by him, without which a fundamental dimension of some works of earlier or later authors would always remain hidden. With an emphasis on the paradox of this literary effect Borges concludes: "*Every* writer *creates* his own precursors. His work modifies our conception of the past, as it will modify the future. In this correlation the identity or plurality of the men involved is unimportant" (1979, 236; emphasis added). As illuminating as Borges's reflection is, and as helpful as his comments are for the insight that literary influence is effected not only via the author but also by way of the reader and the latter's perception and horizon of expectations, both the generalization and the qualification in Borges's conclusions are dubious—quite apart from the ahistorical nature of this theory of influence. The fact that Borges chooses Kafka, before leaping from his work to draw conclusions—somewhat prematurely—about "every writer," is in need of explanation, as is the fact that he talks about an "identity or plurality of *men*" ("la identidad o la pluralidad de los hombres"). Using "men"— the neutral but generally male-inclined *hombres* rather than, say, "authors"—may be (but is, of course, not necessarily) significant here. That male rather than female authors are anticipated in Kafka's sphere of influence is shown by Shimon Sandbank's study *After Kafka: The Influence of Kafka's Fiction* (1989). Sandbank investigates the traces Kafka has left in the work of numerous modern authors— from Sartre to Pynchon—and comes to the conclusion that they are all marked by Kafka's shattering of established dogmas and certainties, but that they nevertheless, in one way or another, mitigate the radical unsettling that underlies his vision. "They are," writes Sandbank, "unable, or unwilling, to write the radically skeptical type of fiction that is Kafka's great contribution to modern literature [. . .] They end with some comfort" (1989, 12). There is not a single woman among the authors Sandbank discusses. Perhaps, however, it is a woman writer, Ilse Aichinger, who, in the few lines of Kafka that she read, experienced the disquieting literary effect that is associated with Kafka's name. And perhaps this effect evoked by Kafka's name is expressed in her work in a form that goes beyond Borges's elucidations, taking Kafka further and carrying him with her not only with respect to common features, but also with respect to historically and gender-determined differences. At the same time, Aichinger's radical rejection of all comforting consolations provides a counterexample to Sandbank's conclusion that we have here a general attenuation of Kafka's legacy.

Balcony Scenes

Whereas the manifestations of Kafka "traces" in the works of authors who could know nothing of him must remain Borges's own projection, Aichinger, in her Kafka Prize speech, precisely where she speaks of her refusal to read more of Kafka than the lines she mentions, provides a clue to an understanding of the relationship between the two authors. The passage which, according to Aichinger, took her breath away and made it impossible for her to read even one more line by Kafka if she wanted to "continue putting on her clothes," "sit down to meals," "come into the garden" (1991d, 106), describes a childhood memory:

> One day when I opened my eyes after a short afternoon nap, not yet quite sure of where I was, I heard my mother call down from the balcony in a natural tone of voice: "What are you doing?" A woman answered from the garden: "I'm having a snack on the grass." At that I was astonished at the firmness with which people are able to bear life.[1]

Kafka incorporated this passage, a childhood memory which he related in a letter to Max Brod, into his early story "Gespräch mit dem Beter" (2002e, 384–94)[2] (Conversation with the Praying Man), making only minor changes. This story presents a confrontation between two men, the first-person narrator and an uncanny, ecstatically praying man, who appears in the church one day. The narrator, who at first embodies the principle of normality and stability, is challenged by the praying man to give up the illusory sense of security that he would like to hold on to. The "balcony scene," the conversation between his mother and her neighbor, constitutes the expression formulated by the praying man of a fundamental existential and ontological doubt that makes a life in stable normality appear unimaginable to him. He concludes his remarks with an urgent, almost imploring challenge to the narrator, who so far has insisted with self-confident certainty on his unshakeable steadiness: "You don't believe people talk like that?" (KGB, 391). The reply of the narrator chimes in with the praying man's perception, and when the narrator assents that such a banal conversation amounts to madness, the praying man is overjoyed. The narrator's reaction leads to a brief, magical moment of a clear-sighted vision, in which the unfathomable madness of the "normal" everyday life embodied by the women is shared by the two speakers: "Ah, but this is good, that you agree with me," the praying man exclaims. "It is true, why should I be ashamed—or rather why should *we* be ashamed—that I don't walk upright, with heavy steps" (KGB, 391–92). In this justification of the praying man's own lack of certainty and self-confidence, the shift from "I" to "we" marks his ultimate moment of bliss when he realizes that his awareness of the madness of normality is shared by his antagonist. Encouraged by his interlocutor's agreement, the praying man continues describing his sense of life with ever-greater intensity. As he unfolds visions of an entirely unstable, threatening, and threatened world, where houses collapse, a storm foretells the end, and death dwells in the houses, the narrator shrinks back and retracts his earlier reply, maintaining now that he can absolutely identify with the banality of the women's balcony-conversation. The story ends with the delighted reaction of the praying man, who sees in this fearful retraction a confirmation that he did not impart his visions in vain and that, once touched by this experience, there is no way back to the cozy illusion of stability.

The disturbing encounter between the two male figures stands in diametrical opposition to the matter-of-course character of the conversation of the two women. The end of the story nevertheless introduces another note. The delighted declaration of love by the praying man, who in the final sentence extols the fine clothes and the "delicate skin" of his interlocutor (which also has a homoerotic content), feminizes the narrator in the most tender way. At the very moment when the latter demonstrates against his will just how profoundly the praying man's vision has seized hold of him—in other words, when he acknowledges the degree to which he has entered the uncanny sphere of the unsecured other—he takes on feminine characteristics. If in the challenge of the praying man the claim of the text itself is recognized as the power to shatter the sense of security of the reader against his desire to retract and flee from these visions, then it may perhaps not be entirely far-fetched to also see Kafka's imaginary interlocutor as a *female* reader—and, given Ilse Aichinger's reaction to the key scene of this meeting, to imagine her as a particularly acute and sensitive recipient of this challenge. Like the narrator's futile attempt to take back his closeness to the praying man, so as to ward off the feeling of insecurity which the latter caused, Aichinger's "revocation," her decision to close the book in order to go on breathing, is the most profound admission of its effect on her. It is in this light, regardless of questions of direct influence, that the shadow of Kafka brushes Aichinger's work.

A closeness to Kafka's work is typically discerned only in Aichinger's early work, but under a different sign it can also be found in her later, experimental, and often obscure prose that, as Heinz Ludwig Arnold writes, "[has] emancipated itself from her own beginnings, where she was close to Kafka" (1995, 258). The greater distance from Kafka in Aichinger's later work, however, represents less a disappearance of his shadow than a changed way of dealing with it. The existential shock of reading Kafka increasingly finds its way into the self-reflexive dimension of her prose and its implicit reflections on language, and leads by this route to an interrogation of the social conditions and power relations hidden behind the illusion of certainties.

Whether Aichinger's story "Zweifel an Balkonen" (Doubt about Balconies, 1991e),[3] written in 1972, eleven years before her prize-acceptance speech, therefore, and certainly after she read the passage in Kafka's letter,[4] relates directly to Kafka's lines, cannot be determined. It is not difficult, however, to demonstrate the relationship between this story, her speech, and Kafka's "Conversation with the Praying Man." As in Kafka so in Aichinger's story the confrontation of someone sure, rooted, firm with one who is strange and unsettling leads to an irreversible recognition of the fundamental instability of existence. "Balconies," writes Elisabeth Pulver in her illuminating interpretation of Aichinger's story, are "something altogether inconsequential, which is not worth talking about [. . .] There is something *petit* bourgeois about them"; they point to a "deceptive security," to "the immovable and innocuous features so central to middle class life" (1995, 273).

Nevertheless, Aichinger makes distinctions. There are the "homeland balconies," which are "more firmly attached" and allow one "to quickly step outside" without a thought, and one can at any time and without impediment withdraw into the living room from them; they are "identical with a dangerous loyalty that does not know itself," with a blind, uninterrogated belonging, and "radiate their own security, which can be seen even from a distance." Like the conversation of the women in Kafka's "balcony scene," homeland balconies are "unaware," are governed by "innocuous" things, and cause a "distraction from thinking" (SW, 20).[5] A further characteristic of the homeland balconies, their certainty of ending up on the "right hand side of the angels" at the Last Judgment, was included by Aichinger in her Kafka speech. There she rejects the idea of finding refuge in religious systems that could protect her from the feeling of insecurity experienced as a result of reading Kafka's lines. In her critique of religious systems and their dynamics of segregation between those who belong and those who do not, she clearly alludes to both Jewish and Christian modes of consolation and offers of comfort. "Should I," Aichinger writes, "expose my heart [. . .] to a power that, at a specific moment, freezes guilt and innocence, to a protection by a love that would draw me to it and yet, when it came to it, divide creatures into some on its right hand side and some on its left side?" (1991d, 105). Aichinger evokes a painting she once saw in the church of Torcello that obviously segregates between followers and "infidels." In the religious representations of this scene, no one had "attempted to go from the right side to the left side, to join his unfortunate brothers" (1991d, 105), those who are excluded from the closed community of the righteous, just as this is also hardly to be expected from the self-satisfied inhabitants of Aichinger's homeland balconies.

In contrast to the homeland balconies, "foreign balconies are insecure." They are separated from the protected interior of the house by a threshold, over which one "stumbles," and they invite only brief sojourns. Unlike the homeland balconies, which are insulated from the outside world, the foreign balconies are shaped according to their surroundings and exposed to every gust of wind. Kafka's praying man has already spoken of threatening gusts of wind that sweep the complacently walking ladies and gentlemen off their feet (KGB, 393). Also his complaint that he was never "convinced of his life through himself" (KGB, 390), that is, never experienced himself as a closed, autonomous unit, places him in opposition to Aichinger's homeland balconies, which are in turn "determined [only] by themselves" (SW, 19). The descriptions of the two kinds of balconies that make up the first part of the story are consistently kept in the impersonal mode. In the subsequent short, self-reflexive passage, there unexpectedly appears a "we," which evidently also includes the narrative instance itself, and which inquires as to the consequences of the distinction between these balconies that has just been made.

This "we" emphasizes that this distinction is a deliberate choice. "No one demanded it of us. Distinctions between foreign and native balconies lead to an unpredictable fragmentation" (SW, 22). Unlike the partition between those on the left and those on the right, those who belong to the community and those who do not, the distinction between balconies introduced in the text raises the awareness of its own arbitrariness, and thereby breaks open the secure, self-contained, and exclusionary identity principle itself. To someone who has gained this awareness, there opens up a view of uncertainty that will never go away: "But can we go back? Can anyone who has ever seen the homeland balconies as homeland balconies, dismiss this knowledge? Place limits on it? [. . .] That is to be doubted. Not even the certain end [. . .] can calm him. He will remain uncertain, he is in his homeland" (SW, 23). These sentences play with tautology and contradiction and run against the laws of logic, but nevertheless, or precisely because they do so, they communicate the effect of the disquieting knowledge. At the same time they register that unsettling feeling Aichinger records in her Kafka speech and here introduces into the language itself.

This disturbance arises from the realization of an instability in the relationship between word and thing. "To recognize homeland balconies as homeland balconies" points to the insight that the new word "homeland balconies" alters the perception of the object, which it purports merely to designate, indeed that such a thing, detached from this invented signifier, does not exist at all. The concept "homeland" (*Heimatland*), which previously still described something certain and rooted, is detached from its signifier and, in conjunction with the one who now has his domicile in uncertainty, is robbed of its meaning. But Aichinger's narrator asks, "who is it, who are they, the homeland balconies?" They are the "great invisible deceivers" (SW, 24), they are words themselves that impose an order on things not inherent in them, creating the pretense that "homeland" is something essential and grounded in itself, that between home and abroad there is a natural distinction rather than one produced by the concept itself. The falling apart of word and thing is here utilized as a source of awareness, which has not only existential but also political consequences. Someone who has "once recognized the homeland balconies as homeland balconies," who has once seen through the deception of words, will "remain uncertain." The fact that in these lines Aichinger presents the slippage of meanings with reference to the politically and historically loaded concept *Heimat* demonstrates a subversive use of the arbitrariness of signs, which she implicitly makes her program in "Schlechte Wörter" (Bad Words), the poetological introductory text to the volume of the same name from which "Doubts about Balconies" is taken.

This Side of Good

"Schlechte Wörter" begins with a rejection of a tradition of poetic speaking that dedicates itself to recovering the lost unity of word and thing. The loss of this unity also appears in Kafka's "Conversation with the Praying Man." There, the first-person narrator attributes the praying man's instability and uncertainty to the arbitrariness of signs, and describes such an unsteady condition as "seasickness on firm ground": "The essence of it is, that you have forgotten the true names of things and now hurriedly empty out chance names over them. Quickly now, quickly now! But hardly have you run away from them, then you have forgotten their names again" (KGB, 389). The loss of a true original language lamented in these lines can be read in light of Walter Benjamin's philosophy of language. For Benjamin, too, the arbitrariness of signs is caused by the loss of an earlier, paradisiacal condition, a fall from a state in which word and thing corresponded. Hence for Benjamin one should now "strive for the right words, the names, *les mots justes*," which "do justice to things" (in Wohlfahrt 1988, 136). "I now no longer use," says Aichinger in the first sentence of "Schlechte Wörter," "the better words" (SW, 11). The better, more precise expression, the "more accurate turn of phrase," is unavailable. "I don't mourn it" (SW, 11). Aichinger shares with Benjamin the concern about the inadequacy of language and the abuse of its powers but draws different conclusions from the diagnosis of the arbitrariness of signs.

> Come on now, it can mean anything. We know that all too well. There are very few who can defend themselves. They come into the world and are immediately surrounded by all the things which are not sufficient to surround them. Before they have been able to turn their heads, they are burdened with designations, beginning with their own names, which do not fit. (SW, 13)

In some ways, this passage corresponds to the description of Benjamin's diagnosis of the language of man after the fall and this language's arbitrary use of words as mere means (2002d, 62–74). However, in "Schlechte Wörter," Aichinger shifts the emphasis of his conclusion. If Benjamin is concerned with reminding us of the lost paradisiacal language of names, pointing to the necessity of a messianic salvation in order to restore the ability to see things as they are, then Aichinger is interested only in making visible the incompleteness of the correspondence between word and thing. Admittedly, men are "burdened with designations that do not fit," in that, as reassurance, these feign the possibility of mastery and vigorous action, order, steadiness, and "home" (*Heimat*). Words, insofar as they pretend control over reality, lend comfort: their existence "in lullabies is easy to prove" (SW, 14). Yet, for Aichinger, these false reassurances should not be countered by "better words," and she commits herself to the "bad words." She, too, knows, that "the best is imperative, but commandments always scare me" (SW, 13). Aichinger's "bad words" are words that are no longer to be measured against absolutes and have given up the open struggle against language that to some extent they were still carrying on in her early poetological text "Meine Sprache und ich" (My language and I, 1978). They are now working *with* language by imperceptibly, "inconspicuously interfering" and watching as "each receives its swift inappropriate designation." "Recently," Aichinger writes, describing her resignation of messianic expectations with quiet irony, "I've even been joining in" (SW, 13). Aichinger commits herself to the "fallen" language, to the "downfall" (*Untergang*) of words, "or rather to the downfalls" (*Untergänge*) that preclude both paradise and redemption. The plural form, which is not to be found in any dictionary, is itself a "bad word," which she now reckons among the "better designations" because "downfalls," like the other bad words, "don't occur in any lullaby" (SW, 13). Aichinger's "bad words" exert a barely perceptible erosion of a language of concepts aimed at stabilizing meaning. They expose the "homeland balconies as homeland balconies," and forever unsettle the former certainties of those brushed by this awareness. For Aichinger, using "bad words" means "to drag the downfall along in front of one" (SW, 13), with all the friction, the dust, and the traces that could disturb the sleep of the occupiers of "heavenly house walls" and "eternal homelands."

Dead Fathers

In Kafka's "The Worry of the Father of the Family" (KSS, 72–73), as in "Conversation with the Praying Man" and in Aichinger's "Doubts about Balconies," someone who imagines himself firmly settled finds himself exposed to a profound feeling of insecurity. The paterfamilias's worry is the possibility that Odradek, a useless thing that lurks in the dark storerooms of the house and looks "like a flat, star-shaped spool for thread," covered with "torn-off pieces of thread of the most various kinds and colors knotted together but tangled up in one another" (KSS, 72), cannot die, because "everything that dies has previously had some sort of goal, some kind of activity, and that activity is what has worn it down; this does not apply to Odradek" (KSS, 73). Hence the "almost painful idea" of the father of the family, that Odradek, "with his bits of threads trailing behind him, he will come clattering down the stairs, [...] at the feet of my children and my grandchildren" (KSS, 73), and outlive him. The father of the family keeps the account books of death: the debit side is activity, purpose, and goal, the credit side a meaningful death, a causal nexus, a deserved wearing-out. To have ground oneself down with activity, such a paternal pride, arisen from the bourgeois work ethic, reconciles with death. The end is not meaningless and death not a scandal but a logical consequence; the links are maintained, the house is secure—if it were not for Odradek.

Because the fact is that "this does not apply to Odradek." Odradek, it is said, cannot be caught. Not as the character of a story, which has been interpreted dozens of times; not as word, since neither of the two explanations of the name proposed in the first sentences of the text is correct and can provide it with a meaning; not as misshapen thing, whose form throws no light on its origin or purpose; not as unruly childlike creature of "no permanent residence." "It is impossible to say anything more definite on it, since Odradek is extraordinarily mobile and impossible to catch" (KSS, 72). Odradek's elusiveness is well known. He—or it— was treated by his readers as "alienated junk" (Hillmann 1967), as commodity, as symbol of universal being, as messenger from another world, at any rate as something "that cannot be categorized using the means of rationality and speech available to the father of the family" (Hillmann 1967, 200). In the course of his transformation from word to living thing, Odradek mutates from an "it," made up of a feminine spool (*die Spule*) and a masculine star (*der Stern*), to a "he," to a small male creature, which, thanks to the worry that he causes the paterfamilias, could also be seen as a rebellious son reminding the father of his mortality, and with it of the impermanence of his order. Odradek, the small, humble being, upsets the self-confidence of the father of the family and thereby unsettles the established, hierarchical power relations.

Aichinger's story "Flecken" (SW, 15–18) (Spots), in which traces of Kafka can only be demonstrated by a detour through Borgesian influence theory, also dramatizes a disturbance by a small misshapen phenomenon of the domestic environment, threatening its hierarchy. In *Schlechte Wörter*, it is placed between the stories "Bad Words" and "Doubts about Balconies" and begins with the discovery that the armchairs have been soiled. "We now have spots on our armchairs" (SW, 15). Such chairs and the settee that goes with them suggest "settledness" and furthermore are covered in "imitation leather," evoking the false security of middle-class life, in which cleanliness is expected and dirt is experienced as a threat. The discovery of the spots leads to detective-like questions, which are not unlike the initial attempts to get a hold on Odradek: where do they come from, what caused them, and when did it happen? These questions as to cause and origin remain unanswered for the time being, and give rise to reflections that overgrow and obscure the questioning. Only the hypothetical question "And would the world be different without these spots?" receives an apodictic answer. "That is a superfluous question. It would be different" (SW, 15). It is true that the spots do not move mountains—"the Rocky Mountains and the Catskills [would be there] nevertheless"—and they neither raise doubts about pleasant promises such as "the handsome house, in which Longfellow watched his handsome daughters grow up," nor provide remedies for "hopelessnesses of every kind," but they do change the "hierarchy of what exists." Because "they cannot be fitted in," the spots, like Kafka's Odradek, cannot be placed in preconceived categories, cannot be further developed. Even "at twilight," that is, as they become less easily perceived—or is it a matter of the fading sight, the diminishing vitality of the beholder?—"the spots don't go away." Might they perhaps outlive the beholder?

The contemplation of Odradek unnerves Kafka's paterfamilias. Of Aichinger's spots it is said: "Perhaps it helps to look at them." Why should paying attention to the spots help? Most likely, it was through carelessness (*Unachtsamkeit*) that they appeared there, through heedlessness (*Achtlosigkeit*), through disregard (*Nicht-beachtung*), through lack of observation? The spots, then, like Kafka's Odradek for Walter Benjamin, would have the "form which things assume in oblivion. They are distorted" (2002b, 811). Aichinger's spots, too, disfigure the armchairs and are themselves "unbearable forms." Which forgetting would they have emerged from and what effect would looking at them have?

To Benjamin, Kafka's Odradek is a relative of the hunchback, this "prototype of distortion," who bears what has been repressed on his back. Because "palpably," he writes in his Kafka essay, "being loaded down is here equated with forgetting" (2002b, 811). This burden corresponds to "what is denied," which, according to Aichinger in "Wisconsin und Apfelreis," we have "on our backs" (SW, 75). To Benjamin forgetting, which distorts things and which is symbolized by Odradek, is linked with the guilt of "believing the fullness of the world to be the only real-ity" (2002b, 810). It is the forgetting of the possibility of another order of things, an order that would be delivered from the oppression of the world of the fathers with their uniforms, which, as Benjamin says in the same essay, "is stained all over" (2002b, 796) ("Die Uniform des Vaters ist über und über fleckig"). This forgetting, and with it the disfigured life, will, Benjamin continues, disappear "when the Messiah comes," who will "merely make a slight adjustment to the world" (2002b, 811). In Aichinger there is no prospect of disappearing; the stains remain: they are themselves the slight thing that "has occurred and was not foreseeable," and could, therefore, almost represent a kind of deliverance.

The stains can liberate because they do not belong, as it says in the middle of "Flecken," to the "incorporated changes such as, for example, death" or "to the cunning evasions of existence, for which a space is kept from the very beginning, even if the dimensions are sometimes too modest. That is the way it has to be. Did you not know that? Will you finally stop trembling" (SW, 16). Why this trem-bling, and who is suddenly, and just once in this story, being addressed? Is the one addressed perhaps trembling because the spots convey to him, as does Odradek to the father of the family, the similarly painful knowledge that the spots, these insufferable spots, could outlive him? That, therefore, like Odradek, they could be witnesses to the death of the father, proofs of the vulnerability of his supremacy and the hierarchy that determines it? Because, so it says in Aichinger's story, "the hierarchy is in danger of collapsing where one least expects it" (SW, 16). It is threat-ened by apparently inconsequential disturbances—by spots, in fact. Why spots?

About the spots it is said: "[They] cannot be depicted in words" (SW, 17).

Spots resist the grasp of language because of the arbitrariness of their forms. It is this arbitrariness that makes them so "unbearable": because the spots cannot be classified, they point to whatever falls out of an order, to that which is excluded by it so that the order together with its hierarchy can be upheld. Consequently they become symbols of what has been repressed. Since, because of the arbitrariness and the specificity of their various shapes, they cannot be pictured using the means of the symbolic order, they reveal the inadequacy of linguistic referentiality and with it the falling apart of word and thing. The call to look at the spots corresponds to Aichinger's programmatic statement that she wanted "to watch as each thing receives its swift inappropriate designation." This knowledge of the inadequacy of words is repressed wherever order is to be maintained. But who then could have challenged this order and the repression on which it depends? Where do the spots come from?

Kafka's Odradek, it is said, is treated like a child because he is so small. Aichinger's spots, likewise, "don't take up much room" and could furthermore have been caused by a child: "Was it not a child after all? These children. One could console oneself with that. Children, just before they find their dead father" (SW, 17). Are the children perhaps the "handsome daughters of Longfellow" in the house of the great poet, but also of the "long fellow," of the great man—the only father, the only house, the only children mentioned in the text? Amid the unanswered questions and fragmentary reflections there emerges just before the end of the story out of its elliptical beginnings a scene like a film sequence, with a blind spot. Carelessly and trustingly the "children, just *before* they find their dead father" cross the threshold, put down the tumbler at armchair height, and knock into it "*before* they take again, what belongs to them and carefully withdraw, step by step, with their back to the threshold and then over it" (SW, 17–18). The children retreat after they have seen something that remains unspoken. Left behind are the dead father and the spots: "No time left to wipe up what was spilled. Not another glance. The dead fathers are victorious. The spots, too" (SW, 18).

The spots that shake the hierarchy must have appeared after the children found the dead father and stumbled with a glass of milk at the sight of horror, just *before* the furtive retreat, before the refused gaze. The children—the daughters?—may then, before their retreat, have seen a world in the condition of "dead fathers." The spots would then have arisen out of the literally shattering experience of this sight, and they would be the witnesses of the dead fathers and to the end of the paternal hierarchy. Have the children perceived this possibility of another, orderless world and then, unable to bear the trembling that came out of the feeling of insecurity, withdrawn cautiously, all too cautiously? The knowledge of the unfoundedness of the hierarchy, of the vertical order, the standards and "elevations" of which were determined by the fathers, would then be repressed and forgotten. "In a moment everything is over, the elevations, the conditions." With the shocked retreat— "not another glance"—with the forgetting and repression of this primal scene of another, both disordered and insecure mode of being, with this retraction out of fear, the fathers are victorious even when dead, and the vertical order has the last word—if it were not for the spots. These spots on the armchairs are the memory traces of what has been repressed. For even this retraction is a clear confession: here, too, there is no way back once the state of insecurity has been experienced. The spots remain, and hence the last words of the story: "they also win" (SW, 18).

Looking at Odradek reminds the father of the family of what he has repressed, everything that is purposeless, disordered, disfigured, but above all his own transience, everything that is a threat to the hierarchy. Kafka's antagonists are clearly recognizable; the opposing camps are marked out. But who is the observer of Aichinger's spots? And is it, for example, a matter of a *male* observer at all? The discovery of spots on the armchairs originates in the female sphere, in "the observation of a housewife," which in the "*we* and *our*" with whom the story begins, "absorbs individual subjectivity into a collective 'family-we'" (Schmidt-Bortenschlager 1999, 22). Significant differences between Kafka's story and Aichinger's become evident here. In Kafka's story about Odradek, the paterfamilias and his "children and children's children" are the only inhabitants of the house; the mother is conspicuously absent. In Aichinger's text, on the other hand, apart from the possibly female children and the dead fathers there is the voice of the observer of the spots—in all probability female, possibly maternal. In the face of a disturbance in the house, her attitude is fundamentally different from that of Kafka's father of the family. In the last sentence of Kafka's story, Odradek triggers in the father the "almost painful idea" of his own mortality. In Aichinger's text the initially somewhat dismayed-sounding speaker ends by accepting the spots: "Perhaps," she says with cautious optimism, "they are actually beginnings of ideas" (SW, 18). What for the father of the family signals the end of his predominance, could for Aichinger's mother of the family be the beginning of a new freedom. Yet Aichinger does not make it as simple as that for her reader—and herself. The spots, it is said, "could be beginnings of ideas. Because there are no beginnings. These spots win. They also win" (SW, 18). Given the possible origin of these spots, then, the enigmatic concluding sentence and its cancellation of the principle of opposition perhaps become comprehensible. These spots are no beginnings, no arbitrary flashes of inspiration, but traces of what went on before and has been repressed. The possibility of beginnings, of other ideas, and of the idea of another order, lies in a changed way of dealing with the spots. Perhaps it helps to look at them.

Kafka's "Worry of the Father of the Family" and Aichinger's "Spots" are governed by similar yet diverging imagery. Spots suggest the feminine sphere of worries about cleanliness. This is not to be equated with the father's concern for order, which is about ensuring that everything is in the right place, that no one is loitering around. About the spots, however, it is said: "If only one could call them loiterers, but one can't do that either." Spots, unlike Odradek, do not appear as independent, autonomous troublemakers, but by persisting where they should not be, they practice a silent, passive, diffuse resistance. In part this form of refusal is already implied in Odradek's small appearance, consisting of numerous pieces of thread, and in his obstinate, taciturn behavior. However, both aspects are radicalized when it comes to Aichinger's spots. The spots are an arbitrarily defined, indeterminable plurality, "the plurality of a removable intermediate existence" ("die Mehrzahl eines entfernbaren Zwischendaseins") (SW, 17). Odradek also suggests an "intermediate existence," which is neither quite object nor quite human and which lurks in the passages and hallways, in the intermediate spaces of the house. Yet the relationship between him and the father of the family, the unsettling of the hierarchy that he causes, and the resistance he embodies differ from the action of the spots, which have no "body" of their own. Unlike in Kafka's story, in which paternal figure and rebellious son, power and resistance, face one another, in Aichinger's story there is no antagonism between two clearly distinguished unities. The spots, with their anarchic effect on the texture, do not have an independent presence: they are inseparably linked to the material they soil. Sugared milk becomes troublesome only when it penetrates the texture of the armchair covers and mingles with it. The annoyance generated by the spots on the armchairs is impure, mixed, confusing like the reaction and the conclusion of the housewife requesting that they be looked at: "The dead fathers win. The spots also win" (SW, 18). Here it is not only the triumph of the paternal victor that is unsettled; the idea of victory itself is soiled. Aichinger's linguistic dissolution of the logical opposition goes beyond an inversion of the power structure in which the paterfamilias could end up being subordinated by Odradek: she disrupts the hierarchy by attacking the structure itself, thereby preventing the possibility that it might rise up again under another power.

Here no "direct political action is propagated, but a specific form of subversion" (SW, 18). In Kafka the father of the family has not yet been overthrown, but his end is in sight. In Aichinger there are *fathers* in the plural, and they are dead. They are in the plural and occupy their position of power in the hierarchy only posthumously, that is, after their effective power has gone. The paterfamilias of Kafka's time may really be dead today, but the hierarchy he built up still exists and can continue, as it says in Aichinger's "Spots," to "cause suffering." Only the appearance of his power has changed: it has become perhaps even more unassailable, for "it cannot be located with the sufferers, who can be glared at," as was still possible for the eerily laughing Odradek in the face of the then "almost painfully" shaken father of the family. Correspondingly, the modality of resistance has also changed. The spots, unlike Odradek, do not remain out of reach; rather they "intervene" like Aichinger's "bad words" in the order of language.

In the last lines of the story Aichinger warns, "Just don't overdo the efforts at consolation" (SW, 18). Euphemistically, she fends off those appeasements which Shimon Sandbank has identified in Kafka's successors and which could also perhaps be read from her trust in the effect and resistance of the spots. Benjamin's hope that the disfigured creature Odradek could really outlive the father of the family is no longer shared by Aichinger. Instead her inclusion of the inconspicuous spots in the "hierarchy of what exists" expresses the sober vision of a world in the "vacuum of the overthrown fathers" (Von Matt 1995, 334), in which "in relationship to power there is not the *one* place of the *great* refusal—the soul of revolt, the focus of all rebellions, the *pure* law of the revolutionary" (Foucault 1999, 477). Instead there is a diversity of resistances, which, like the spots on homely armchairs, do not have predetermined shapes.[6] The contours of this profile are already suggested in the small, multifarious, impure figure of Kafka's Odradek. Perhaps one might cautiously say that he is the beginning of Aichinger's idea.

The Gap between
Hannah Arendt and Kafka

Because it was only passed down as a rumor, we shall "never, never" know for certain what the imperial message in Kafka's story of the same name contains (KCS, 5). We can assume that this message, which the Emperor on his deathbed wished to convey to his humble subject, who had fled to the remotest parts of the land, was his testament. The Emperor would not have made such a commotion about anything less than the disposal of his last will, nor repeatedly and in the presence of the most venerable witnesses of the Empire assured himself of the correctness of its wording when he sent off the messenger with it. That this tireless courier never arrives at his destination can hardly be ascribed to a lack of determination, since over the millennia the obstacles in his way grow beyond all bounds. In the end, he bears only the message of a dead man and fails to reach his addressee. As a result, no testament accompanies the Emperor's legacy. When evening comes, the evening of life or the end of time, the one for whom the message was intended sits expectantly at the window and imagines it. And because the message is passed down to us only as literature, we shall never know whether the man at the window is looking into the past or the future, whether he is gazing at its origin and is imagining *it, the* message of the Emperor, or if, in order to go on living and to be able to pass something on, he only dreamt it all up, the Emperor, the message, and the messenger, the inheritance itself.

These two possibilities assign different roles to the message imagined by the man at the window, and, by extension, to literature. In the first case, there is an original message and the man knows of its existence, but since its transmission has been interrupted he has to use his imagination to fill in its content. Although the truth of this imaginative reconstruction of the message must by necessity be speculative, it remains in a continuum with the aims and purposes of the original. So, while its truth value is uncertain, its values depend on its closeness to the Emperor's intent as to what he could have wanted to impart to his subject. In this reading, the end of Kafka's parable depicts the man's attempt to figure out the task that was commanded to him by the Emperor, probably an assignment concerning the man's role in the empire after the ruler's death. In a world bereft of tradition and the guidance of a superior authority, literature, like the Emperor's message imagined by the man at the window, becomes the substitute of the Emperor's directives. In the second reading of Kafka's parable, the very existence of such a message—its origin, authority, and destination—is itself part of what the man "dreams up" (literally, "erträumt er sich"). His expectancy of *the* message and his attempt to figure out its content are replaced by an awareness that the entire scene is a figment of his "dream" and that the message can therefore be imagined without regard for a preceding and ulterior authority. There is a rupture at the level of narration: the Emperor and the man at the window no longer belong to the same plane of reality. In this second reading, the gap between the messenger who does not arrive and the man sitting at the window defines the autonomy of literature in modernity, its limitations in conveying "messages," and its freedom to "dream them up." In the first reading, the story still contains a message; in the second, the message itself is a story. In the light of this latter possibility, we may ask: what can a message that is nothing but a story, that consists of literature, transmit? Is it legitimate to argue that Kafka's story contains a message, that it transmits directions *about* politics and social configurations, about Jews and communities?

Hannah Arendt thought so. In "The Pariah as Rebel," the first part of *The Jew as Pariah: A Hidden Tradition,* written in 1944, Arendt describes Kafka's novel *The Castle* as the perfect representation of the existential condition of the pariah and a powerful "illustration of the dilemma of the modern, would-be assimilationist Jew" (1978, 84). In her reading of the novel, the land surveyor K. is the man of goodwill who wants nothing else but the right to live a decent life and to blend into a society that persists in excluding him. However, in the village dominated by the opaque powers of the castle he remains an outsider and is powerless to bring about any significant change. Alone in his hopeless, endless struggle, he ultimately dies of exhaustion. "What he strove to achieve lies beyond the strength of any man" (1978, 88), because he cannot fulfill this task on his own. However, he left behind among the villagers the sense that rebellion is possible, though not for one man alone: neither the isolation of a pariah—or a secluded community of pariahs—nor the parvenu's lone attempt to be accepted in society can come to terms with the present situation of the Jew surrounded by a hostile environment. This interpretation of Kafka's novel leads Arendt to find in Kafka an implicit but inevitable commitment to Zionism and to conclude with her famous affirmation of Jewish national solidarity: "For only within the framework of a people can a man live as a man among men" (1978, 90).

Arendt's reading of Kafka as defender of national cohesion derives from the possibilities she believes Jews faced in the early twentieth century. She describes two ways in which the pariah used to deal with his exclusion from mainstream society in the nineteenth century: the gathering of people in the same situation at the outer margins of society, and the flight into the seemingly timeless values of "nature and beauty." Arendt considers the first solution an "utter detachment from reality" and the second an "escape mechanism" (1978, 84). For Arendt, Kafka, the twentieth-century man, offered an alternative. Believing neither in the retreat into marginality nor in the consolations offered by nature and art like the disillusioned pariah, but also rejecting the temptation of seeking an exceptional access to society like the parvenu, he understood that the only possibility of survival for the one excluded from society was to use "thinking as a new weapon." Arendt derives from literature, and from Kafka in particular, instructions for the right way of behaving politically in a world in which the transmission of the original message has been disrupted.

Nearly ten years later, in her *Between Past and Future,* first published in 1954, Arendt reflects on the role of thinking in circumstances in which no testament specifies how one is to deal with the inheritance of the past. In the course of her argument she once more turns to Kafka, but this time around she no longer has faith in his particular mode of thinking. Arendt introduces her foreword to *Between Past and Future* with a reflection on the words of the French poet and Résistance fighter René Char that "our inheritance was left to us by no testament" (1968, 3).[1] Char laments that the shared experience of a moment lived in the years of the Résistance, when the narrowness of private interests was overcome by a collective, public freedom, can neither be carried on nor handed down because modernity has abolished the traditional means of transmission. For Arendt, however, although the wealth of such moments—the "treasure of the revolutions" (AB, 5)—cannot be transmitted, that impossibility can be compensated for and turned into a potentially positive "fact of political relevance" (AB, 14). It may indeed be impossible for such concrete experiences of freedom to be passed on, but Arendt believes that their effect can nevertheless be kept alive. This can occur in the transference of the structure of these experiences to a space of thinking (*Denkraum*). The liberating interruption of the "inexorable flow of time" experienced in revolutionary moments can—by analogy—live on in the equally beneficial interruption of accepted ways and habitual attitudes that occurs in thinking. It is therefore not so much the content of the revolutionary moments as their potential for new beginnings that can be adopted and transmitted. In this way it becomes possible for "each new generation, indeed [. . .] each new human being" (AB, 13) to experience anew the heritage of the struggles of liberation.

Arendt illustrates her idea of the space of thinking as an "interval in time" with the help of Kafka's parable "He."[2] In it she finds a representation of the difficulty Char laments, the near impossibility of transmitting the inheritance of the past and of passing it on to the future by way of a space of thought that is structured in accordance with the experience he had in the Résistance. Kafka's parable describes a scene in which a man is hemmed in by two opponents:

> He has two antagonists: The first presses him from behind, from the origin. The second blocks the road ahead. He gives battle to both. To be sure, the first supports him in the fight with the second, for he wants to push him forward and in the same way the second supports him in the fight with the first, since he drives him back. But it is only theoretically so. For it is not only the two antagonists who are there, but he himself as well, and who really knows his intentions? [His dream, though, is that some time in an unguarded moment—and this would require a night darker than any night has been yet—he will jump out of the fighting line and be promoted, on account of his experience in fighting, to the position of umpire over his antagonists in their fight with each other.] (AB, 7)[3]

In the version of Kafka's parable used by Arendt—a version adopted from Max Brod that disregards the fact that Kafka crossed out this ending[4]—all that is left to the man is the dream of leaping out of the battle line between past and future. Arendt reads Kafka's parable as a figure of thought describing modern man, who has lost his groundings. Struggling against determination by the past, which pushes the man forward in a direction governed by his origins, by given conditions and events, and against the obstacles that block his way to a future no longer defined by the past, he experiences paralysis and disorientation and is thrown back on himself. In his despair he dreams, as the only escape, of the possibility of leaping out of the continuum of time, out of history. Much as she admires Kafka for the sharpness of his diagnostic eye, Arendt interprets this dream critically as nostalgia for a return to a metaphysical "timeless, spaceless, suprasensuous realm" (AB, 11). This critique is in perfect accord with her former negative assessment of the pariah's "escape mechanisms," but while her earlier readings saw in Kafka an ally and found in his literature a political message against such a detachment from reality, she now detects in the man's dream the limits of Kafka's political commitment.

Arendt outlines a corrective to this dream and boldly proposes going "a step further" than Kafka, replacing the location at which, in the parable, past and future collide, with a *space* that she visualizes as a "parallelogram of forces" (AB, 12). Within this gap that has now assumed spatial dimensions, man might intervene in the course of history. In this way, his thinking turns into a resistance against the frontal clash of the two opposing forces. At the spot where past and future meet, a space has come into existence, a gap of freedom within the linear course of time where thinking "as it were, can go forward in slow, ordered movements" (AB, 12) and can change the course of events. In this way the place where man is inserted into history does not break apart the continuum between past and future, but bends it in a way that marks his presence and his agency. This space allows him to discover "what was most his own, what had come into being only with his own self-inserting appearance" (AB, 12), yet remains sufficiently removed from both past and future to offer him a position from which to "judge the forces fighting with each other with an impartial eye" (AB, 12). In this transformation of Kafka's image Arendt opens up a space for thinking in which opinions can be formed without denying either the shaping force of history or the identity and agency of the individual who is inserted into it.[5] Had he been aware of this possibility, Kafka's protagonist, according to Arendt, "would not have jumped out of the fighting line" and "be above the mêlée as the parable demands" (AB, 12). Arendt's hope is based on the possibility of creating a space of freedom from historical determination *within* history and compensating for the interrupted tradition with the development of a sphere in which the awareness of history makes political thinking possible. Whether Arendt thereby succeeds in going "a step further" than Kafka without, as she believes, "distorting [his] meaning" (AB, 11), is doubtful. Kafka's "he" is likely to have other dreams.

Does Kafka's nocturnal hope, as Arendt thinks, really consist of becoming an "umpire," a referee who can judge the opposing forces of past and future with a non-partisan eye? His original—and ultimately dismissed—text talks of a "judge" (*Richter*), not an umpire or referee. Unlike a referee, who always remains on the field of play and decides *between* the parties, Kafka's judge rises above both antagonists. His dream of leaping out of the line of battle does not imply a better epistemological point of observation, but another form of existence. Kafka's specification of an "unguarded moment" in a "night darker than any night has ever been yet" is absent in Arendt commentary. This night echoes Kafka's nocturnal "perhaps dangerous, perhaps redeeming" activity of writing, which, in his diary, he also describes as a "leap out of murderers' row" (D, 406) (*Totschlägerreihe*). Admittedly, Kafka, in this diary entry, again understands the perspective gained in this writing as a place "of a higher kind of observation," but this does not designate, as Arendt thinks, a place won by the capacity for neutral judgment, and hence another, no longer "thoughtless" attitude to history, but something else than history altogether. Arendt is not quite getting the measure of Kafka when she accuses him of holding on to the old, metaphysical dream of a leap out of history instead of creating a space of freedom *within* it.[6] Kafka's protagonist, hard-pressed by inexorable history, dreams the metaphysical dream, but meanwhile the writer Kafka himself is to be found in a room nearby, looking out onto a free space where he imagines emperors and messages, men and their dreams. It is the space of literature.

Both Arendt and Kafka aim at a realm "where freedom could appear." Yet, while Arendt, in what she calls thinking, still wants to hear, however indirectly, what the emperor would say, Kafka enacts the freedom of inventing possibilities that are disconnected from this narrow definition of the political realm. With Arendt's "step beyond" Kafka, the two seem to part ways. But this is "only theoretically so." In a letter from 1956 addressed to her husband, Heinrich Blüchner,

Arendt writes: "One of these days—when? It doesn't matter when, let's say at some point—I will be able to describe the actual domain of political life, because no one is better at marking the borders of a terrain than the person who walks around it from the outside" (in Baehr 2002, 4). Undoubtedly, even as she dreams of "jumping out of the fighting line," Arendt's gaze remains fixed on the public world, but, once out there, it is not unthinkable that on her walk she may encounter someone coming from the other direction who refuses to be inserted in time and prefers to think of "human history as a second between two steps of a wanderer" (Kafka 1977, 161).

If Arendt and Kafka were to meet, a gap would nevertheless remain between them. Kafka himself would hardly have let himself be placed in Arendt's parallelogram, where thinking goes "forward, in slow, ordered movements." Out of the "murderer's row" of history he jumps only with his "perhaps dangerous, perhaps saving comfort of writing" (D, 406). In "a night, dark as no night has ever been yet," where perhaps no light at all even suggests the exit, he imagines an exit and a light when the evening comes. When it grows dark, he sits by the window in a room adjoining history and writes imagined and transmissible stories that reach an uncommon community of readers with texts that, in the best case, generate new stories about messengers and messages, about the Emperor, and about the reigning figure of this book, Kafka himself.

Notes

Introduction

1. Further page references are given as D.
2. All translations, unless otherwise indicated, are mine.
3. For different approaches to this grouping and the corresponding definition of modern German-Jewish literature in recent scholarly works, see Gilman and Zipes 1997; Kilcher 2000; Gilman and Steinecke 2002; Lamping 1998; Witte 2007; for a recent important intervention in the field, see Gelber 2008, 165–84.
4. Kafka has been discussed in terms of both paradigms. While some critics situate him squarely in the continuum of Jewish writers, others minimize or even deny the relevance of his Jewish background for his work. See especially Haring 2001, 310–24. See also Baioni 1994, 9–11.
5. All translations, unless otherwise indicated, are mine.
6. Kilcher calls for a scholarly analysis of German-Jewish literature that would explore "the argumentative"—and, one ought to add, literary—"strategies of constructing and interpreting the irreducibly polyvalent intercultural space of German-Jewish literature in each particular writer, in each particular text" (1999, 511).
7. The persistence of this view into the twenty-first century is confirmed by Yuri Slezkine's book *The Jewish Century,* which starts with the provocative sentence "The Modern Age is the Jewish Age" and contends that "modernization," understood as "becoming urban, mobile, literate . . . flexible" is, "in other words, about everyone becoming Jewish" (Slezkine 2004, 1).

1. When Kafka Says We

1. The translators of the English edition of the *Diaries* have mistranslated the German original "Gemeinschaft" as "fellowship."
2. Gustav Janouch reports a remark Kafka supposedly made in one of their conversations. When Janouch asked, "You are so lonely?" Kafka nodded, and Janouch continued: "Like Kaspar Hauser?" Kafka laughed and replied, "Much worse than Kaspar Hauser. I am lonely—like Franz Kafka" (1968, 35).
3. Further page references are given as KSS.
4. Stanley Corngold rightly corrects an older English version in which the term "Reigen des Volkes" is wrongly translated as "a ring of brothers," which does not convey the

political dimension of the idyllic—suspiciously idyllic—union suggested in *Volk*. See Kafka 1976, 238.

5. For a similar reading, see Casanova 2004, 271.

6. Corngold corrects the older English translation by Willa and Edwin Muir which misses some crucial nuances: the German word "Volkskreis" is incorrectly rendered as "social circle," a translation that again obfuscates the political dimension of Kafka's text. Furthermore, the word "unwiderstehlich" (irresistibly), characterizing the force that drives the dog out of the circle, is translated as "as though by sheer force," a mistake also corrected by Corngold. See Kafka 2002b, 488. The Muirs' translation is found in Kafka 1976, 283.

7. Ritchie Robertson (1985, 156) interprets this passage as Kafka's suspicion and general critique of Catholicism and other religions that claim to be intermediaries between the individual and the divine and promise that confession will be rewarded by immediate forgiveness. The words "untersuchten, beurteilten" (analyzed, judged) indicate that this process is not necessarily limited to religious communities, but also includes communities based on scientific or legal foundations.

8. Further page references are given as KCS.

2. Shooting at the Audience

1. For references see "Speech on the Yiddish Language," below, from which this and all further quotations are taken (emphasis added).

2. Most recently, Pascale Casanova refers to this speech and describes Kafka's "whole literary enterprise as a monument raised to the glory of Yiddish" (2004, 269).

3. On the reception of Kafka's "Speech on Yiddish," see Bruce 2007, 6–7. Bruce, who defines her study's aim as an attempt "to lay out the formative influences [. . .] that led Kafka to become engaged in [cultural] Zionist activities," interprets the speech as a "tactically astute" means of conveying to his "enlightened" audience "a vision of self-regeneration through Yiddish" (2007, 47). This interpretation perfectly fits her impressively documented thesis about Kafka's interest in cultural Zionism and her intention to show "how much Kafka identified with other Jews and Jewish culture" (2007, 4), but it reduces the importance of the literary and rhetorical force of the speech to a mere means directed at a political end, the revival and strengthening of Jewish identity and culture. A different stance is taken by Bernhard Stiegert in a deconstructive reading of Kafka's speech. Stiegert equates the Yiddish language evoked by Kafka with "a process of geographic/linguistic deterritorialization" and a repressed and subversive threat *inside* the audience's own German language. However, Stiegert neglects the ambivalence in Kafka's own attitude toward Yiddish and his audience that he displays in the speech (Stiegert 1990, 225).

4. In light of Kafka's essay on minor literatures, in which Yiddish literature serves as a model for the literature of other small nations standing in the shadow of dominant ones, one might argue that Kafka's interest in Yiddish is driven by a desire to affirm a strong national identity. In this essay—a five-page diary entry written in 1911—Kafka indeed hails "the unity and solidarity [das einheitliche Zusammenhalten] of national consciousness" whence arises "the pride and support which the nation gains for itself in the face of a hostile environment" (D, 114). Stanley Corngold rightly remarks that this point is "by no means easily assimilated in a contemporary climate favoring the fragmentation of integral personality, the radical entitlement of what is left, and the cultivation of difference" (2004, 149). However, according to Corngold, Kafka also points out the limitations in scope and quality when literature is put into the service of a strengthening of national identity (2004, 155–56).

3. An Alliance of Foes

1. See also Torton Beck 1983, 567.

2. Further page references given as LW. Some quotations have been slightly modified.

3. See Stanley Corngold's convincing description and analysis of this movement in Kafka's writing as "chiastic recursion" (Corngold 2004, see *inter alia* 125).

4. On gesture in Kafka see Benjamin 2002b, 802, 808; Adorno 1955, 248–49; Agamben 2000, 49–62; Corngold 2004, 173.

4. A Vision out of Sight

1. Robert Alter, quoted in Joseph Lowin, "Basket Case Yehuda Amichai's 'Tourists,'" http://www.google.be/search?q=cache:wOFgwmbhKSwJ:www.ivrit.org/html/literary/tourists.htm+Amichai+Robert+Alter+roman+arch&hl=en&ie=UTF-8, accessed 17 March 2004.

2. Further page references are given as T.

3. On 2 May 1901, a disillusioned Herzl wrote in his diary: "Today I am forty-one years old [. . .]. Almost six years ago I started this movement that made me old, tired, and poor" (1976, 189).

4. Theodor Herzl, *Feuilletons;* the four tales are quoted here from the second volume of the third edition of 1921: "Epaphroditus," 1900, "Däumerle und Bäumerle oder die Zukunft," 1902, "Die linke Glocke," 1901, "Die Brille," 1902. Further page references are given as F.

5. See the postface to Brude-Firnau 1976, 283–344.

6. A clear proof is Herzl's reference to the battle of Fidentia, literally taken from Plutarch's "Life of Sylla [*sic*]." Plutarch writes that Sulla "dared to face fifty cohorts of the enemy with only sixteen of his own" and was "crowned by flowers blown by a gentle gale of wind [. . .] from the neighboring meadows" on the "shields and helmets" that gave the soldiers "the appearance of being crowned with chaplets." This is echoed verbatim in Herzl's story, where Sulla remembers the "days of Fidentia [. . .] when you were only sixteen cohorts at the seige of Fidentia, facing fifty cohorts of the enemy" upon which a "gentle wind blew flowers onto the helmets and shields" (250). See http://ancienthistory.about.com/library/bl/bl_textplutarch_sylla.htm, accessed 17 March 2004.

5. Diverting the Lineage

1. These aspects of the legend have been brought into question before. Angelika Koch (1971, esp. 25), for example, attempts to free Lasker-Schüler "from the myth of naive childishness," but her interpretation of Lasker-Schüler's motif of play as a sign of inner emigration does not reach far enough; Sigrid Bauschinger reveals the emotional ardor in Max Herrmann-Neiss's homage to Lasker-Schüler as "mater dolorosa and holy Miriam," as a "Circe of religious transfiguration" (Bauschinger 1980, 318) ("Circe der Verklärung"); Dieter Bänsch's (1971) critique of the "established image" of the poet is entirely directed at exposing the myth of Lasker-Schüler as figure of reconciliation and redemption.

2. Else Lasker-Schüler, *Hebräische Balladen,* first published in 1913. All the poems are quoted from Lasker-Schüler 1980. Further page references are given as HB.

3. Meir Gertner, for example, describes the biblical figures in the *Hebrew Ballads* as bearers of a "solemn and exalted vision" (1969, 177).

4. See, for example, Klaus Weissenberger, for whom the poet's messages of love and healing are indeed feminine, but in whose view the poet requires male identifications in order to lend her messages sufficient potency, as it is this that enables transcendence and the realization of exaltation. He speaks, for example, about the "male powers of mental collection and the female powers of intuitive surrender" in Lasker-Schüler's poetry. His interpretations of the poems of the *Hebrew Ballads* emphasize such clichés of the feminine—capacity for devotion, experience of suffering, and inwardness—without critical reflection, and form the matrix of a "basic structure of feminine imaginative force" (1983, 202). Mary-Elizabeth O'Brien's article "Ich war verkleidet als Poet, ich bin Poetin" (1992), unlike Weissenberger's, is intended to represent a feminist approach, yet O'Brien repeats nearly verbatim Weissenberger's presumption that Lasker-Schüler attempted to overcome the powerlessness and inferiority of her femininity by way of identification with male personae.

5. This is the poem's final version. In the interpretation presented here only one of the differences in relation to the earlier version is taken into account.

6. In the Bible story, Saul is not Abigail's father; he becomes her father-in-law after David takes her as his wife out of gratitude.

7. The poem "Abraham and Isaak," which recounts this event, ends with the verses "And carried the only son bound to his back / To be faithful to his great lord— / But he loved his servant."

8. Karl Jürgen Skrodzki, one of the editors of the critical edition of Lasker-Schüler's collected works, argues that it is less their biblical content than their worldview that characterizes these poems as "Hebraic": "Weniger ihr biblischer Inhalt als vielmehr die Weltsicht des lyrischen Subjekts weist die Gedichte als 'hebräische' aus." http://www.kj-skrodzki.de/Dokumente/Text_012.htm, accessed 24 January 2008. Similarly, Marina Krug (2000) situates Lasker-Schüler's *Hebrew Ballads* in the context of a "Jewish Renaissance" and cultural Zionism. Such readings, which place these poems squarely into the Jewish tradition, risk neglecting the rebelliousness and syncretism of these poems.

6. Saving Confusions

1. Sigrid Bauschinger, quoted in *Frankfurter Allgemeine Zeitung,* 29 October 1993, 35.

2. Jakob Hessing, quoted in *Frankfurter Allgemeine Zeitung,* 29 October 1993, 35.

3. References to *Die Nächte* are to the first edition: Lasker-Schüler 1907. All translations, unless otherwise indicated, are mine. Further page references are given as N.

4. Some recent studies still insist on Lasker-Schüler's conciliatory attitude. A recent analysis of the function of biblical references in her work describes it as a "utopian and optimistic call for reconciliation" ("utopisch-hoffnungsvoller Versöhnungsappell") directed at Jews and Christians. This view omits the provocative and blasphemous, occasionally even aggressive, aspects of her work and the specific kind of community—comprising the young, the artists, the strangers—that is united here against those who invoke the authority of the Bible in a more traditional sense. See Hennek-Weischer 2007.

5. The period between 1907 and 1914 following the publication of *The Nights* is regarded as her most productive time, when she was also part of Berlin bohemian life and indeed one of its central figures. The time when *The Nights* was being written corresponds to the early years of her break with her bourgeois environment and, even more than the later works, conveys a liberating transgressiveness.

6. Here one may be reminded of the later polemical essay by Lasker-Schüler, "Ich

räume auf!" (I'm clearing up), in which she accuses her publishers of selling out their authors and attacks the principle of patronage. There she writes: "We poets who daily rise up with the oppressed of every class are and remain small-minded in the face of our own fate. We are only demanding what is necessary in order to maintain the treasure that has been entrusted to us, let us call it reprieve. Especially as getting rich, as the example shows, all too often means complete impoverishment" (1986, 313). And: "It would do us as artists, that is, all poets and writers, good to take a deep breath! We can get what we want. Let us organize ourselves like the workers, put our art under public control. Our art doesn't belong to moneybags, it belongs to mankind" (1986, 325).

7. In Hebrew script Balak can also be read as Baloch. It is Balak who orders Balaam's curse, which the latter transforms into a blessing.

8. The poem "Elbanaff" is preceded by Lasker-Schüler's comments that her early poems were written in a "primordial language (*Ursprache*) from the time of Saul, the royal wild Jew. I still can speak this language which I probably breathed in my dreams. My poem Weltflucht is written in this mystical Asiatic language" (1986, 350).

9. It can be assumed that Lasker-Schüler knew Hugo von Hofmannsthal's "Chandos Letter," which was published in the Berlin periodical *Der Tag* in 1902. The alleged loss of speech of the "Grand Mogul of Philippopel" is possibly a direct reference to this text, in which Lord Chandos laments about having lost the ability "to think or speak coherently about anything." The context, too, in which Lord Chandos finds himself in a linguistic crisis is similar to that of the Grand Mogul. So Lord Chandos writes: "I found it inwardly impossible to utter any judgment about affairs of the Court, occurrences in Parliament or anything else whatsoever." Does Lasker-Schüler, with her speech-robbing insect, take Lord Chandos's complaint at its word when he writes: "[D]ie Worte lassen mich wiederum im Stich?" (The words desert me again). A literal translation might be, "The words leave me in the lurch again": the German word *Stich* here also means "sting" or "bite." Hugo von Hofmannsthal, quoted in Karthaus 1977, 146–48. In her "novel" *Mein Herz*, Lasker-Schüler is sharply critical of Hofmannsthal's play *Jedermann* (Everyman).

7. A Counter-Prayer

1. Further page references are given as CG.

2. "In Front of a Candle," *Poems of Paul Celan: A Bilingual German English Edition*, trans. Michael Hamburger (New York: Persea Books, 2002), 55. The translation has been slightly adjusted.

3. Definitions of *beschwören* in *Bedeutungswörterbuch* (Mannheim: Dudenverlag, 1970), 121: "*Beschwören*: 1. beeiden: seine Aussagen (vor Gericht) beschwören [to affirm by oath; to swear to one's statements (in court)]; 2. eindringlich bitten [to implore, entreat]; 3. durch Zauber Gewalt erlangen [to achieve power through magic]."

4. Translation here taken, slightly altered, from Celan 2001, 401–13. Further page and volume references to Celan's *Gesammelte Werke* are given as CGW.

5. *Gebete der Israeliten* (Frankfurt, 1974), 429.

6. "The Menorah," *Encyclopedia Judaica* (1974, 11:1368), s.v. "Kabbalah."

7. See Celan's Bremer Prize Speech, CGW, 3:185.

8. The tower and the dove may also allude to Hölderlin.

9. *Gebete der Israeliten*, 423; emphasis added.

10. "Isaiah describes mourners as beating their breasts." *Encyclopedia Judaica* (1974, 7:486).

11. *Encyclopedia Judaica* (1974, 11:630; emphasis added), s.v. "Kabbalah."

8. Roots against Heaven

1. The German word *Pappel,* poplar, is derived from the Latin *populus.* André Gide (1927), in his contribution to *La Querelle du peuplier,* consistently refers to this etymology. Although it is not certain that the actual etymology of *Pappel* derives from the meaning of *populus,* people, it is clear that Celan plays on this link. In one of his notes to the "Meridian" speech, Celan writes, "Es gibt auch dieses Etymon: nicht als das vom längst nicht mehr sichtbaren, nicht von der Wurzel abgeleitete, sondern das am Zweig wahrgenommene" (1999, 106) (There is also this kind of etymological link: not what is derived from a no longer visible root, but what is perceived from the branch).

2. See Hamacher 1988, 81–126. Hamacher's important essay carries the analysis of the figure of inversion in Celan's poetry to its most radical conclusion and demonstrates that the inversion enacted in Celan's poetry incessantly performs its own defeat. It is no coincidence that Hamacher devotes a considerable part of his analysis to Celan's poem "Radix, Matrix," in which the root metaphor plays a central role.

3. In several preliminary notes to the "Meridian" speech touching on the topic of Jewishness and remembrance, Celan thematizes the encounter with the "eye" of the witness as the viewpoint defying all recuperation. In some of these notes he evokes this "eye" in very different terms from those of the poem that associates it with "Adel," with aristocratic nobility. In one of these notes Celan explicitly writes that the one who mourns only for the beauty of this eye, "kills it anew." Instead, "den Krummnasigen, Kielkröpfigen, den Einwohnern der stinkenden Judengassen, den Mauschel-Mäulern—ihrer gedenkt das gerade Gedicht—das Hohe Lied" (1999, 127). The discrepancy between this unusual evocation of anti-Semitic stereotypes in the notes Celan neither used nor published, and the insistence on the eye's nobility in the published poem possibly reveal Celan's fear that these images of the Jews as "crooked-nosed creatures" could be misunderstood or misused when brought out into the open.

9. The Voice of Israel

1. The Swedish writer Selma Lagerlöf intervened with the Swedish royal family on her behalf. Sachs and her mother finally escaped on one of the last flights leaving Nazi Germany for Sweden, a week before Sachs was scheduled to be deported.

2. See also: "As [my poetry] happens in order to make the voice of Israel heard, I am happy" (Sachs 1984, 72); "Because it is considered a voice of my people, I am happy" (Sachs 1984, 68); and many similar statements.

3. This also gave rise to statements such as the following: "God himself must have guided the author's pencil so that she may bear witness for her people." Quotation from an article published in *Kasseler Zeitung* in 1947, in Fritsch-Vivié 1993, 90.

4. Ehrhard Bahr writes that Sachs's poetry before 1943 was described as "neo-Romantic," a poetry that "consciously avoids the surrealist and expressionist tendencies of contemporary art and instead resorts in imagery and form to the traditional canon of German Romanticism" (Bahr, 1980, 41).

5. Domin explicitly refers to the "great catharsis" (in Aichinger et al. 1961, 192).

6. Letter to Nelly Sachs from 4 November 1966. In Frisch-Vivié 1993, 91.

7. Nelly Sachs herself repeatedly referred to her own work in a similar way. However, Franz Josef Kuschel quite rightly remarks that Sachs's "letters and poems are two different kinds of texts," and her poetic texts shouldn't be reduced to "the [. . .] illustration of what

has long since been established even without her poetry: [. . .] that she believed in God, Israel and love" (1994, 204).

8. "The voice of this poetry, almost disembodied because of the absence of a lyric I, lacks the concrete accusation, the question of individual responsibility and the awareness of guilt associated with it" (in Dinesen 1985b, 136).

9. Enzensberger 1959, 770–75. Here quoted from Aichinger et al. 1961, 50.

10. Lermen 1995, 47–63.

11. Numerous critics, and Sachs herself, have pointed out this development from a Jewish identification in her earlier work—mainly her first collections of poetry written after the war, *In den Wohnungen des Todes* (1947) and *Sternverdunklung* (1949)—toward a general human orientation in the poetry of her later years. On 25 August 1959 Sachs wrote in a letter to Johannes Edfelt: "The destiny of my people is simply attached to my name, and even though the last two collections of poetry have long meant all of mankind—the 'Dwellings' have not been forgotten" (1984, 228). "Dwellings" refers to *In den Wohnungen des Todes* (In the Dwellings of Death).

12. In some instances, this articulates itself in the most hackneyed clichés of German romanticism, as in the poem "Chorus of the Wanderers": "Behind it the doe, the orphan-eyed Israel among the animals / Disappears into its murmuring forest / And the lark re-joices above the golden fields" (Sachs 1988, 52).

13. Ruth Dinesen explicitly refers to her "Jewish Poetry" and reads these poems as manifestation of Sachs's newly gained "Jewish identity" (in Bathi and Fries 1996, 32).

14. This gatherer of traces is related to Benjamin's rag-picker, who, in a messianic gesture, wants to resurrect the dead of history by gathering the remnants of a previous, destroyed time (Benjamin 1999, 349–50).

15. Possibly the reversed writing in the mirror is an allusion to Hebrew, read from right to left, which is to be recognized in the mirror reflection of the German poem.

16. Celan began to take an interest in Nelly Sachs's poems in 1953.

17. He continues: "Nelly Sachs, a daughter of the Berlin bourgeoisie, probably also worked on this machinery of idealization in which the Wilhelmine bourgeoisie translated esoteric and hermetic traditions into a kind of Gnostic idealism of cleansing which raises up, per aspera ad astra, from the dark matter of dust to the redeeming light of the stars" (1996, 353).

18. For an outstanding interpretation, see West 1996, 77–104, esp. 100.

19. See Geoffrey Hartman's elucidating interpretation of the star motif in Sachs's and Celan's poetry. Hartman distinguishes Sachs's simultaneously religious *and* historic meaning of the star, which is nevertheless based on traditional nature symbolism, from Celan's image of the star as a product of poetry, "the work of human hands," "an artificial, hopeful, tactile, verbal compound." Sachs "barely suspends the childlike expectation for a redemptive crowning event. For Celan there is no pattern that goes from figure to fulfillment, or toward a truth (*Wahrsagung*) that transcends language." In light of the final verse of "Voice of the Holy Land," however, this distinction may well be less significant than Hartman assumes (1996, 14–15).

20. Celan and Lestrange 2001, 205.

21. Celan and Lestrange 2001, 205.

10. A Broken Ring

1. This situation changed in the 1990s with the publication of several important studies about the attitude of the German literary and cultural establishment toward Jewish

writers in the aftermath of the war. See, for example, Briegleb 1997; Briegleb 2002; Braese 2005.

2. Further page references given as AE.

3. Briegleb also mentions Peter Weiss in this context. Weiss, who in *Meine Ortschaft* (1964) dealt with the Frankfurter Auschwitz trials, had, according to Briegleb, been chided "aus der Mitte der Gruppe heraus" (from within the core of the group) (1997, 32).

4. Urs Widmer shows in his article "So kahl war der Kahlschlag nicht" that there were more than traces of national socialist language in the early writings of the group. With significant irony he describes how later on Hans Werner Richter, Wolfdietrich Schnurre, Heinrich Böll, und Alfred Andersch were "cleaning out" the German language. The ambivalence of this activity, captured in Widmer's tone, becomes particularly evident when it is compared to those writers who, like Paul Celan, felt that they needed to forever inscribe into language the "world-historical wound" (Stéphane Mosès).

5. "[E]ine geschlossene Form, die Rückgewinnung des heilenden Erzählens, mit dessen Hilfe man sich zu neuer Werthaftigkeit vorzutasten hoffte" (Arnold 1980, 57).

6. In 1965 Rolf Schroers described the group's reaction to Celan's reading in the following terms: "Paul Celan's visionary diction did not fit the style of the group, his bathos seemed inappropriate" (in Lettau 1967, 384). See also Briegleb's detailed description of H. W. Richter's attempts to keep Celan away from the group, in Briegleb 1997, 51–54. Some of the members appreciated Celan's poems, called them "*poésie pure*," and praised the power of his language and the precision of his images (Lettau, 1967, 76).

7. "Man lud beispielsweise die Emigranten nicht ein, die das später sehr beklagten und dachten, die Gruppe 47 sei gar antisemitisch. Man lud aber auch die älteren deutschen Autoren nicht ein. Richter wäre nie auf die Idee gekommen, sagen wir mal, den Ernst Jünger [. . .] einzuladen, die ja weiß Gott auch zur deutschen Literatur gehörten." Interview with J. Kaiser in the catalogue of the Deutscher Taschenbuch Verlag, 1997, 3.

8. "Ganz emphatisch gesagt: In der Gruppe 47 trafen sich zeitgeschichtlich geschlagene Leute, die . . . vielleicht noch beim Arbeitsdienst waren, oder Soldat und sich—wenn sie Glück hatten—in Kriegsgefangenenlagern in Amerika wiedertrafen" (ibid.). Briegleb mentions the banalization ("Verharmlosungs-Politik") of issues related to the Nazi past in an article written by Joachim Kaiser in 1962 ("Ein Sturm im Wasserglas"—"A Storm in a Glass of Water") following a discussion about a play by an ex-Nazi poet ("[Diskussion über] was dagegen spreche, das Pro und Contra zur Inszenierung des Dramas eines Ex-Nazidichters mit einem pro-Artikel zu eröffnen" (1997, 61–62).

9. Briegleb writes that Richter himself masked his own past: "Richter selbst ging voran, nicht nur seine Fragebogen–Biographie ist entsprechend geschönt" (Richter himself went ahead, not only his [de-nazification]-forms were embellished appropriately). He refers to Schutte 1988 (Briegleb 1997, 75).

10. At fifteen, Grass volunteered for the submarine corps but was not accepted. Two years later he was enlisted in the Waffen SS and was happy to oblige. Grass made this confession public in 2006, over sixty years after the facts. Briegleb, who published his book-length study about the *Gruppe 47* in 2002, could not have known about Grass's participation in the SS, but he does count him among the younger generation of the *Gruppe 47* who paid lip service to anti-fascism but did not truly face the Nazi crimes or their own past.

11. Martin Walser declared after the readings of Aichinger, Celan, and Bachmann in 1952 that modern literature in post-war Germany had started with these texts. It may not be a coincidence that the ways in which these authors inscribed the Holocaust into the language of literature coincided with certain anti-realistic developments in modernism.

II. After the Silence

1. "Ein verpflichtendes, aber kein verschlingendes Verhältnis [zur Vergangenheit]" (Schindel 1992, 300). Further page references given as SG. Whenever possible, the quotations from Schindel's *Gebürtig* are taken from *Born-Where,* the English translation by Michael Roloff. Most of the time, however, they had to be considerably modified. Roloff translates "verpflichtend" as "dutiful" instead of "committed" or "responsible." He thereby mistakenly adds a negative connotation to Schindel's term. See Schindel 1995a. Further references to the Roloff translation given as SBW.

2. Elfriede Jelinek's novel *Die Kinder der Toten* (Children of the Dead) features "Untote," souls that cannot find rest and that embody a past that has never been fully faced. In the afterword to *Born-Where,* the English translation of *Gebürtig,* Michael Roloff calls Schindel's book a "generational novel of ghosts" (SBW, 288).

3. In his essay "Schweigend ins Gespräch vertieft," Schindel writes: "Daher kann es keine Normalität geben."

4. In his autobiographical sketch "The Two Lives of Paul Celan," Schindel retraces his own development away from a realist and explicit mode of writing toward a more elliptic and elusive one. In the same text, Schindel describes the impact of Celan on his own writing, but also his own path toward a different form of "indirectness" (2004, 125).

5. Further page references given as RS.

6. "Man soll die Antisemiten doch statieren lassen. Sollen sie nicht anderthalb Stunden, sondern, sagen wir, drei Stunden so sitzen und stehen bei Minus zweiundzwanzig Grad. Andererseits, wenn die frieren, werden Unsereins doch nicht erwärmt, damals nicht, und heut tut's ein Tee auch" (SG 352). Roloff translates the last sentence of this passage as: "On the other hand, if we freeze, our kind still won't warm up, not then and not today—the tea won't do it either." This translation conveys the exact opposite of the original. See SBW, 284.

7. "Ich bist du, wenn du im Nichtich bist" (SG, 48). Roloff misses the point when he translates "Ich bist du" as "I am you" (SBW, 36).

8. Further page references given as ME. All translations mine.

I2. Jewish Voices, Human Tone

1. "Is there a Jewish voice in Europe?" Quoted from http://www.paideia.eu.com.
2. See Iris Radisch, "Reden im Eden," in *Die Zeit,* 4 October 2001, 10.

I3. Of Language and Destiny

1. See Celan's last letter to Ilana Schmueli of 12 April 1970, written six days before his death (Schmueli and Sparr 2004, 140).

2. The most important early studies on traces of Kafka in Celan's work are Perels 1973; Sparr 1988; Colin 1986; and Günzel 1995; Amir Eshel (2002) discusses the Kafka-Celan relationship with respect to Hebrew and Yiddish; Dieter Lamping's book (1998) about Jewish-German authors of the twentieth century bears both names in its title, but he is more concerned to indicate a period of time or a literary epoch than to establish direct links between the two writers. The most fertile and reliable secondary source of numerous references to Kafka in Celan's work is the commentary-appendix by Barbara Wiedemann in Celan 2003.

3. "Eine kaiserliche Botschaft" (An Imperial Message), in Kafka 2002e, 280–82. (Not marked by Celan in his edition of Kafka's *Beim Bau der chinesischen Mauer* [The Great Wall of China].)

4. Marked by Celan with a stroke in the margin in Kafka, *Tagebücher 1910–1923*, ed. Max Brod (New York: Fischer Verlag, 1951), 585.

5. From "Ich sehe nur Verfall" (I see only decline) to "erregt" (stirs us) is marked with a single stroke in the margin; from "Hie und da hören wir" (Here and there we catch) to "Last der Jahrhunderte" (the weight of centuries upon us) is marked with triple strokes in the margin. At the lower edge of the same page: "x Vorbilder? Welche?" (models? Which?), and below that, "x Schlüssel zu Kafka selbst?" (Key to Kafka himself?). Kafka, "Forschungen eines Hundes," in *Beim Bau der chinesischen Mauer* (The Great Wall of China), ed. Max Brod and Hans Joachim Schoeps (Berlin: Kiepenheuer, 1948), 177. See KSS, 148.

6. Marked with a bracket in the margin in Kafka, *Beschreibungen eines Kampfes: Novellen Skizzen Aphorismen aus dem Nachlass* (Description of a Struggle: Posthumous Novellas Sketches Aphorisms), ed. Max Brod (New York: Schocken Books, 1946 [1936]), 102. See KCS, 228.

7. Remark in the margin in Kafka, "Der Jäger Gracchus," in *Beschreibungen eines Kampfes: Novellen Skizzen Aphorismen aus dem Nachlass* (Description of a Struggle: Posthumous Novellas Sketches Aphorisms), ed. Max Brod (New York: Schocken Books, 1946 [1936]), at the bottom of 104: "cf. letters from Riva to Brod and Weltsch!" Beside the letter to Max Brod, 28 September 1913, from the sanatorium, once "Jäger G." (Hunter G.), beside "In comparison to that nothing is of importance and I am really only travelling around in these caves." And once "J. Gr." (H. Gr.) with an arrow from the sentence "I cannot live with it (reality) and I cannot live without it." In Kafka, *Briefe 1902–1924*, ed. Max Brod (New York: Schocken Books, 1975), 122. On the same page under the first sentence of the letter to Felix Weltsch of September 1913, likewise from the sanatorium in Riva, written out in full: "Jäger Gracchus" (Hunter Gracchus). Strokes in the margin also in Kafka, *Hochzeitsvorbereitungen auf dem Lande* (Wedding Preparations in the Country), ed. Max Brod (New York: Schocken Books, 1953), 81; in the Third Octave Notebook, triple strokes in the margin from "Ein erstes Zeichen beginnender Erkenntnis" (A first sign of initial knowledge) to "Er kommt zu mir" (He comes to me).

8. Kafka, "Vom Scheintod," in *Beim Bau der chinesischen Mauer* (The Great Wall of China), ed. Max Brod and Hans Joachim Schoeps (Berlin: Kiepenheuer, 1948); at the bottom of 433: "Jäger Gracchus?" (Hunter Gracchus?).

9. In northern German towns in the late medieval period *fehme*-courts were from time to time instituted outside the normal legal procedures. The accused faced judges who were masked and therefore anonymous. It was a kind of formalized lynch law—subsequently praised by the Nazis as an expression of popular justice.

10. See Celan's line "Weisst du noch, dass ich sang" (Do you still remember, that I sang), in his poem "Bei Wein und Verlorenheit" (CG, 126). See also Celan's statement "Auch musiziere ich nicht mehr wie zur Zeit der Todesfuge" (in Hamacher and Menninghaus 1988, 320) (Nor do I make music any more as I did at the time of Fugue of Death).

11. It is noteworthy that Kafka published his first eight prose works in *Hyperion*, a bimonthly literary journal published in Munich between 1908 and 1910.

12. This storm, it is said, "not only snapped all the trees [. . .] it uprooted everything, tore everything down which stood in its way [. . .] until there was nothing left that resisted it. But for one tree, a powerful stag moss, 115 feet high, which remained standing, everything else was leveled to the ground [. . .]. The smashed trees lying on the ground around it suffocated all life beneath them, rotted, [. . .] poisoning the soil, so that any kind of vegetation

became impossible. Rainfalls washed this sludge away, the earth eroded, more was washed away, until only the bare rock was left." See http://www.museumderunerhoertendinge.de/dinge/baum/stein.htm, accessed 24 October 2004.

13. Marked by Celan with a stroke in the margin. The passage continues: "Yes, that is the burden of my complaint; that is the kernel of it. Where are they? Everywhere and nowhere? Perhaps my next-door neighbor, only three jumps away, he calls on me sometimes [. . .]. Is he my real colleague?" Next to this sentence there is the marginal comment "Brod." In Kafka, *Beim Bau der chinesischen Mauer* (The Great Wall of China), ed. Max Brod and Hans Joachim Schoeps (Berlin: Kiepenheuer, 1948), 175. See KSS, 147.

14. "Born from wordblood" can also refer to the words used by Kafka to express his affinity and bond with his own precursors: "I consider Grillparzer, Dostoevsky, Kleist and Flaubert to be my true blood-relations" (1982, 460).

15. In the earliest detailed discussion of the poem Christoph Perel emphasizes "the trial nature of my efforts" (1973, 58). In an essay that appeared as late as 1988 Thomas Sparr, for whom the poem "Frankfurt, September" is the only poem which contains "exogenous traces of Celan's reception of Kafka," stresses that there is "something provisional, a lack of hard knowledge" about his paper (1988, 141). Even Rainer Nägele, who presents a rich interpretation of the poem, writes: "We can only speculate as to what Celan knew about these relationships [the Freud-inspired father-son relations he had uncovered] when he wrote the poem," yet his apology is much less modest than those of other interpreters and he concludes with a polemic against philological decodings in general: "as all literary criticism, which explains the literary text by way of the inferred motivations and intentions of the author, can ultimately only produce simile-jackdaws." This legitimation of his own speculative approach causes him, however, to give up too quickly: "The fact, that this particular jackdaw is breakfasting, displaces it to the end of a night about which we know nothing" (1987, 237–65). Meanwhile we know more.

16. Marked by triple strokes in the margin in Kafka, "Betrachtungen über Sünde, Leid, Hoffnung und den wahren Weg" (Reflections on Sin, Suffering, Hope and the True Way), in *Beim Bau der chinesischen Mauer* (The Great Wall of China), ed. Max Brod and Hans Joachim Schoeps (Berlin: Kiepenheuer, 1948), 232.

17. According to Barbara Wiedemann, "Simili-Dohle" is borrowed from "Simili-Burkhardt," an expression Celan found in a work by the novelist Albert Vigoleis Thelen (CG, 752).

18. See Sparr 1988, 142. Sparr refers to a dream dreamt by Raban in Kafka's *Hochzeitsvorbereitungen auf dem Lande* (Wedding Preparations in the Country), 10.

19. See the passage marked by Celan in *Der Hungerkünstler* (The Hunger Artist), 34; see also Barbara Wiedemann's commentary in CG, 752.

20. Kafka, *Hochzeitsvorbereitungen auf dem Lande* (Wedding Preparations in the Country), 12 (not marked by Celan). See KCS, 56.

21. See commentary by Wiedemann in CG, 752.

22. Some of the sources in the Eddas describe these goddesses as guides of the dead. See http://www.aberhallo.de/lexikon/index.php/Dise, accessed 12 July 2004.

23. Kafka, *Beim Bau der chinesischen Mauer* (The Great Wall of China), 222, marked by Celan with a double stroke in the margin.

14. A Permanent Shadow

1. Aichinger is quoting from Kafka 1958, 29.
2. Further page references given as KGB.

3. Further page references given as SW.

4. Aichinger writes in her speech that she learned of Kafka's existence "shortly after the end of the war" and refers indirectly to the point in time when she read the passage with the words "just then, when I had escaped the hangmen of this world" (1991d, 104).

5. In the slightly altered version of the "balcony scene" in "Gespräch mit dem Beter" (Conversation with the Praying Man) Kafka has added after the reply of the neighbor, "I'm having a snack on the grass," the sentence: "They said it *without thinking* and not very loudly, as if anyone should have expected it" (KGB, 14; emphasis added).

6. Foucault's "deconstruction of the revolutionary," Peter von Matt writes in *Verkommene Söhne, missratene Töchter,* "describes exactly the diffuse profile of resistance of children around the toppled father" (1995, 335).

15. The Gap between Hannah Arendt and Kafka

1. Further page references are given as AB.

2. For Arendt the "gap in time" is a dimension of the temporality of thinking in general, but it became a question of political significance in modernity when it no longer concerned a small elite of thinkers but each and every individual.

3. Arendt quotes this text from the translation by Willa and Edwin Muir in *The Great Wall of China* (New York: Schocken Books, 1946), adding that she slightly adapted the translation where she deemed it necessary to do so. In a footnote she adds the original German text (AB, 283).

4. In Kafka's manuscript the text stops after "[. . .] his intentions?" The rest of the parable quoted by Arendt has been crossed out by Kafka. The edition consulted by Arendt— and all the previous editions of the *Diaries* before the Fischer edition of 2002—follow Max Brod's reinsertion of this continuation. The passage can be found in the "apparatus" volume of the Fischer edition, which describes the material shape of the manuscripts (2002d, 398). I am grateful to Stanley Corngold for sharing this discovery with me.

5. In a later chapter from *Between Past and Future* entitled "Truth and Politics" Arendt describes what the "gap between past and future" makes possible when it is imagined as a space generating thinking as its own, "third" force. This force results from a process in which man, faced with history and its inevitable, "tyrannical nature of factual truth," can nevertheless find his own position thanks to the process that is set in motion through the insertion of what is "most his own" into the flow of historical time. "This process," Arendt writes, "does not blindly adopt the actual views of those who stand somewhere else and hence look upon the world from a different perspective, nor of counting noses and joining a majority, *but of being and thinking in my own identity where actually I am not*" (AB, 241; emphasis added). These lines powerfully articulate a position that neither acclaims nor dismisses "identity." The space of thinking harbors the conditions that allow me to transport my own, particular interests and concerns elsewhere, to a place "where I am not." As a result, my viewpoint will be neither independent of what I carry with me from the past— history as well as my specific background and origins, that which makes up what is "most my own," nor is it determined by it. Rather, this viewpoint is the result of the journey that my self has undergone on its way to "elsewhere."

6. In the passages crossed out by Kafka, the end of the parable comes in two versions and shows multiple hesitations. In the words of Stanley Corngold this "shows Kafka wrestling with the precise formulation of the sentence he ultimately rejected. Kafka's adjustments aim to attenuate the idea that these are *his* 'opponents, battling one another' by referring to them only as 'the' opponents, battling one another." Corngold's point is

crucial because it situates Kafka's protagonist outside and above the battle line. Corngold continues: "In a word, if any story might be drawn from Kafka's semantic and syntactical battle with his thought, he could not decide how high above the contestants he ought to locate the agency of elevation—is it an affair of his elevating himself over his opponents or an affair of a merciful intervention from above judging him qualified to be raised up above (the) opponents?" Corngold's conclusion that "this battle has to be regarded as itself undecided" is utterly convincing. Arendt's critical comment on this sentence nevertheless remains an important reflection on Kafka's thought despite Kafka's having finally dismissed it. It is possible (but in no way certain) that he was motivated by scruples similar to Arendt's when he crossed out the "dream" of "jumping out" of history. Kafka's hesitation reveals that this issue may have been one of his interior "battle lines" and therefore should not be disregarded. I thank Stanley Corngold for allowing me to quote him verbatim from a private communication (31 October 2007).

Bibliography

Adorno, Theodor W. 1955. "Aufzeichnungen zu Kafka." In *Prismen: Kulturkritik und Gesellschaft,* 248–49. Frankfurt am Main: Suhrkamp.

———. 1981. "Rede über Lyrik und Gesellschaft." In *Noten zur Literatur,* ed. Rolf Tiedemann, 49–68. Frankfurt am Main: Suhrkamp.

Agamben, Giorgio. 1993. *The Coming Community.* Minneapolis: University of Minnesota Press.

———. 2000. "Notes on Gesture." In *Means without End.* Minneapolis: University of Minnesota Press.

Aichinger, Ilse. 1978. "Meine Sprache und ich." In *Meine Sprache und ich: Erzählungen,* 219–22. Frankfurt am Main: Fischer Verlag.

———. 1991a. "Der Engel." In *Eliza, Eliza: Erzählungen 2 (1958–1968),* 113–21. Frankfurt am Main: Fischer Verlag.

———. 1991b. "Das Erzählen in dieser Zeit." In *Der Gefesselte,* 9–11. Frankfurt am Main: Fischer Verlag.

———. 1991c. *Der Gefesselte.* Frankfurt am Main: Fischer Verlag.

———. 1991d. "Die Zumutung des Atmens." In *Kleist, Moos, Fasane,* 102–107. Frankfurt am Main: Fisher Verlag.

———. 1991e. "Zweifel an Balkonen." In *Schlechte Wörter,* 19–25. Frankfurt am Main: Fischer Verlag.

Aichinger, Ilse, et al. 1961. *Nelly Sachs zu Ehren: Gedichte, Prosa, Beiträge.* Frankfurt am Main: Suhrkamp.

Amichai, Yehuda. 1967. "Tourists." In *Jerusalem 1967.* See http://www.google.be/search?q=cache:wOFgwmbhKSwJ:www.ivrit.org/html/literary/tourists.htm+Amichai+Robert+Alter+roman+arch&hl=en&ie=UTF-8, accessed 17 March 2004.

Arendt, Hannah. 1968. *Between Past and Future.* New York: Viking Press.

———. 1978. *The Jew as Pariah: Jewish Identity and Politics in the Modern Age.* New York: Grove Press.

Arnold, Heinz Ludwig. 1995. "Schlechte Wörter." In *Ilse Aichinger: Leben und Werk,* ed. Samuel Moser, 255–59. Frankfurt am Main: Fischer Verlag.

———, ed. 1980. *Die Gruppe 47.* Munich: Text und Kritik.

Avineri, Schlomo. 1999. "Theodor Herzl's Diaries as a Bildungsroman." *Jewish Social Studies* 5, no. 3: 1–46.

Bachelard, Gaston. 1984. *La Flamme d'une chandelle.* Paris: Quadrige.

Baehr, Peter. 2002. "A Wheel That Has Come Off." *The Times Literary Supplement,* April 12.

Bahr, Ehrhard. 1980. *Nelly Sachs.* Munich: Edition Text und Kritik.

Baioni, Giuliano. 1994. *Kafka: Literatur und Judentum.* Stuttgart: Metzler.

Bänsch, Dieter. 1971. *Else Lasker-Schüler: Zur Kritik eines etablierten Bildes.* Stuttgart: Metzlersche Verlagsbuchhandlung.

Bathi, Timothy, and Marilyn Sibley Fries. 1996. *Jewish Writers, German Literature: The Uneasy Examples of Nelly Sachs and Walter Benjamin.* Ann Arbor: University of Michigan Press.

Bauschinger, Sigrid. 1980. *Else Lasker-Schüler: Ihr Werk und ihre Zeit.* Heidelberg: Stiehm.

Beck, Evelyn Torton. 1971. *Kafka and the Yiddish Theater: Its Impact on His Work.* Madison: University of Wisconsin Press.

Bein, Alex. 1942. *Theodor Herzl.* Trans. Maurice Samuel. Philadelphia: Jewish Publication Society.

Benjamin, Walter. 1999. *The Arcades Project.* Ed. R. Tiedemann, trans. H. Eiland and K. McLaughlin. Cambridge, Mass.: Harvard University Press.

———. 2002a. "The Destructive Character." In *Selected Writings II,* ed. Michael W. Jennings, Howard Eiland, and Gary Smith, 541–42. Cambridge, Mass.: Harvard University Press.

———. 2002b. "Franz Kafka." In *Selected Writings II,* ed. Michael W. Jennings, Howard Eiland, and Gary Smith, 794–818. Cambridge, Mass.: Harvard University Press.

———. 2002c. "Eduard Fuchs, Collector and Historian." In *Selected Writings III,* ed. Howard Eiland and Michael W. Jennings, 260–302. Cambridge, Mass.: Harvard University Press.

———. 2002d. "On Language as Such and on the Language of Man." In *Selected Writings I,* ed. Marcus Bullock and Michael W. Jennings, 62–74. Cambridge, Mass.: Harvard University Press.

Bhabha, Homi K. 1995. "Unpacking My Library Again." *Journal of the Midwest Modern Language Association* 28, no. 1: 5–18.

Biller, Maxim. 1997. *Land der Väter und Verräter.* Munich: Deutscher Taschenbuch Verlag.

Binder, Hartmut. 1979a. *Kafka-Handbuch I.* Stuttgart: Kröner Verlag.

———. 1979b. *Kafka-Handbuch II.* Stuttgart: Kröner Verlag.

Blanchot, Maurice. 1983. *The Unavowable Community.* Trans. Pierre Joris. Barrytown, N.Y.: Station Hill Press.

Bollack, Jean. 1994. "Paul Celan und Nelly Sachs: Geschichte eines Kampfes." *Neue Rundschau* 105, no. 4: 119–34.

———. 2000. *Poetik der Fremdheit.* Vienna: Zolnay.

Borges, Jorge Luis. 1979. "Kafka and His Precursors." In *Labyrinths,* 234–37. London: Penguin.

Braese, Stephan. 2005. *Die andere Erinnerung: Jüdische Autoren in der deutschen Nachkriegsliteratur.* Vienna: Philo Verlag.

Brieglob, Klaus. 1997. "Ingeborg Bachmann, Paul Celan: Ihr (Nicht-)Ort in der Gruppe 47 (1952–1964/65): Eine Skizze." In *Ingeborg Bachmann und Paul Celan: Poetische Korrespondenzen,* 29–84, ed. Bernhard Böschenstein and Sigrid Weigel. Frankfurt am Main: Suhrkamp.

———. 2002. *Mißachtung und Tabu: Eine Streitschrift zur Frage: Wie antisemitisch war die Gruppe 47?* Vienna: Philo Verlag.

Bruce, Iris. 2007. *Kafka and Cultural Zionism: Dates in Palestine*. Madison: University of Wisconsin Press.

Brude-Firnau, Gisela. 1976. *Vision und Politik: Die Tagebücher Theodor Herzls*. Frankfurt am Main: Suhrkamp.

Casanova, Pascale. 2004. *The World Republic of Letters*. Cambridge, Mass.: Harvard University Press.

Celan, Paul. 1983. *Gesammelte Werke*. 5 vols. Frankfurt am Main: Suhrkamp.

———. 1999. *Der Meridian: Endfassung, Vorstufen, Materialien*. Frankfurt: Suhrkamp.

———. 2001. *Selected Poems and Prose of Paul Celan*. Trans. John Felstiner. New York: W. W. Norton.

———. 2002. *Poems of Paul Celan: A Bilingual German English Edition*. Trans. Michael Hamburger. New York: Persea Books.

———. 2003. *Die Gedichte*. Ed. Barbara Wiedemann. Frankfurt am Main: Suhrkamp.

Celan, Paul, and Gisèle Lestrange. 2001. *Briefwechsel*. Vol. 1. Ed. Bertrand Badiou. Frankfurt am Main: Suhrkamp.

Chalfen, Israel. 1983. *Paul Celan: Eine Biographie seiner Jugend*. Frankfurt am Main: Suhrkamp.

Colin, Amy. 1986. "Words as Weapons: Celan Reading Kafka." In *Kafka's Contextuality*, ed. Alan Udoff, 145–75. New York: Gordian Press and Baltimore Hebrew College.

Corngold, Stanley. 2004. *Lambent Traces*. Princeton, N.J.: Princeton University Press.

Deleuze, Gilles, and Félix Guattari. 1986. *Kafka: Toward a Minor Literature*. Minneapolis: University of Minnesota Press.

Derrida, Jacques. 1986. *Schibboleth pour Paul Celan*. Paris: Galilée.

Didi-Huberman, Georges. 2004. *Images malgré tout*. Paris: Editions de Minuit.

Dinesen, Ruth. 1985a. "Naturereignis—Wortereignis: Übereinstimmung und Nicht-Übereinstimmung in Gedichten von Nelly Sachs und Paul Celan." *Text und Kontext* 13, no. 1: 119–41.

———. 1985b. "Verehrung und Verwerfung: Nelly Sachs: Kontroverse um eine Dichterin." In *VII Kongress der Internationalen Vereinigung für Germanistische Sprach- und Literaturwissenschaft*, vol. 10, ed. Karl Pestalozzi, 130–37. Göttingen: Niemeyer.

———. 1996. "The Search for Identity: Nelly Sachs's Jewishness." In *Jewish Writers, German Literature: The Uneasy Examples of Nelly Sachs and Walter Benjamin*, ed. Timothy Bathi and Marilyn Sibley Fries, 23–43. Ann Arbor: University of Michigan Press.

Donne, John. 1896. "Songs and Sonnets." In *Poems of John Donne*, vol. 1, ed. E. K. Chambers. London: Lawrence and Bullen.

Dor, Milo. 1973. "Paul Celan." In *Über Paul Celan*, ed. Dietlind Meinecke, 281–85. Frankfurt am Main: Suhrkamp.

Encyclopedia Judaica. 1974. Jerusalem: Keter Publishing House.

Endres, Elisabeth. 1995. "Ilse Aichinger." In *Ilse Aichinger: Leben und Werk*, ed. Samuel Moser, 114–20. Frankfurt am Main: Fischer Verlag.

Enzensberger, Hans Magnus. 1959. "Die Steine der Freiheit." *Merkur* 13: 770–75.

Eshel, Amir. 2002. "Von Kafka zu Celan: Deutsch-Jüdische Schriftsteller und ihr Verhältnis zum Hebräischen und Jiddischen." In *Jüdische Sprachen in deutscher Umwelt: Hebräisch und Jiddisch von der Aufklärung bis ins 20. Jahrhundert*, ed. Michael Brenner, 96–127. Göttingen: Vandenhoeck und Ruprecht.

Felstiner, John. 1995. *Paul Celan: Poet, Survivor, Jew*. New Haven, Conn.: Yale University Press.

Foucault, Michel. 1999. *The History of Sexuality*. New York: Random House.

Freud, Sigmund. 1961. *Die Traumdeutung,* ed. Anna Freud. Frankfurt am Main: Fischer Verlag.

Friedländer, Saul. 1994. "Trauma, Memory and Transference." In *Holocaust Remembrance: The Shapes of Memory,* ed. Geoffrey Hartman, 252–63. Cambridge: Blackwell.

Fritsch-Vivié, Gabriele. 1993. *Nelly Sachs.* Reinbek bei Hamburg: Rowohlt.

Gadamer, Hans-Georg. 1973. *Wer bin Ich und wer bist Du? Ein Kommentar zu Paul Celans Gedichtfolge "Atemkristall."* Frankfurt am Main: Suhrkamp.

Geissner, Helmut. 1968. "Nelly Sachs." In *Deutsche Literatur seit 1945 in Einzeldarstellungen,* ed. Dietrich Weber, 15–37. Stuttgart: Alfred Kroner Verlag.

Gelber, Mark H. 2008. "German-Jewish Literature and Culture and the Field of German-Jewish Studies." In *The Jewish Contribution to Civilization: Reassessing an Idea,* ed. Jeremy Cohen and Richard I. Cohen, 165–84. Oxford: The Littman Library.

Gertner, Meir. 1969. "Biblische Spiegelbilder." In *Else Lasker-Schüler: Ein Buch zum 100. Geburtstag der Dichterin,* 166–82, ed. Michael Schmid. Wuppertal: Peter Hammer Verlag.

Gide, André. 1927. *Prétextes.* Paris: Mercure de France.

Gilman, Sander L., and Jack Zipes, eds. 1997. *Yale Companion to Jewish Writing in German Culture 1096–1996.* New Haven, Conn.: Yale University Press.

Gilman, Sander L., and Hartmut Steinecke, eds. 2002. *Deutsch-jüdische Literatur der neunziger Jahre: Die Generation nach der Shoah.* Berlin: Erich Schmidt Verlag.

Glaser, Hermann, Jakob Lehman, and Arno Lubos, eds. 1984. *Wege der Deutschen Literatur.* Frankfurt am Main: Ulstein.

Glenn, Jerry. 1973. *Paul Celan.* New York: Twayne.

Goldstein, Fanni. 1936. "Der expressionistische Stilwille im Werk Else Lasker-Schülers." Ph.D. thesis, Vienna.

Grass, Günther. 2006. *Beim Häuten der Zwiebel.* Göttingen: Steidl.

Günzel, Elke. 1995. *Das wandernde Zitat: Paul Celan im jüdischen Kontext.* Würzburg: Königshausen und Neumann.

Hamacher, Werner. 1988. "Die Sekunde der Inversion: Bewegungen einer Figur durch Celans Gedichte." In *Paul Celan,* ed. Werner Hamacher and Winfried Menninghaus, 81–126. Frankfurt am Main: Suhrkamp.

Hamacher, Werner, and Winfried Menninghaus, eds. 1988. *Paul Celan.* Frankfurt am Main: Suhrkamp.

Haring, Ekkehard W. 2001. "Wege jüdischer Kafka-Deutung: Versuch einer kritischen Bilanz." In *Das jüdische Echo: Europäisches Forum für Kultur und Politik,* 310–24.

Hartman, Geoffrey. 1996. "Breaking with Every Star: On Literary Knowledge." *Comparative Criticism* 18: 3–20.

Heidegger, Martin. 1976. *Sein und Zeit.* Tübingen: Max Niemeyer.

Hennek-Weischer, Andrea. 2007. "Die tiefsten Erinnerungen [. . .] im Glanze meines Blau: Die Bibelrezeption Else Lasker-Schülers." *Jahrbuch für Internationale Germanistik* 1: 153–83.

Herbrechter, Stefan, and Michael Higgins. 2006. *Returning (to) Communities: Theory, Culture and Political Practice of the Communal.* Amsterdam: Rodopi.

Herzfelde, Wieland. 1969. "Else Lasker-Schüler." *Sinn und Form* 21, no. 6: 13–15.

Herzl, Theodor. 1900. *Philosophische Erzählungen.* Berlin: Gebrüder Paetel.

———. 1911. *Feuilletons,* vols. 1 and 2. Vienna: Wiener Verlag.

———. 1976. *Vision und Politik: Die Tagebücher Theodor Herzls,* ed. Gisela Brude-Firnau. Frankfurt am Main: Suhrkamp.

———. 1985. *Zionistisches Tagebuch 1899–1904.* Berlin: Propyläen.

Herzog, Todd. 2002. "'New York Is More Fun': Amerika in der zeitgenössischen deutsch-jüdischen Literatur—die zeitgenössische deutsch-jüdische Literatur in Amerika." In *Deutsch-jüdische Literatur der neunziger Jahre: Die Generation nach der Shoah,* ed. Sander L. Gilman and Hartmut Steinecke, 204–14. Berlin: Erich Schmidt Verlag.

Hillmann, Heinz. 1967. "Das Sorgenkind Odradek." *Zeitschrift für deutsche Philologie* 86: 197–210.

Hoffer, Klaus. 1993. "Der Beginn der Aktion." In *Ilse Aichinger,* ed. Kurt Bartsch and Gerhard Melzer, 88–101. Graz: Droschl Verlag.

Höltgen, Karl-Joseph. 1955. "Untersuchungen zur Lyrik Lasker-Schülers." Ph.D. thesis, Bonn.

Holthusen, Hans Egon. 1995. "Im Rücken des Todes." In *Ilse Aichinger: Leben und Werk,* ed. Samuel Moser, 194–97. Frankfurt am Main: Fischer Verlag.

Isenberg, Noah. 1999. *Between Doom and Redemption: The Strains of German-Jewish Modernism.* Lincoln: University of Nebraska Press.

Ivanovic, Christine. 1999. "All Poets Are Jews: Paul Celan's Readings of Marina Tsvetayeva." *Glossen* 6. http://alpha.dickinson.edu/departments/germn/glossen/supertite12.html, accessed 27 January 2008.

Janouch, Gustav. 1968. *Gespräche mit Franz Kafka.* Frankfurt am Main: Fischer Verlag.

Jeziorkowski, Klaus. 1996. "Nelly Sachs." In *Deutsche Dichter des 20. Jahrhunderts,* ed. Hartmuth Steinecke, 530–62. Berlin: Erich Schmidt Verlag.

Kafka, Franz. 1958. *Briefe 1902–1924.* Ed. Max Brod. Frankfurt am Main: Fischer Verlag.

———. 1975. *Diaries.* New York: Schocken Books.

———. 1976. *Complete Stories.* Ed. Nahum N. Glatzer. New York: Schocken Books.

———. 1977. *Das Kafka Buch.* Ed. Max Brod. Frankfurt am Main: Fischer Verlag.

———. 1982. *Briefe an Felice.* Frankfurt am Main: Fischer Verlag.

———. 1983. *Briefe an Milena.* Ed. Jürgen Born and Michael Müller. Frankfurt am Main: Fischer Verlag.

———. 1992. "A Little Woman." In *Metamorphosis and Other Stories: Works Published during Kafka's Lifetime,* trans. and ed. Malcolm Pasley, 202–209. London: Penguin Books.

———. 1995. *The Metamorphosis and Other Stories.* Ed. Joachim Neugroschel. New York: Scriber.

———. 2002a. *Nachgelassene Schriften und Fragmente I.* Frankfurt am Main: Fischer Verlag.

———. 2002b. *Nachgelassene Schriften und Fragmente II.* Frankfurt am Main: Fischer Verlag.

———. 2002c. *Tagebücher.* Frankfurt am Main: Fischer Verlag.

———. 2002d. *Tagebücher (Apparatband).* Frankfurt am Main: Fischer Verlag.

———. 2002e. *Drucke zu Lebzeiten.* Frankfurt am Main: Fischer Verlag.

———. 2007. *Selected Stories.* Trans. and ed. Stanley Corngold. New York: Norton.

Karthaus, Ulrich, ed. 1977. *Impressionismus, Symbolismus und Jugendstil.* Stuttgart: Reclam.

Kaus, Rainer J. 2002. *Eine kleine Frau: Kafkas Erzählungen in literaturpsychologischer Sicht.* Heidelberg: Universitätsverlag C. Winter.

Kilcher, Andreas. 1999. "Was ist deutsch-jüdische Literatur? Eine historische Diskursanalyse." *Weimarer Beiträge* 45, no. 4: 485–517.

———, ed. 2000. *Lexikon der deutsch-jüdischen Literatur: Jüdische Autorinnen und Autoren deutscher Sprache von der Aufklärung bis zur Gegenwart.* Stuttgart: Metzler.

Kimmich, Dorothee. 1996. "Kalte Füsse: Von Erzählprozessen und Sprachverdikten bei Hannah Arendt, Harry Mulisch, Theodor W. Adorno, Jean-François Lyotard, und

Robert Schindel." In *Shoah: Formen der Erinnerung; Geschichte, Philosophie, Literatur, Kunst,* ed. Nicolas Berg, Bernd Stiegler, and Jess Jochimsen, 93–106. Munich: Wilhelm Fink Verlag.

Kittler, Wolf, and Gerhard Neumann, eds. 1990. *Franz Kafka: Schriftverkehr.* Freiburg im Breisgau: Rombach.

Koch, Angelika. 1971. *Die Bedeutung des Spiels bei Else Lasker-Schüler im Rahmen von Expressionismus und Manierismus.* Bonn: Bouvier.

Korhonen, Kuisma. 2006. "Textual Communities: Nancy, Blanchot, Derrida." *Culture Machine* 8. http://culturemachine.tees.ac.uk/Cmach/Backissues/j008/Articles/korhonen.htm, accessed 23 February 2008.

Kraft, Werner. 1951. *Else Lasker-Schüler: Eine Einführung in ihr Werk und eine Auswahl.* Wiesbaden: Steiner.

Krämer, Michael. 1994. "'Wir wissen ja nicht, was gilt': Zum poetischen Verfahren bei Nelly Sachs und Paul Celan—Versuch einer Annäherung." In *Nelly Sachs: Neue Interpretationen,* ed. Michael Kessler and Jürgen Wertheimer, 35–69. Tübingen: Stauffenburg Colloquium.

Kröll, Friedhelm. 1979. *Gruppe 47.* Stuttgart: Metzlersche Verlagsbuchhandlung.

Krug, Marina. 2000. *Die Figur als signifikante Spur: Eine dekonstruktive Lektüre zu den Gedichten "Esther" sowie "David und Jonathan" aus dem Zyklus "Hebräische Balladen" von Else Lasker-Schüler.* Frankfurt am Main: Peter Lang Verlag.

Kuschel, Karl-Josef. 1994. "Die Gedichte der Nelly Sachs als theologische Herausforderung." In *Nelly Sachs, Neue Interpretationen,* ed. Michael Kessler and Jürgen Wertheimer, 203–25. Tübingen: Stauffenburg Colloquium.

Lamping, Dieter. 1998. *Von Kafka bis Celan: Jüdischer Diskurs in der deutschen Literatur des 20. Jahrhunderts.* Göttingen: Vanderhoeck und Ruprecht.

Lange-Kirchheim, Astrid. 1986. "Kein Fortkommen: Zu Franz Kafkas Erzählung 'Eine kleine Frau.'" In *Phantasie und Deutung: Frederick Wyatt zum 75. Geburtstag,* ed. Wolfram Mauser, Ursula Renner, and Walter Schönau, 180–93. Würzburg: Königshausen und Neumann.

Langer, Lawrence L. 1986. "Kafka as Holocaust Prophet: A Dissenting View." In *Kafka's Contextuality,* ed. Alan Udoff, 113–45. Baltimore, Md.: Gordian Press and Baltimore Hebrew College.

Lasker-Schüler, Else. 1907. *Die Nächte Tino von Bagdads.* Berlin: Axel Juncker Verlag.

———. 1980. *Hebrew Ballads and Other Poems.* Trans. and ed. Audri Durchslag and Jeanette Litman-Demeestère. Philadelphia: Jewish Publication Society of America.

———. 1986. "Ich räume auf! Meine Anklage gegen meine Verleger." In *Der Prinz von Theben und andere Prosa, Gesammelte Werke in acht Bänden,* ed. Friedhelm Kemp, 301–52. Munich: DTV.

———. 1996. *Werke und Briefe.* Frankfurt am Main: Jüdischer Verlag.

———. 1998. "Sternendeuterei." In *Werke und Briefe: Prosa 1903–1920,* kritische Ausgabe, 162–68. Frankfurt: Jüdischer Verlag.

Leer, Joachim, and Georg Guntermann. 1995. *Brauchen wir eine neue Gruppe 47? 55 Fragebögen zur deutschen Literatur.* Bonn: Reinhard Nenzel Verlag für Literatur und Wissenschaft.

Lenk, Elisabeth. 1983. *Kritische Phantasie.* Munich: Matthes und Seitz.

Lermen, Birgit. 1995. "Stimmen vom Nesselweg her: Gedichte nach Auschwitz." *Theologie und Glaube* 85, no. 1: 47–63.

Lermen, Birgit, and Michael Braun, eds. 1998. *Nelly Sachs. An der letzten Atemspitze des Lebens.* Bonn: Bouvier Verlag.

Lettau, Reinhard, ed. 1967. *Die Gruppe 47: Bericht, Kritik, Polemik.* Neuried/Rhein: Luchterhand.

Levinas, Emmanuel. 1990. *Difficult Freedom.* Baltimore, Md.: Johns Hopkins University Press.

Lévy, Bernard-Henri. 1979. *Le Testament de Dieu.* Paris: Grasset.

Lingis, Alphonso. 1994. *The Community of Those Who Have Nothing in Common.* Bloomington: Indiana University Press.

Lorenz, Dagmar. 1981. *Ilse Aichinger.* Bodenheim: Athenaeum.

———. 1997. *Keepers of the Motherland: German Texts by Jewish Women Writers.* Lincoln: University of Nebraska Press.

Meinecke, Dietlind. 1970. *Wort und Name bei Paul Celan: Zur Widerruflichkeit des Gedichts.* Bad Homburg: Gehlen.

Menasse, Robert. 2001. *Vertreibung aus der Hölle.* Frankfurt am Main: Suhrkamp.

———. 2002. "Igel, Hase und die Lehre des Rabbi: Dankrede zum Hölderlin-Preis der Stadt Bad Homburg." *Frankfurter Allgemeine Zeitung,* 15 June 2002.

Meschonnic, Henri. 1973. *Pour la poétique II: Épistémologie de l'écriture, poétique de la traduction.* Paris: Gallimard.

Munk, Elie. 1976. *La Voix de la Thora.* Paris: Fondation Lévy.

Nägele, Rainer. 1987. "Paul Celan: Konfigurationen Freuds." In *Argumentum e Silentio: International Paul Celan Symposium,* ed. Amy D. Colin, 237–65. Berlin: Walter de Gruyter.

Nancy, Jean-Luc. 1986. *La communauté désoeuvrée.* Paris: Christian Bourgois.

Neumann, Peter Horst. 1995. "Genauigkeit im Ungewissen." In *Ilse Aichinger: Leben und Werk,* ed. Samuel Moser, 259–60. Frankfurt am Main: Fischer Verlag.

Nicolai, Ralf R. 1996. "'Eine kleine Frau' im Motivgeflecht Kafkas." In *Neues zu Altem: Novellen der Vergangenheit und der Gegenwart,* 89–115. Munich: Wilhelm Fink Verlag.

———. 1997. "Ilse Aichinger's Response to Kafka: 'The Bound Man.'" In *The Legacy of Kafka in Contemporary Austrian Literature,* ed. Frank Philipp, 44–61. Riverside, Calif.: Ariadne Press.

Nietzsche, Friedrich. 1959. *Die Fröhliche Wissenschaft.* Munich: Goldmann.

Norris, Pamela. 1998. *The Story of Eve.* London: Picador.

Novalis. 1985. *Hymnen and die Nacht und Heinrich von Ofterdingen.* Munich: Goldmann.

O'Brien, Mary-Elizabeth. 1992. "'Ich war verkleidet als Poet, ich bin Poetin': The Masquerade of Gender in Else Lasker-Schüler's Work." *The German Quarterly* 65, no. 1: 1–17.

Parkes, Stuart, and John J. White. 1999. *The Gruppe 47 Fifty Years On: A Re-Appraisal of Its Literary and Political Significance.* Amsterdam: Rodopi.

Pazi, Margarita. 1994. "Jüdische Aspekte und Elemente im Werk von Nelly Sachs und ihre Wirkungen." In *Nelly Sachs, Neue Interpretationen,* ed. Michael Kessler and Jürgen Wertheimer, 153–69. Tübingen: Stauffenburg Colloquium.

Perel, Christoph. 1973. "Zu Paul Celans Gedicht 'Frankfurt September.'" *Germanisch-Romanische Monatsschrift* 54: 56–67.

Piontek, Heinz. 1995. "Über die Poesie in Ilse Aichingers Prosa." In *Ilse Aichinger: Leben und Werk,* ed. Samuel Moser, 224–26. Frankfurt am Main: Fischer Verlag.

Pöggeler, Otto. 1986. *Spur des Wortes: Zur Lyrik Paul Celans.* Freiburg: Alber.

Pulver, Elisabeth. 1995. "Genaue Ahnungen." In *Ilse Aichinger: Leben und Werk,* ed. Samuel Moser, 269–78. Frankfurt am Main: Fischer Verlag.

Rabinovici, Doron. 2000. *The Search for M.* Trans. Francis M. Sharp. Riverside, Calif.: Ariadne Press.

Reichmann, Eva. 2001. "Identität als Problem: Leben als Jude in Österreich im Werk von Doron Rabinovici, Robert Menasse und Robert Schindel." *Aspekte jüdischer Literatur,* ed. Armin A. Wallas and Werner Wintersteiner, 25, no. 2: 40–48.

Richter, Hans Werner. 1997. *Briefe,* ed. Sabine Cofalla. Munich: Carl Hanser Verlag.

Robert, Marthe. 1979. *Seul, comme Franz Kafka.* Paris: Calmann-Lévy.

Robertson, Ritchie. 1985. *Kafka: Judaism, Politics, and Literature.* New York: Oxford University Press.

Robin, Régine. 1989. *Kafka.* Paris: Pierre Belfond.

Rosenbaum, Ron. 1998. *Explaining Hitler.* London: Random House.

Rothmann, Klaus V., ed. 1978. *Kleine Geschichte der deutschen Literatur.* Stuttgart: Reclam.

Sachs, Nelly. 1965. *Das Leiden Israels. Eli. In den Wohnungen des Todes. Sternverdunkelung.* Frankfurt am Main: Suhrkamp.

———. 1984. *Briefe der Nelly Sachs.* Ed. Ruth Dinesen and Helmut Müssener. Frankfurt am Main: Suhrkamp.

———. 1988. *Fahrt ins Staublose.* Frankfurt am Main: Suhrkamp.

Sandbank, Shimon. 1989. *After Kafka: The Influence of Kafka's Fiction.* Athens: University of Georgia Press.

Schindel, Robert. 1992. *Gebürtig.* Frankfurt am Main: Suhrkamp.

———. 1995a. *Born-Where.* Trans. Michael Roloff. Riverside, Calif.: Ariadne Press.

———. 1995b. *Gott schütz uns vor den guten Menschen: Jüdisches Gedächtnis—Auskunftsbüro der Angst.* Frankfurt am Main: Suhrkamp.

———. 2004. *Mein liebster Feind: Essays, Reden, Miniaturen.* Frankfurt am Main: Suhrkamp.

Schmidt-Bortenschlager, Sigrid. 1999. "Poetik der Negation." In *Verschwiegenes Wortspiel,* ed. Heidy Margrit Müller, 21–31. Bielefeld, Germany: Aisthesis Verlag.

Schmueli, Ilana, and Thomas Sparr. 2004. *Paul Celan und Ilana Schmueli: Briefwechsel.* Frankfurt am Main: Suhrkamp.

Scholem, Gershom. 1970. "Juden und Deutsche." In *Judaica* 2: 20–46. Frankfurt am Main: Suhrkamp.

Schulze, Joachim. 1976. *Celan und die Mystiker.* Bonn: Bouvier Verlag.

Schutte, Jürgen. 1988. *Dichter und Richter: Die Gruppe 47 und die deutsche Nachkriegsliteratur.* Ausstellungskatalog. Berlin: Akademie der Künste.

Segev, Tom. 2001. *Elvis in Jerusalem: Post-Zionism and the Americanization of Israel.* Trans. Haim Waitzman. New York: Metropolitan Books, Henry Holt.

Slezkine, Yuri. 2004. *The Jewish Century.* Princeton, N.J.: Princeton University Press.

Sparr, Thomas. 1988. "Celan und Kafka." *Celan-Jahrbuch* 2: 140–54.

Steiner, George. 1967. "A Kind of Survivor." In *Language and Silence.* London: Faber.

Steinwendtner, Brita. 1993. "Sammle den Untergang: Zu Ilse Aichingers Kurzprosaband 'Schlechte Wörter.'" In *Ilse Aichinger,* ed. Kurt Bartsch and Gerhard Melzer, 138–47. Graz, Germany: Droschl Verlag.

Stiegert, Bernhard. 1990. "Kartographien der Zerstreuung: Jargon und die Schrift der jüdischen Tradierungsbewegung bei Kafka." In *Franz Kafka: Schriftverkehr,* ed. Wolf Kittler and Gerhard Neumann, 222–47. Freiburg im Breisgau: Rombach.

Stumpp, Gabriele. 2004. "Zu einigen Aspekten jüdischer Tradition in Robert Menasses *Vertreibung aus der Hölle.*" In *Robert Menasse,* ed. Kurt Bartsch and Verena Höller, 59–78. Vienna: Literaturverlag Droschl.

Torton Beck, Evelyn. 1971. *Kafka and the Yiddish Theater: Its Impact on His Work.* Madison: University of Wisconsin Press.

————. 1983. "Kafka's Traffic in Women: Gender, Power and Sexuality." *The Literary Review* 26, no. 4: 565–76.

Ury, Marian. 1992. "Poems of the Five Mountains: An Introduction to the Literature of the Zen Monasteries." Michigan Monographs in Japanese Studies 10. Ann Arbor, Mich.: Center for Japanese Studies, University of Michigan.

Von Matt, Peter. 1995. *Verkommene Söhne, missratene Töchter: Familiendesaster in der Literatur.* Munich: Carl Hanser Verlag.

Weissenberger, Klaus. 1983. "Else Lasker-Schülers Anverwandlung des Joseph-Mythos." *Colloquia Germanica* 16: 201–16.

West, William. 1996. "The Poetics of Inadequacy: Nelly Sachs and the Resurrection of the Dead." In *Jewish Writers, German Literature,* ed. Timothy Bathi and Marilyn Sibley Fries, 77–104. Ann Arbor: University of Michigan Press.

Widmer, Urs. 1967. "So kahl war der Kahlschlag nicht." In *Die Gruppe 47: Bericht, Kritik, Polemik,* 328–35, ed. Reinhard Lettau. Neuwied, Berlin: Luchterhand.

Witte, Bernd. 1981. "Zu einer Theorie der hermetischen Lyrik am Beispiel Paul Celans." *Poetica* 13: 133–48.

————. 2007. *Jüdische Tradition und literarische Moderne: Heine—Buber—Kafka—Benjamin.* Munich: Hanser.

Wohlfarth, Irving. 1988. "Die Willkür der Zeichen: Zu einem sprachphilosophischen Grundmotiv Walter Benjamins." In *Perspektiven kritischer Theorie,* ed. Christoph Türcke, 124–72. Lüneburg, Germany: zu Klampen.

Young-Bruehl, Elisabeth. 1982. *Hannah Arendt: For Love of the World.* New Haven, Conn.: Yale University Press.

Index

Vivian Liska

is Professor of German Literature and Director of the Institute of Jewish Studies at the University of Antwerp, Belgium. Among her published works are *The Night of the Hymns: Paul Celan's Poems, 1938–1944* and *Giorgio Agamben's Empty Messianism* (in German), as well as numerous articles on modern German and contemporary Jewish literature. She is editor (with Thomas Nolden) of *Contemporary Jewish Writing in Europe* (Indiana University Press, 2007) and (with Astradur Eysteinsson) of *Modernism*.